The Evaluation and Application of Survey Research in the Arab World

About the Book and Authors

At a time when survey research is increasingly being conducted in the Arab world, there is also growing concern about the degree to which research assumptions and methods developed in the West are appropriate for use in the study of Arab society. This book assesses the application and limits of survey research performed in the Arab world, reviews the surveys currently being used to study public attitudes and behavior patterns, and discusses epistemological, methodological, and ethical issues associated with these studies. Readers are alerted to normative and empirical considerations bearing on the quality of survey research and given practical suggestions for innovation in the design and execution of survey research and in the analysis of survey data. The book raises intellectual issues of concern to all who seek to better understand Arab society and provides extensive information about attitudes and behavior in the Arab world.

Mark A. Tessler teaches political science at the University of Wisconsin–Milwaukee and is faculty associate of the Universities Field Staff International. **Monte Palmer** teaches political science at Florida State University. **Tawfic E. Farah** is director of the Middle East Research Group and editor of the *Journal of Arab Affairs*. **Barbara Lethem Ibrahim** is a program officer with the Ford Foundation in Cairo.

The Evaluation and Application of Survey Research in the Arab World

Mark A. Tessler,
Monte Palmer,
Tawfic E. Farah, and
Barbara Lethem Ibrahim

Westview Press / Boulder and London

Westview Special Studies on the Middle East

Published in 1987 in the United States of America by Westview Press, Inc.; Frederick A. Praeger, Publisher; 5500 Central Avenue, Boulder, Colorado 80301

Library of Congress Cataloging-in-Publication Data
The Evaluation and application of survey research
  in the Arab world.
  (Westview special studies on the Middle East)
  Chiefly papers from a conference held in Bellagio,
Italy, in June 1983 which was sponsored by the
Rockefeller Foundation.
  1. Social sciences—Research—Arab countries—
Congresses. 2. Evaluation research (Social action
programs)—Arab countries—Congresses. 3. Social
surveys—Arab countries—Congresses. 4. Arab
countries—Research—Congresses. I. Tessler, Mark A.
II. Rockefeller Foundation. III. Series.
H62.5.A65E94 1987   300'.723   86-28097
ISBN 0-8133-0023-1

Printed and bound in the United States of America

10   9   8   7   6   5   4   3   2   1

Contents

vii

PART TWO
ISSUES OF RELEVANCE, METHODOLOGY,
AND CUMULATIVENESS

Tables and Figures

Acknowledgments

Many individuals and institutions helped to make this book possible. Much of the book is based on information presented at an international conference supported by generous grants from the Ford Foundation and the Rockefeller Foundation. The Rockefeller Foundation hosted the six-day meeting in June 1983 at its Study and Conference Center in Bellagio, Italy, which is certainly one of the finest conference facilities anywhere. A grant from the Ford Foundation in Cairo, administered by the American University in Cairo, supported attendance by Arab scholars residing in the Middle East. The Ford Foundation also provided important administrative support during the planning of the conference and the preparation of this book. The generosity of each of these institutions is gratefully acknowledged.

The conference was planned by a six-member committee composed of Tawfic Farah, Barbara Ibrahim, Saad Eddin Ibrahim, Ann Lesch, Monte Palmer, and Mark Tessler. Various members of this working group prepared the grant proposals and organized and convened the Bellagio conference. Special thanks are due to Saad Eddin Ibrahim and Ann Lesch, whose other commitments prevented them from coauthoring this book but who made critical contributions to the planning and administration of the meeting at Bellagio. The success of the conference is also the result of the valuable contributions of the twenty-four Arab and U.S. social scientists who attended the meeting. These individuals are identified in Appendix A.

The planning of the conference and preparation of the book were also made possible by Fulbright grants from the U.S. Information Agency. Conference proceedings were transcribed by Princess Palmer and Monte Palmer, whose work was supported by the Middle East Research Group. Under a Fulbright Islamic Civilization grant, Mark Tessler then edited the proceedings and assumed principal responsibility for assembling the present collection. Valuable suggestions concerning several aspects of the project were offered by the Office of Research of the U.S. Information

Agency. The support and assistance of each of these agencies is acknowledged with sincere appreciation.

Mark A. Tessler
Monte Palmer
Tawfic E. Farah
Barbara Lethem Ibrahim

Introduction:
Survey Research in Arab Society

Mark A. Tessler

Survey research, which involves administration of a questionnaire or interview schedule to a sample of respondents and subsequent analysis of the data collected, is one of the most important instruments of systematic social inquiry in the United States and Europe.[1] It is the foundation of most studies of individual attitudes and behavior, and it is also widely used to acquire information about social aggregates.

Although in recent years survey research has become common in the Arab world and in other developing areas, its use is still in an early stage and there are many obstacles to its full and proper employment. The present book deals with the ways that surveys can and should be utilized to study social reality in the Arab world. Its goal is to contribute to more and better quality survey research in the future, and it examines the kinds of problems that must be solved if such research is to achieve its potential. Relevant problems are present in areas related to methodology, epistemology, cumulativeness, ethics, and the general context of social research in the Arab world. In addition, the book explores the limits as well as the applicability of survey research as an investigatory tool for the study of Arab society. As elsewhere, surveys conducted in the Arab world can be and sometimes have been of poor quality. Thus, this book discusses not only the ways that surveys can be used productively but also the conditions under which they are unlikely to produce findings that are relevant or accurate.

Survey research often needs to be combined with other research procedures to be maximally useful. Further, on occasion, surveys should be eschewed entirely in favor of methodologies better suited to the investigation of a particular topic. Nevertheless, survey research is establishing itself as a standard and widely used tool in the research arsenal of social scientists practicing their craft in the Arab world. The frequency of surveys is increasing, and many have been carried out with care and have produced important results. Such studies demonstrate that survey research can contribute meaningfully to the twin goals of understanding Arab society better and providing information that will assist in solving practical problems and achieving development-related goals.

Maximizing these kinds of contributions and reducing the amount of poor quality or irrelevant survey research were the goals of twenty-four Arab and U.S. social scientists who met at the Rockefeller Foundation Study and Conference Center in Bellagio, Italy, in June 1983. During the six-day conference they explored many aspects of the evaluation and application of survey research in the Arab world, and their contributions constitute the foundation of this book. This introduction deals with the following topics: (1) the contribution that survey research can make to the study of the Arab world and other developing areas; (2) problems associated with the conduct of survey research in Arab society; (3) the structure and content of the Bellagio conference; (4) the contents and organization of the present book; and (5) the various audiences to which this book is addressed.

The Contribution of Survey Research

To appreciate the potential contribution of survey research we must understand the importance of studying individual attitudes and behavior patterns in the Arab world and other developing societies. There are important connections between individual orientations on the one hand and societal development on the other. Such connections are found in the political, economic, and social realms, and in each there are many substantive and theoretical issues that deserve study not only by those seeking to understand development and change but also by those with responsibility for managing the evolution and transformation of their societies. In these areas, knowledge about the distribution, determinants, and consequences of various patterns of thought and action can make both a scientific and a practical contribution. Much more research is needed in order to gather and analyze the data from which this knowledge may be derived, however. Information about individual attitudes and behavior patterns is usually best collected by survey research, often in conjunction with other research methodologies and sometimes as the only appropriate investigatory tool.

The important relationship between individual orientations and societal development is recognized by political leaders as well as scholars. The chief executive of one Arab state depicted this relationship when describing his country's development program, saying that "underdevelopment in the final analysis stems from intellectual causes. It is man's mind which is the driving force in improving the human condition, and . . . a psychological revolution is therefore necessary to assure the success of our national development plan."[2] Other Arab regimes have also made the transformation of popular attitudes and behavior patterns a major preoccupation. Although attempts to effect a radical and wholesale transformation of traditional norms and behavioral codes are certainly not the only approach to national development, a country's character and potential are greatly influenced by the way its citizens think and act. Development may require social-structural change and the establishment of appropriate national institutions. In addition, however, development can be neither understood nor pursued unless attention is also paid to problems and processes operating at the individual level of analysis.

One area in which this conclusion emerges with particular clarity, and which is thus useful for illustrative purposes, concerns population growth and family planning. Popular attitudes toward family size and birth control are of critical concern in most developing countries because unchecked population growth has the potential to wipe out development gains. These attitudes and the behavior patterns to which they lead are shaped by government policies and by the aggregate social and economic environment within which people reside. At bottom, however, they are microlevel phenomena, whose character and variation can best be understood through investigations conceived and executed at the individual level. Survey research has thus been widely employed in studies related to fertility, family planning, and population dynamics. Indeed, it may be in this substantive area that survey research has been employed with the greatest frequency and effectiveness in the Arab world.

More and better quality survey research is needed in order to understand the causes and consequences of many critical political, economic, and social attitudes and behavior patterns. In the political arena, for example, it is important to investigate political participation, including levels of political interest and knowledge and citizen concern with civic affairs beyond the local level. Among the many economic orientations relevant for societal development are attitudes toward work and occupational status, norms about achievement and productivity, and receptivity to economic innovation. In the social realm, the course of societal development is shaped by values pertaining to childrearing and to relations between the sexes, by patterns of language use and conceptions of ethnicity, and by attitudinal and behavioral norms associated with religion.

These kinds of individual orientations not only influence the ability of a people to achieve its collective goals, they are also consequences of change at the societal level. In other words, they are significant and deserve study as responses to social change and societal development, as well as developmental stimuli. Individual opinions, beliefs, and patterns of conduct define the evolving political, economic, and social ethos of a society, and they are thus among the most important ways that society's normative order is changing as a result of development processes operating at the system level. In addition, attitudes and behavior patterns at the individual level give meaning to a changing present and an emerging future. They define the lifestyle and culture of a national community. They also express its identity, ideology, and collective spirit.

Although the importance of individual-level orientations for system-level development processes is generally recognized, two legitimate caveats are often expressed by students of development. First, it would be erroneous to assume that change is synonymous with Westernization. Attitudes and behavior patterns derived from a people's own traditions may be no less conducive to societal development than social codes imported from the West or elsewhere. Also, conversely, social change and societal development do not necessarily involve the replacement of indigenous norms with foreign values and patterns of behavior. As both a stimulus and a response to macrolevel change, emerging normative configurations are likely to reflect a balance of traditional and nonindigenous elements, the precise nature and distribution of which can be determined only through empirical investigation.

Second, aspects of underdevelopment derive from the international political and economic order, such that development usually cannot be achieved solely by seeking to inculcate suitable values among a country's people and by creating correspondingly appropriate national institutions. Restructuring international relationships to increase equity and enhance the autonomy of developing countries parallels domestic needs (at both the individual and the system level) as a critical arena for development efforts.

These observations place inquiries about the relationship between individual orientations and societal development into proper perspective. They in no sense reduce the importance of this relationship for developing societies, however: The attitudes and behavior patterns of a country's citizens remain essential ingredients in the process of development. Individual orientations are affected by change at the societal level and constitute a vital link in the interactive chain by which systemic policies and institutions make their influence felt and produce conditions that in turn shape the evolution of the entire society. These orientations are also critical inputs, determining the kinds of issues to which political leaders and development planners devote attention and either facilitating or constraining development initiatives at the systemic level. In short, societal development cannot take place, or be properly understood, without attention to the nature, causes, and consequences of popular attitudinal and behavioral configurations.

No single overarching theory integrates all relevant individual orientations and unites them with other aspects of development in a comprehensive, compelling, and generally accepted analytical model. Nor is such a theory attainable at present. But progress can be and is being made at the level of middle-range theory. The result is a growing understanding of how many political, economic, and social orientations affect and in turn are affected by the character, performance, and evolution of a society's institutions and policies. A partial list of the issue areas that can be profitably pursued at the level of middle-range theory is given below. In each area, both scientific and practical knowledge can be acquired by conducting survey research with a view toward discovering the determinants and consequences of individual level norms and behavior patterns, and thereafter toward establishing the distribution over space and time of generalizable variable relationships.

There has already been a considerable quantity of survey research dealing with a few of these issues in the Arab world. Examples of such surveys and their findings will be presented later in this book. In most instances, the amount of knowledge thus far acquired is much more limited. The purpose of the present discussion is neither to summarize findings nor identify gaps, however; it is to illustrate the kinds of political, economic, and social issues that are amenable to investigation through survey research and from whose importance the significance of this investigatory technique is derived.

The Political Realm

Whatever its form of government, a country cannot be considered politically developed if its people possess little information about or attachment to the national political system, if the bulk of its citizens neither consider themselves united in a political community nor are tied in any meaningful fashion to national institutions. The emergence of appropriate citizen orientations, which tend to covary and constitute a syndrome often referred to as participant citizenship, is thus a major concern in most developing countries. Governments frequently devote substantial resources to programs of socialization and political education, designed to inculcate positive and participatory norms among the populace. Survey research can shed light on the extent and locus of participant citizenship in developing countries, as well as on associated dimensions of mass political culture. It can also provide valuable information about the conditions and experiences that either promote or retard the growth of this important aspect of political development.

Religions, communalism, and ideological diversity are sources of conflict in many developing countries, including a number of Arab states. Divisions based on these factors reflect competing views about how society should be organized and how the boundaries among political communities should be drawn. They also frequently differentiate among groups that compete for political and economic resources, thus giving rise to tensions based on instrumental as well as expressive considerations. The playing out of these conflicts, as well as their evolution and ultimate resolution, will determine the structure and the policies of many political systems in future years. Survey research can provide data with which to analyze the social underpinnings of normative differences based on religion, communal identity, and ideology. It can shed light on the tensions that often flow from competing political identities and values, and it can produce insights that may help to limit the severity of such conflicts.

Students are the most volatile population category in many developing countries. Because their schools are concentrated in the major political centers of the state, students' protests and demonstrations have become a source of grief to numerous governments. Indeed, it has become commonplace for leaders in the Arab world and elsewhere to close universities during periods of political turmoil. However, today's students are tomorrow's leaders. The political values of the young men and women enrolled in a nation's universities and colleges will soon be carried into the highest levels of government. Today's students constitute a new political generation, whose arrival on the political scene a few years hence will have the potential to alter radically the character of the nation's elite. Survey research can investigate the underlying causes of student unrest and trace the link between student discontent and present-day tensions. It can also suggest how today's students may affect the nation in the future, in such important domains as political leadership and ideological change.

The Economic Realm

Established hierarchies of professional status and prevailing attitudes about the kinds of jobs that are desirable not only shape the career decisions of individuals; they also affect the ability of a developing society to meet its human resource needs. Further, popular orientations toward economic life are a major component in the success or failure of development initiatives and economic reforms. The interface between such attitudes and national development is thus an important subject for survey research. Such research can explore the character and origins of economic and work-related values among various population categories. It can also assess the implications of these orientations for aggregate economic performance.

Some oil-producing states of the Middle East and elsewhere have gained parity with the United States and Western Europe in terms of per capita income. Unfortunately, their wealth is based almost entirely upon rents derived from the exportation of raw materials. The industrial (and agricultural) production of many major oil-producing states is minimal. Also, in many cases, a majority of both skilled and unskilled workers must be imported from abroad. This situation raises the possibility that some oil-producing states, once their petroleum resources are exhausted, will be left without a viable productive sector to sustain their economies. In the meantime, rentier economies face myriad problems as they struggle to translate their wealth into development and to lay a foundation for self-sustaining growth. Survey research can be used to examine the frequent reluctance of citizens to become involved in the productive sectors of their nation's economy and to investigate various social and cultural dimensions of rentier economic status. It can also be employed to study the domestic and international labor migrations stimulated by oil-producing economies.

Public administration is often the weakest link in the economic and political system of a developing country. The bureaucracy, for example, must implement development programs; what it cannot execute usually does not get done. Moreover, the bureaucracy is the primary link between political leaders and the general population. If the bureaucracy is ineffective in meeting the needs of the people, the political leadership may lose its claim to legitimacy. Survey research permits examination of public administration in the context of development from two perspectives: the values and behavior patterns of public servants and popular attitudes toward bureaucracies.

The Social Realm

Governments and citizens in the Arab world and elsewhere are concerned with defining and institutionalizing appropriate social and cultural values. The sense of identity provided by these values joins political and economic development as a major national objective. For the society as a whole, these values define a valued historic legacy and a unique present-day personality. They also inspire and give meaning to the quest for a better future. For the individual citizen, these values offer continuity and a sense of psychological security amid rapid changes. Survey research can shed light on these issues by examining social and cultural values, both describing the character and distribution of normative orientations and investigating the ways that changing conditions strengthen some values and modify others.

Overpopulation is increasingly detrimental to social and economic development in the Arab world. In many states, spiraling population growth has undermined otherwise significant economic gains and has reduced the quality of life for many citizens to bare subsistence. Survey research is a major investigatory tool for both scholars and government agencies seeking to examine the extent and determinants of fertility levels and to monitor the effectiveness of family planning programs.

Few aspects of social change in the Arab world have been more dramatic or more controversial than the changing status of women. Many governments seek to foster women's emancipation, arguing that it is necessary not only for reasons of civil rights and social equity but also because inequality between the sexes hinders development in other areas. Such views are supported by a growing women's movement in many countries. The results of such policies are visible in many areas, including the rapidly expanding education of women. On the other hand, considerable opposition remains on the political level, and the changing status of women often produces strains and ambivalence at the level of the individual and the family. Survey research can assess the attitudes of women toward their changing circumstances and can investigate the nature and determinants of men's attitudes toward the prospect of women's emancipation. Surveys can also be used to explore some of the problems women encounter as they attempt to forge new roles for themselves in male-dominated societies.

Problems of Survey Research in Arab Society

The issues identified are familiar to students of development, and all have been the subject of survey research and other investigations in the Arab world and elsewhere. Thus the extent of present-day ignorance about the relationship between individual orientations and societal development should not be overstated. Nevertheless, information about the kinds of issues discussed previously remains sparse, particularly with respect to the Arab world, an area that is obviously important in its own right and from which may be derived insights of even broader applicability. Discrete studies have made important contributions in a number of fields. Also, several recent anthologies synthesize existing knowledge about attitudes and behavior in one domain or another. For example, *Political Behavior in the Arab States,* edited by Tawfic Farah, brings together a number of political studies. Similarly, *Population Factors in Development Planning in the Middle East,* edited by Frederick Shorter and Huda Zurayk, is a collection of contributions dealing with such areas as population growth, fertility, and women's economic participation.[3] On the whole, however, the kind of information about the Arab world that can be provided by survey research remains in short supply.

Thus Arab society is being inadequately studied in important respects. The incorporation of information about Arab society into broader, more integrative and cross-cultural inquiries is also seriously hampered. In the political realm, for example, a major investigation of the state of research on the Arab world in 1976 concluded that very few surveys of political attitudes and behavior patterns had been conducted. The author of the report, a senior scholar, complained that "the critical mass of research [in the field of political behavior] has been done outside the Middle East." "Data generation and analysis in the region remain to be done," he concluded, adding that "it is time to begin some systematic study in this area."[4] More recent writers have made the same point. For example, one distinguished scholar observed in 1983 that the "missing dimensions" in the study of Arab political life are those associated with political psychology and political sociology, "particularly as represented in survey research." Although he applauded a few recent initiatives, including survey research by three of the authors of the present book, his overall assessment was that "much more is needed in order to bring a healthier perspective to our understanding of Arab politics and so that we may see it less as a reflection of formal cultural norms or contemporary world ideological currents and more as [the behavior] of ordinary individuals."[5]

It is important to identify the principal obstacles to survey research and the production of knowledge about individual orientations responsible for this situation. Several sets of interrelated problems and needs are particularly relevant and a brief introduction to each is provided in the following sections. Most of these problems and needs have general significance; though they involve obstacles to the production and utilization of survey data that are particularly pronounced in Arab society, they also limit the systematic and scientific study of individual attitudes and behavior in many other developing societies.

Data Resources

More and better quality survey research is needed in the Arab world. Nevertheless, survey research is by no means unknown, and valuable expertise and data resources are already very much in existence. One problem is the lack of systematic factual information about the locus and extent of such resources: No directories or publications identify the individuals and institutions regularly engaged in such research. There is also only limited and scattered information about existing data sets and about the degree to which topics amenable to study by survey research have in fact been investigated. An inventory of survey research personnel and activities in the Arab world is thus required.

A related problem is limited access to existing survey data sets from the Arab world. Although there are widely used data archives in the United States and Europe and in a few other areas, no comparable facilities exist in the Arab world. Nor is there more than a small and unrepresentative sample of data sets involving Arabs in archives outside the Middle East. As the Inter-University Consortium for Political and Social Research reported to the authors of this book, for example, "the need for these data resources is quite obvious . . . [but] to date we have been unsuccessful in our attempts to acquire survey data from the Arab world." There are available data sets based on survey research in the Arab world, but these tend to be held by individuals and are cumbersome and difficult to acquire. As a result, the kind of analysis and reanalysis that promotes full utilization of existing data resources is virtually unknown as far as research on Arab society is concerned.

Methodological and Contextual Considerations

Methodological problems focus attention more specifically on the conduct of survey research, on obstacles both to the collection and analysis of survey data pertaining to Arab society and also to the maintenance of scientific rigor in the execution of these operations. Among such problems are (1) obstacles to the construction of appropriate representative and analytical samples; (2) considerations of validity, reliability, and standardization in measurement, and of measurement equivalence in comparative studies; and (3) issues relating to the development and administration of survey instruments, including matters of language, respondent cooperation, response set, and interview bias.

Although these concerns are all standard in survey research, they are accentuated in Arab society because much of the work is new and because it lacks the cumulative character of survey research in the United States and Europe. A related contributing factor is that many survey research procedures routinely employed in the West cannot be applied in the Arab world without modification. It is necessary, in the latter connection, to discover the conditions under which these procedures can be used elsewhere with confidence; to develop original and innovative approaches to methodological problem-solving, in order to permit meaningful survey research when the aforementioned conditions are not fulfilled; and, finally, to chart the locus of applicability of any innovations or adapations that are developed, thereby advancing further the quest for methodological cumulativeness both within and across societies.

Contextual, rather than methodological, problems also impinge upon the conduct and use of survey research. These include opposition by those who regard survey research as an investigatory procedure that cannot be detached from its Western origins and who thus believe it inevitably produces inaccurate information; resistance based on political or special-interest considerations, from governments and others who fear that surveys will provide information detrimental to their interests; and structural limitations relating to high costs, excessive complexity, the absence of suitable data processing facilities, and so forth. These and other contextual problems discourage the conduct of survey research and limit utilization of existing data. An understanding of the nature and consequences of such problems is essential to an assessment of the state of survey research in Arab society. Knowledge about these problems and about approaches to dealing with them will also enhance the quality and utility of future surveys.

Epistemology and Issues of Paradigm

Inadequate information is available about the degree to which social science theories and methods developed in the West are applicable in Arab society. On one hand, concepts routinely investigated in surveys conducted in the United States and Europe may take on different meanings in the Arab world. On the other, the epistemological and methodological assumptions on which survey research is based may in some cases be inapplicable in the Arab world. Empirical research is necessary to chart the parameters of cross-cultural equivalence in these areas. In areas in which concepts and methods cannot be transferred, it is also necessary to develop and empirically validate alternative canons of research. Although some Arab scholars concerned with these problems have called for the creation of an indigenous social science, to be used in tandem with universal aspects of the scientific method, there has been little progress toward the construction of new analytical frameworks and research methodologies. Nor even has agreement been reached on the scope of this task.

Ethical Considerations

Attention should be paid to ethical considerations in all social research. Areas of concern include the impact on the research of the investigator's values and the consequences of the research for those who are studied. As far as survey research in the Arab world is concerned, these concerns are sometimes made more problematic by the fact that much research is carried out by foreign scholars and institutions. Moreover, even Arab social scientists are often remote from the populations they study. Ethical questions may be magnified if respondents are not sufficiently familiar with survey research to give informed consent to those who collect data about them or if they are unable to participate in determining how the data collected will and will not be used. Social scientists must struggle to deal responsibly with these and similar questions if survey research is to achieve its potential and if abuses are to be kept to a minimum.

Analytical Integration and Cumulativeness

The adequacy of research findings is limited by the paucity of replication, comparative research, and integrated studies based on multiple data sets. These latter types of research increase the accuracy, completeness, sophistication and generalizability of information produced by social research. To achieve these goals one can proceed in at least three different ways. First, an investigator can replicate one or several earlier surveys. If possible, data from the initial surveys should be obtained as well, so that an integrated data file may be constructed for analytical purposes. Second, programs of comparative survey research can be designed, based on the predetermined construction of intersocietal and/or longitudinal data files. A third approach involves secondary analysis based on a careful merging of existing and separate data sets. In each case, the research design permits inclusion in the analysis of system-level attributes that vary over space and time, thereby contributing to the production of social science knowledge possessing greater explanatory power and broader applicability. Work of this type is all too rare, even in societies where survey research is common; and in the Arab world and most other developing areas, replications and integrated studies based on the construction of compound data files are in even shorter supply. This constitutes an important limit on the quality of scientific and practical knowledge about individual orientations in the context of development.

The Bellagio Conference

The generosity of the Ford Foundation and the Rockefeller Foundation made it possible to convene an international conference devoted to the Evaluation and Application of Survey Research in the Arab world. The six-day conference was held in June 1983 at the Rockefeller Foundation Study and Conference Center in Bellagio, Italy. The purpose of the gathering was to assess the utility and limits of survey research as a tool for the study of Arab society. Participants sought to take stock of the contribution that survey research has already made to the study of the Arab world and to assess the contribution that it can make in the future. They also sought to identify possible solutions to problems associated with the collection and analysis of survey data in Arab countries. The Bellagio meeting was attended by twenty-four senior scholars, almost all of whom had had extensive experience in the conduct of survey research in the Arab world and elsewhere. A substantial number of the participants had had experience in research administration as well. The scholars assembled at Bellagio came from seven Arab countries and the United States; many of those from the United States were of Arab origin. These scholars were drawn from seven academic disciplines: anthropology, business administration, demography, economics, political science, psychology, and sociology. The names and institutional affiliations of the seventeen men and seven women who took part in the Bellagio conference are given in Appendix A.

Some of the sessions of Bellagio were devoted to substantive issues, at which one or two scholars reported on survey work they had carried out in connection with a particular research topic. Presentations of this sort were made at a session on political issues, at another on economic issues, and at a third session dealing with social issues. Following each presentation and related comments, other participants joined in an extended discussion and made contributions based on their own research experiences. The goal of these sessions was not to take inventory of research findings in a given substantive area but to shed light on the ways that surveys have been used effectively to investigate various topics, to consider how they might be used with even greater success in the future, and to identify any important limitations associated with their application. Further, the sessions provided an opportunity for participants to exchange views about priorities for future research in particular substantive areas and to explore the possibility of collaborative research endeavors.

Methodological issues were also discussed in general and with special reference to the Arab world. Major problems associated with conduct of survey research in Arab society were identified, and participants were invited to think about possible solutions. Methodological issues frequently emerged during the sessions devoted to substantive topics. In addition, however, there were separate round-table sessions for focused consideration of measurement, sampling, and survey administration issues. At these sessions, participating scholars identified some of the special problems they had encountered in the course of their own research. They also presented information on the research strategies they had developed to deal with these problems and offered an assessment of the degree to which their strategies had been successful. Finally, the scholars assembled at Bellagio sought to distill from their collective experiences some ideas about possible methodological innovations, suggesting approaches that might be tried in future survey research and thereafter evaluated and refined.

Another category of issues discussed at length concerned the kinds of contextual problems enumerated in the preceding section. For example, much attention was given to obstacles to survey research created by governments concerned about political opposition and hesitant to permit the unrestricted expression of opinion. Similar problems were discussed in relation to opposition from local officials, who often feared that they might somehow be embarrassed by the results of a survey. Even more attention was paid to the difficulty of dealing with respondents who are unfamiliar with surveys or unclear as to their purpose. Finally, there was much discussion of the problems that result from resource limitations, from inadequate facilities, and from a lack of institutional support for practitioners of survey research in the Arab world. Some of this discussion took place at a concluding roundtable session devoted to the topic of cumulativeness, at which the importance of establishing communications networks and research support structures was stressed. Appropriate institutional structures can unify research endeavors, promote innovation in many areas, lobby on behalf of a scholarly community, and mobilize social scientists so that they may more fully integrate their individual research efforts.

No less important were normative issues and problems, which constituted a final topic discussed by the social scientists meeting at Bellagio. Under this heading fell concerns of ethics, relevance, and epistemology. Such concerns surfaced repeatedly in all of the panels, and they usually provoked lively discussions. In addition, however, normative questions were also the subject of focused discussions at three round-table sessions. Among the ethical considerations that received attention were the establishment of research priorities, related questions concerning the intended and actual beneficiaries of survey research, the need to protect subjects from exploitation by researchers, the delineation of sensitive or inappropriate topics, and guidelines for sharing available survey data. Among the issues discussed under the heading of relevance were the appropriate balance of theoretical and applied research, the relationship between survey research and other approaches to social inquiry, and the audience(s) to which research findings should be directed.

Epistemological considerations, often described as issues of paradigm, focused both on the degree to which assumptions underlying survey research are applicable in the Arab world and on the possibility of using surveys to investigate concepts derived from the Arab experience rather those drawn from studies conducted elsewhere. One question about the assumptions of survey research, for example, concerned the possibility of focusing on units of analysis other than the individual. With respect to the matter of appropriate concepts, there were animated discussions about whether surveys in the Arab world have properly treated concepts like social status, modernization, and religious militancy.

Few of these issues were treated in isolation from one another. Most of the presentations and discussions dealt with a wide range of issues, often focusing on patterns of interaction among a battery of questions and problems. Further, although a number of problem-solving strategies were suggested, attention was devoted principally to the articulation of relevant issues and to the related concern of raising the consciousness and sensitivity of those who conduct survey research in the Arab world. Participants generally agreed that the most important contributions of the conference lay in forcing survey researchers to become more aware of the nature, assumptions, and consequences of their scholarly activities and in providing an opportunity for the experienced social scientists brought together at Bellagio to exchange insights and stimulate one another's thinking.

The conference and the record of its deliberations contained in this book are thus intended as a stimulus to more and better quality survey research in the future. Such work should not only become more theoretically compelling and methodologically rigorous; it should also increase in relevance and stand out by virtue of its respect for high ethical standards and its attention to the specificity of Arab society. The scholars assembled at Bellagio did not spell out in detail how progress toward achieving these goals should be made. Indeed, though they did offer practical suggestions for dealing with some immediate problems and long-term needs, they disagreed among themselves on many key points. They were united, however, by a belief that the community of scholars of which they are a part must look more closely and self-consciously at the investigatory procedures it employs and must strive to address the kinds of issues previously summarized when designing and executing future survey projects. If practitioners of survey research in the Arab world respond to this stimulus, both in their individual research endeavors and as a community of concerned and committed social scientists, their efforts will contribute in an incremental fashion to improving the quality of their collective enterprise. In this manner, problems can be solved and progress made.

The Bellagio conference did not attempt to fashion a precise blueprint for solving problems associated with the conduct of survey research in the Arab world. Participants recognized that such a blueprint cannot be established by intellectual fiat and then imposed on a scholarly community. The growth and improvement of social research, they concluded, must be built from below. New canons and practices must emerge incrementally, in response to the cumulative efforts of social scientists who are not content to apply uncritically the research procedures they have inherited but who instead will experiment, innovate, and otherwise struggle to deal with the special problems confronting them. Only in response to such a cumulative commitment and effort, sustained over the long term, can progress be expected. The goal of the Bellagio conference was not to provide definitive answers to substantive, methodological, contextual, and normative questions; it was rather to raise questions, to heighten awareness, and, above all, to motivate individuals to make the kind of effort and commitment that are necessary if the scientific and practical contributions of survey research are to be realized more fully in the future.

This Book

The present book seeks both to communicate some of the information presented at Bellagio and to convey the general spirit of the discussions in order to provide the kind of stimulus described. In Part One, a number of the presentations made at Bellagio are reproduced. In some cases, part or all of a working paper prepared for the conference is presented; in others, oral remarks have been transcribed. Finally, several of the papers in Part One were prepared after the conference, by participants who sought to make an additional contribution.

Although none of the chapters in Part One deals with all the issues discussed at the conference, all but one or two consider a variety of topics and problems, and it is thus impossible to classify them in terms of methodological preoccupations, epistemology, or any other single category of concerns. It is thus probably best to regard Part One as a partially integrated battery of contributions that, taken as a whole, illustrates and invites further thought about all the issues discussed at Bellagio.

The contribution by Saad Eddin Ibrahim discusses the modern origins of social research in the Arab world and then provides an overview of the topics that have been most frequently studied and the location of major research centers. Thereafter, Ibrahim focuses on the interplay of epistemology and methodology, asking whether the assumptions underlying survey research are valid in the Arab world and inquiring about the possibility of fashioning a social science that is better suited to Arab society.

M. O. El Sammani and Naiem Sherbiny, both economists, report on various aspects of major survey research projects that they helped direct. Sammani's chapter focuses on the role of surveys in rural development studies and describes a project in the southern Sudan. He discusses many of the practical problems encountered in administration of the project. He also deals in detail with relations between the research team and the local community, raising important issues pertaining to ethics and relevance. Sherbiny's contribution deals with innovations in the area of sampling and measurement made during a labor survey conducted by the World Bank in Saudi Arabia. In addition to describing how problems were dealt with and how proposed solutions were evaluated, the chapter illustrates a general approach to recognizing and dealing with many kinds of obstacles.

A general approach to problem-solving is also illustrated by Huda Zurayk, in a chapter that deals with questions of measurement. Zurayk devotes attention to conceptual as well as the methodological aspects of measurement, including an uncritical borrowing of conceptual and operational definitions from surveys done in the West. A number of her arguments are illustrated with examples based on research about women's social and economic behavior.

Michael Suleiman describes the evolution of a sequential and multisociety study of political socialization among Arab school children. Suleiman explains how research that began in Egypt evolved as it progressed to Sudan, Morocco, and Tunisia. In addition to discussing the expanding scope and complexity of the project, Suleiman also describes how his research was affected by the political circumstances in each country. He discusses his successes and failures in obtaining official permission for his study and in securing local cooperation in carrying out the project.

Iliya Harik's contribution concludes Part One. It discusses some of the political and cultural characteristics of the present-day Arab world that present obstacles for those seeking to conduct survey research. In addition to limited resources and inadequate institutional support, Harik suggests that the absence of democracy in most Arab countries constitutes an important obstacle, not only to survey research but to social inquiry in general. Harik also discusses the role played by foreign scholars and institutions in studying Arab society, reviewing and assessing some Arab criticisms of investigations conducted or sponsored by foreigners. Finally, he considers the arguments of those who believe that social scientific research, including survey research, leads to distorted conclusions when applied to Arab culture. His general conclusion is that the intellectual foundations of the scientific method transcend cultural boundaries, but applications may not be successful unless accompanied by sensitivity to local norms and values.

These chapters, illustrated by examples from projects in many countries and spanning a large number of academic disciplines, reflect the diversity of the contributions made at Bellagio. Taken together, they convey something of the tone as well as the content of the conference and provide a point of departure for those scholars who in the future will conduct survey research in the Arab world. Although not all the topics examined at Bellagio are discussed in these papers, Part One will have achieved its purpose if researchers are motivated to seek greater sensitivity to the surroundings in which they conduct their investigations and to make themselves more aware of the normative assumptions and practical consequences associated with their work. To this can only be added the hope that they will also be alert to the ethical implications of social research and that they will be stimulated to experiment and innovate in order to improve the quality and relevance of future survey research in Arab society.

The chapters in Part Two are more integrative, synthetic, and self-consciously prescriptive. They were written by four of the individuals who organized and convened the Bellagio conference. Farah, Ibrahim, Palmer, and Tessler were part of a six-member team of Arab and American scholars who conceived the idea for a conference on the evaluation and application of survey research in the Arab world and who subsequently planned the project and administered the grants that made it possible. Following the conference, each undertook to prepare a general contribution dealing with an interrelated set of issues raised at Bellagio. These chapters were given thematic unity, not only in that issues selected for analysis were themselves interrelated but also though their examination in relation to a specific problem area. Finally, beyond seeking to provide this kind of focus and coherence, each author was encouraged to draw widely on previous research and to utilize his or her intellectual creativity to clarify needs and to point the way toward plausible solutions. Thus, in one focused area bearing on survey research, each author was charged with pulling together some of the major concerns that had surfaced during a week of wide-ranging discussions and with laying a foundation for efforts to deal with relevant issues more satisfactorily in the future.

The chapter by Barbara Ibrahim is organized around the general theme of relevance, which was the focus of one of the round-table sessions at Bellagio. Ibrahim's chapter suggests some of the topics that may be profitably examined through survey research, as was done earlier in this Introduction. This dimension of relevance is not her principal concern, however; she seeks rather to raise broad questions that should guide social scientists seeking to decide whether survey research is the most appropriate technique to use when investigating a particular topic. This approach is important because investigators sometimes decide to conduct a survey without an adequate appreciation of the strengths and weaknesses of the technique they have chosen and without having thought seriously about whether such an approach to data collection is the most appropriate for the research problem at hand. Ibrahim raises three broad questions under the general heading of relevance: Who is the intended audience for the study and how will the results be used? What is the scope and depth of information needed to address the research problem? What is the appropriate sampling unit to target? In discussing these questions, the author devotes attention to practical problems, methodology, ethical considerations, and issues of paradigm.

Monte Palmer deals with a series of conceptual and methodological issues in relation to measurement and the construction of survey instruments for use in the Arab world. Among the many problems he seeks to clarify are abstract conceptual considerations bearing on epistemology and cross-cultural equivalence and operational concerns such as scale construction and questionnaire length. Taken together, the points he discusses offer valuable guidance for those concerned with designing and evaluating survey instruments, especially those who seek to measure variables possessing high levels of conceptual abstraction. For scholars who determine that survey research is relevant to their data collection and analysis needs, Palmer's chapter contains many specific recommendations. He illustrates most of his points with examples from actual surveys conducted in the Arab world. Therefore, the chapter will also be useful to readers wishing more information about how survey research can be and has been used to study Arab society.

Tawfic Farah's chapter on selecting a sample and interacting with respondents seeks to accomplish two purposes. On the one hand, it summarizes basic information on sample construction and offers suggestions and examples concerning the application of sampling techniques to Arab society. On the other, Farah focuses on two problems of survey administration of special concern in the Arab world. The first concerns gaining the trust and confidence of persons to be sampled, a topic much discussed at Bellagio and treated by several other contributors to this book. An associated consideration is the need for proper understanding of the interview situation by persons unfamiliar with opinion sampling. Discussion of these issues raises a number of methodological questions, among them matters of reliability, response set, and interview bias. It also raises important issues of ethics and epistemology. Farah's second concern is the delineation of appropriate units of analysis. Reflecting further on a topic treated by Barbara Ibrahim, Farah considers the possibility that in some cases it may be more appropriate to sample small groups than individuals.

Mark Tessler's first chapter on scientific cumulativeness summarizes briefly the intellectual and practical importance of integrating findings from diverse programs of research in order to advance the accuracy, completeness, and generalizability of social science knowledge. In this way, the quality of explanations and guides to action derived from systematic social research can steadily improve. Thereafter, Tessler deals with obstacles to scientific cumulativeness in three areas. First, it is necessary to collect and make available descriptive information about the research that has already been done in the Arab world, to bring together the results of previous work and to identify gaps and set priorities for future research. Second, replications, complementary studies, and coordinated intersocietal research are essential because of their direct contribution to scientific cumulativeness and analytical integration. Tessler gives examples of a few areas in which such programs of research have taken place. Third, researchers need to develop institutionalized data archives and to encourage secondary data analysis and fuller exploitation of existing survey data resources. In each of these areas, Tessler offers strategies for meeting practical needs and for dealing with related normative considerations. He emhasizes both the role that can be played by major research institutions and the action that can be taken by individual researchers working alone or in small groups.

Tessler's second chapter provides an introduction to the scientific method as it applies to the conduct of social research in the Arab world. It also discusses those aspects of the scientific method from which derive considerations of cumulativeness. The chapter is intended, in part, for those who have had some practical experience with survey research but have not had an opportunity to master the intellectual and conceptual foundations of systematic social inquiry. Many at Bellagio felt that it was not unusual to find such individuals involved in survey work in the Arab world and elsewhere. The chapter is also addressed to those familar with scientific social research in general but not with its application in the Arab world. Since most points are illustrated with examples from surveys conducted in various Arab countries, the chapter, like several other contributions, provides a substantive introduction to the ways that survey research has been employed in Arab society. Attention is paid to the distinction and interrelationship between scientific and nonscientific knowledge, to the quest for generalizable research findings, and to the role of both descriptive and explanatory studies. Attention is also paid to both theoretical and applied research objectives.

The Audience

This book is addressed to a number of audiences, both Arab and Western. Intended as a stimulus and guide to more relevant and better quality survey research, it is aimed first at practitioners of survey research in Arab society. By calling attention to the value of the information that surveys can provide and by offering ideas about how obstacles to such research can be identified and overcome, the book attempts to permit a wider audience of concerned social scientists to share the information and enthusiasm generated by the Bellagio conference. As stated earlier, definitive solutions to existing problems are not possible. Specific techniques and guidelines are suggested at many points throughout this volume. Nevertheless, it is impossible to anticipate all major needs, to say nothing of proposing useful solutions in all or most research settings. Thus, the present book seeks to encourage an awareness and a sensitivity that will assist individual scholars in making informed decisions about the application and limits of survey research in the Arab world, and in this connection it identifies general approaches and strategies for improving the quality and relevance of surveys.

Many of the intellectual and practical issues examined in this book are relevant to the conduct of survey research in other parts of the world, especially in developing areas where surveys are not yet widely used and where some of the same methodological, ethical, and epistemological challenges are faced. Thus the book may also be a source of ideas and information for social scientists and other practitioners of survey research in Africa, Asia, Latin America, and elsewhere. In these areas, too, there is a scarcity of the kind of information about individual attitudes and behavior patterns that survey research can provide. Present as well are contextual problems and difficulties associated with the transfer from one culture to another of assumptions, concepts, and methodological procedures.

Some of the concerns and insights that emerged at Bellagio are of particular relevance to foreign scholars wishing to conduct surveys in the Arab world. As many of the chapters make clear, it is not enough for a researcher to understand the essentials of social science research in general and of survey research in particular. Many specific pitfalls and problems would be unfamiliar to a U.S. or European scholar without considerable experience in the Arab world. An additional set of problems is posed by the presence of a foreign researcher, including a number of ethical issues. Again, however, an investigator unfamiliar with the Arab world might not even be aware of these concerns. Solid training in the theory and method of social science research is thus a necessary but not a sufficient condition for conducting research in an unfamiliar cultural and political environment. The present book is not offered as a substitute for familiarity with Arab society, of course. On the contrary, it points up clearly the critical importance of substantial cross-cultural experience and offers foreign scholars both general guidance and specific suggestions to assist them in using to advantage their knowledge about the society in which they are conducting survey research.

The distinction between foreign and indigenous scholars is not always clear cut. For example, some of the contributors to this book are permanent and long-time residents of the United States who are of Arab origin; thus they possess some of the advantages of an indigenous scholar but also face some of the problems of a foreign researcher. A similar instance arises for social scientists from one Arab environment working in another Arab environment, a situation that can occur either when an Arab scholar from one country carries out research in another or when an investigator works in an unfamiliar part of his or her own country. Sammani's account of his research in southern Sudan is an excellent example because his research team was certainly "foreign" in the eyes of the local population. Other examples were given at Bellagio, and there are also several published accounts of Arab social scientists who have been in this position.[6] At least some of the issues associated with research conducted by foreigners are also present when persons of one religion, gender, or social class conduct research about persons of another religion, gender, or social class.

The book is intended not only for indigenous and foreign social scientists who conduct survey research in the Arab world; it deals with issues important to those whose concern with survey research is less direct and it will thus be useful to consumers as well as practitioners of such research. Leaders and development planners must understand the scientific and practical importance of collecting and analyzing survey data. They must also understand the limits of such research and be able to judge the relevance and quality of any available survey data. An ability to make such determinations is also critical for other consumers of survey data, including scholars, journalists, and political observers. The appropriateness and utility of survey data must be evaluated not only in terms of standard assessments of internal and external validity but also with reference to the kinds of specialized methodological, normative, and practical considerations that impinge on the conduct of survey research in the Arab world.

Many of the problems discussed in this book will have special significance for men and women involved in research administration, including those who participate in running universities, foundations, institutes, and other agencies charged with sponsoring or coordinating research programs. Such individuals are in a position to encourage the conduct of needed survey research. They can also play a critical role in improving the quality of future surveys and in mobilizing the resources and support necessary to deal with contextual problems. Finally, such institutions can take the lead in fashioning a collective response to the kinds of ethical and epistemological problems that are difficult for individual social scientists to address on their own. They can help to establish standards of conduct, and they can provide structures for survey researchers to come together and participate in identifying and solving various kinds of problems. Thus, the book is self-consciously addressed to those who sponsor and support the conduct of survey research in the Arab world and who have an important institutional contribution to make in improving the quantity and quality of such research.

Although concerned with the evaluation and application of survey research, many of the issues discussed in this book are relevant to other kinds of social inquiry. Students, practitioners, and administrators of social science research in general, as well as those concerned with survey research in particular, thus constitute another audience to which these chapters are directed. Although some methodological and substantive aspects of survey research may not be of more general interest, most of the concerns discussed are relevant for other forms of social investigation. This is the case for issues of epistemology and paradigm that bear on the application in one culture of concepts and modes of inquiry developed in another; it is also very much the case with ethical considerations, including both the importance of dealing responsibly and honestly with communities studied and considerations associated with the use and dissemination of information collected. Finally, many of the practical and contextual concerns discussed in relation to survey research are of general relevance. These include problems posed by a political environment that is at least partly closed and in which familiarity with social research and its purposes may be limited.

Finally, some chapters of this book are addressed to social science students, especially those in the Arab world. Following the Bellagio conference, a number of Arab and Western social scientists who teach at Arab universities urged that the book be written with a view toward meeting some of the needs of their students. They pointed out that materials for teaching about the theory and practice of research in the Arab world are in short supply and that Western textbooks on survey research and other kinds of social inquiry are not adequate for their pedagogic needs. Also, faculty members from social science departments at the American University in Cairo (AUC) met with two of the authors and offered suggestions about topics, language, examples, and so forth.[7] The need for a work that will be useful to students preparing to conduct research in the Arab world has also been expressed by some U.S. professors. Though basic works about the logic of inquiry are readily available, guidance on how to apply intellectual principles and methodological procedures in a foreign setting is much more limited.

The suggestions offered by faculty members at AUC and elsewhere have been followed to the extent possible. In particular, sections have been added to several of the chapters in Part Two to meet student-related needs. Students wishing to prepare themselves to conduct survey research in the Arab world should not rely entirely on the present book. Although some theoretical and methodological material has been added to provide a more comprehensive introduction to systematic social research, most of the information found in basic texts on survey research has not been repeated. Nevertheless, the authors have attempted to provide a work that Arab university students may profitably read in conjunction with a basic text. They have also sought to prepare a book that will be useful to U.S. and European students being trained to carry out research in the Arab Middle East. Even if such students will not be conducting surveys, they must be instructed in the general problems of transferring research methodologies from one culture or another, and they must acquire a sensitivity to some of the ethical, epistemological, and contextual problems discussed at Bellagio.

Notes

1. A useful introduction is provided by Herbert F. Weisberg and Bruce D. Bowen, *An Introduction to Survey Research and Data Analysis* (San Francisco: Freeman, 1977). Among the many other recommended works are Charles Backstrom and Gerald Hursh, *Survey Research* (Evanston, Ill.: Northwestern University Press, 1963); Leslie Kish, *Survey Sampling* (New York: Wiley, 1965); C. A. Moser and Graham Kalton, *Survey Methods in Social Investigation* (New York: Basic Books, 1972); Earl Babbie, *Survey Research Methods* (Belmont, Calif.: Wadsworth, 1973); and Donald Warwick and Charles Lininger, *The Sample Survey: Theory and Practice* (New York: McGraw-Hill, 1975). A collection that shares some of the special concerns of the present book is William O'Barr, David Spain, and Mark Tessler, eds., *Survey Research in Africa: Its Applications and Limits* (Evanston, Ill.: Northwestern University Press, 1973).

2. Speeches by Habib Bourguiba in 1961 and 1963, quoted and discussed in Mark Tessler, William O'Barr, and David Spain, *Tradition and Identity in Changing Africa* (New York: Harper & Row, 1973), p. 221. This book also presents a general discussion of the relationship between individual orientations and societal development.

3. Tawfic Farah, ed. *Political Behavior in the Arab States* (Boulder, Colo.: Westview Press, 1983), and Frederick C. Shorter and Huda Zurayk, eds., *Population*

Factors in Development Planning in the Middle East (New York and Cairo: Population Council, 1985).

4. I. Wm. Zartman, "Political Science," in Leonard Binder, ed., *The Study of the Middle East: Research and Scholarship in the Humanities and Social Sciences* (New York: Wiley, 1976), p. 305; see also pp. 272–273. Similar conclusions are drawn in the Binder book's chapter on sociology by Georges Sabbagh; see, for example, pp. 546–553.

5. Malcolm Kerr, "Foreword," in Farah, *Political Behavior.* For an extended discussion of this point, see Gabriel Ben Dor, "Political Culture Approach to Middle East Politics," *International Journal of Middle East Studies* 8 (January 1977): 43–63.

6. See, for example, Jean Duvignaud, *Change at Shebika: Report from a North Africa Village* (New York: Pantheon, 1970). Duvignaud reports on the experiences of social science students from Tunis who carried out research in a remote oasis in southern Tunisia.

7. The authors are currently seeking to arrange for an Arabic-language edition of this book.

PART ONE

The Bellagio Conference

1

The Agony and the Ecstasy
of Social Research
in the Arab World

Saad Eddin Ibrahim

We do not often talk about the ecstasy of doing research, about why it is exciting. As a practitioner of social research, I take great pleasure in discovering that some of the things happening in our society are qualitatively and quantitatively different than those occurring elsewhere in the Third World and in the rest of the world. Great transformations have taken place during my lifetime and during the time that I have been an active researcher. These changes are political, economic, demographic, and social; they occur in education, class, and social stratification throughout the region. However, these transformations do not come about without a heavy price or without pain. There have been birthpangs, delivery, and false pregnancies. Changes have involved bloodshed, violence, and misery. Those residing in the region cannot escape being afflicted by some of these pains, not only as affected citizens and as human beings but also as social scientists who cannot always work the way they would like, the way they know social research should be done. Between the ecstasy and the agony, we must take stock of what has been accomplished, of what has not been accomplished, and of where we go from here.

In its crudest form, social research is not new to the Arab world. There is a tradition dating from Pharaonic times of conducting surveys of sorts, of stock-taking, and of crude data gathering for administrative purposes. Such exercises were conducted whenever a great empire-builder was in the area until the nineteenth century. But really systematic social research only began when French scholars in the Napoleonic expedition gathered data in accordance with an implicit paradigm. Their work was later published in the multivolume book, *Description of Egypt*. This book was followed by other works in the nineteenth century. French scholars did much work in North Africa, and the British and other Europeans did similar work in Egypt, the Sudan, and the Arab East. Some of this work, in retrospect, was conducted in preparation for colonialism; it heralded the ingress of foreign powers into the Arab world. Although these scholars may not have been aware that what they were doing would later be helpful to the colonialists, their writings were used by the colonial powers.

When the actual military penetration of the Arab world took place, there was a second wave of scholarly interest in Arab society, this time intentional and deliberate. This wave lasted from the late nineteenth century until World War II. During the interwar period, traditional studies were carried out by colonial powers and indigenous social science research began. Works in the latter category were exemplified by those of scholars at the American University of Beirut, such as *Social Relations in the Middle East* by Stewart Dodd and his students. Even though directed by a foreigner, this study was conducted by native students and scholars in Syria, Lebanon, and Palestine. If read today, the study looks very rudimentary and unsophisticated, but in its time it represented a kind of breakthrough. The tradition of "joint venture" research continued and was exemplified in the 1950s by the works of Morroe Berger (*Bureaucracy in Modern Egypt* and *The Arab World Today*) and Daniel Lerner (*The Passing of Traditional Society*). An avalanche of this kind of joint research continued through the 1950s and then was interrupted in the 1960s by political upheavals and the influence of the Arab national movement. Then for ten to fifteen years foreign participation in research was minimal while national involvement in the research enterprise grew. By the end of the 1960s, several research centers had been established in the Arab world, along with universities that had social science departments and supported social research.

Current Social Research Efforts

The current effort in social research can be summarized by noting who is doing research and what kind of research is being done.

- Lebanon was one of the first countries where modern social research was conducted. The American University of Beirut (AUB) was the focal point for this kind of research; to a lesser extent, St. Joseph University was an important center as well. More recently, several private institutes have been established, some of which are doing research for commercial and consulting purposes. Nevertheless, these institutes produce usable social science data.

- In Tunisia, CERES (Centre d'Etudes et de Recherches Economiques et Sociales) was set up in the early 1960s and has had a good program of research. Even though it has had its ups and downs, it remains one of the bulwarks of social research in the Arab world.

- In Iraq, there is the National Center for Criminological Research and a Center for Gulf Studies.

- In Jordan, there is the Royal Scientific Society and the Jordan Center for Studies and Information.

- The Palestine Liberation Organization has set up its own centers, the Planning Center and the Palestine Research Center. These centers carry out some survey research, with varying degrees of conformity to the canons of social research.

- Two key centers in Egypt have carried out important and extensive research programs since the late 1950s. The national governmental center—the Center for Sociological and Criminological Research—was established in 1956–1957 and since that time has been the leading institution for conducting survey research. Some of its studies have been published, but most of its work has not been well disseminated. Even the published work frequently has not found its way to everyone in the Arab world or to scholars elsewhere. The second important center is private—the Social Research Center at the American University in Cairo. Set up in 1953, it has carried out longitudinal research, especially on Nubian settlement. Recently, it has devoted a great part of its effort and energy to demographic, population, and family planning research.

- In Kuwait, there is the Center for Gulf Studies.

In addition to these institutions, some pan-Arab centers conduct surveys and carry out other social research. Many of these are part of the specialized agencies of the League of Arab States. Some are part of the UN agencies located in the Arab world, such as the International Labor Organization, UN Educational, Scientific and Cultural Organization, UN Development Programme, and the World Bank. Private Arab organizations are also doing pan-Arab research; the most notable of these is the Center for Arab Unity Studies in Beirut.

At the present time, there also are a number of foreign research organizations, which represent the third wave of foreigners doing research in the Arab world. After the lull of the late 1950s and the 1960s, foreign researchers began to return in the 1970s, particularly in key countries like Egypt, the Sudan, Iraq, and Syria. Although many of these are not extensively engaged in survey research, some of their work includes the gathering and analysis of quantitative social science data. In the 1970s, the open door policy of Egypt meant an open door for social research, which has been carried out not only by scholars but also by consulting firms and funding agencies and in the form of social impact studies associated with U.S. and European development aid. There has been a great increase in the number of foreign scholars, particularly doctoral and postdoctoral students. Foreign centers have also located in the Arab world and have funded survey research. Among them are the International Development Research Council of Canada, the Konrad Adenauer Foundation, and the Ford Foundation.

The Focus of Social Research

What kind of survey research has resulted from this situation? Several topics have received disproportionate attention, both from native social scientists and from foreign scholars.

1. The first area (and one of the safest in which to do research) has been population and family planning. Research on this issue is authorized and supported by most governments. The topic is important because of the relationship between development efforts and the problem of overpopulation. Among the subaspects of this field of research are rural-urban migration, adjustment to city life, and the impact of birth control methods and programs.

2. Another important area is agrarian transformation. Research in this area is also tolerated by the state, and much is even state supported. This research centers on change in the rural areas and especially on the impact of land reform or other rural development programs. In Egypt, Iraq, Syria, and Yemen, land reform has been an important aspect of agrarian transformation. There has also been much interest in the impact of the mechanization of agriculture and of changes in the class structure in the rural areas.

3. Class structure and social stratification constitute another important area, but these sensitive topics and their study are often frowned upon by governments. Research has usually been done in one of two discrete ways: on a micro level by masters and doctoral students, who take a single neighborhood or village and study its class structure and social stratification system; or in a veiled manner, as through the conduct of family budget surveys. Data from such surveys are sometimes analyzed in a secondary fashion to get a picture of class structure and income distribution. Family budget surveys have been conducted in Tunisia, Egypt, the Sudan, and Iraq in the last twenty years. In some of these surveys, social scientists have been able to smuggle in questions that give direct clues about income distribuion and class structure. Finally, in several Arab countries, including Egypt, researchers have been able to carry out some small-scale surveys dealing with these issues.

4. Topics pertaining to women, family, and marriage define another area in which it is fairly safe and easy to do research without encountering government opposition. Some controversy may develop when the results of such studies are published. There may also be some criticism from conservative elements and religious leaders. Only at the publication stage, when there may be a conflict between the findings of the research and certain prevailing values, is controversy possible.

5. Social impact studies have flourished in the last five years. Such studies are instrumental, applied, and action oriented. For the most part

they are motivated and funded by foreign donor agencies—especially by the U.S. Agency for International Development (USAID), for which they are mandated by U.S. congressional directive. After USAID's experience in Iran, there has been growing awareness in the United States that foreign assistance decisions should be based on both economic considerations and social feasibility. Therefore, before a project is implemented, a social impact study is made. Some of the questions addressed are who is going to benefit from the proposed project, how is it going to affect the existing configuration of income distribution and class structure, and what will be its overall fallout. Such studies have flourished in recent years in countries receiving substantial U.S. aid, especially Egypt, the Sudan, Jordan, and Yemen.

6. Every political subject is sensitive and there is much suspicion on the part of the government and even the respondents if they realize that political issues are being investigated. For this reason, politics is the most difficult topic on which to conduct research. One exception is state-sponsored public opinion research. Shrewd governments have sometimes authorized public opinion research on the condition that findings not be made public. Only a few top government officials receive the results. A second exception is when political research is disguised by placing it within a different framework, such as that of modernization studies. The word *modernization* is generally neutral and even has some positive connotations, so research dealing with it is generally accepted. An area unrelated to survey research concerns events data. A project to gather such data was begun several years ago by Edward Azar in the United States. Azar is of Arab origin and has trained a number of Arab students in the methodology of this kind of research—which involves maintaining a file of important events taking place in the Arab world, especially political ones. A few Arab institutions have followed Azar's lead and established their own events files; one is in Amman and another in Cairo, at the al-Ahram Center for Political and Strategic Studies.

Problems with Social Research

Many problems are associated with the conduct of survey research and other kinds of social inquiry in the Arab world. Among them are such meta-sociological problems as (1) the lack of trained researchers, (2) the lack of research funds, and (3) the absence of academic freedom. These considerations have nothing to do with the substance of the research, but they nevertheless condition, restrict, and affect directly the ability to carry out programs of research.

A different category of problems concerns the theoretical paradigm that guides the research. A lot of talk has been devoted to issues of paradigm in the last decade or so, but very little has been done to deal with this issue creatively. The central problem is that almost all Arab social scientists have received Western training and, therefore, use imported Western paradigms, such as the positivist or the Marxist paradigm, when designing and carrying out research. Although there have been strong reactions against foreign paradigms, these negative reactions have not translated themselves into the creation of alternate models and frameworks. In fact, researchers do not really know whether they can create alternative paradigms, although some have been laboring to do so. Even when Western paradigms are criticized, Western terms and concepts are often used. For example, someone who borrows from C. Wright Mills criticisms' of the paradigms guiding Western research echoes the ideas of a Western scholar. The same is true when one draws upon the Frankfort school of social science to critique the positivist and functionalist paradigms. Yet some Arab scholars reject all Western approaches and aspire to create an authentically Arab paradigm.

In practice, alternative paradigms cannot just be thought up by a couple of scholars or invented by a group of social scientists sitting in an air-conditioned office. Progress must be made by carrying out research activities. The conduct of research on one's own society may enable one to derive "indigenous" theories in an existential manner. New paradigms can be slowly built on the foundation of accumulated research findings about the specificity of the Arab world. Unfortunately, however, many of the Arab social scientists who are the most vocal critics of Western paradigms are not active in carrying out research. In other words, a category of professional critics has developed, who do nothing but criticize and who do not really carry out research. Although many of the criticisms are valid, they have been repeated over and over during the last ten years. The only way to come up with a satisfactory alternative to the suspect paradigms is to conduct research; from research findings, researchers can add to, subtract from, and otherwise modify existing approaches, models, and assumptions.

A final category of problems concerns issues of methodology, especially the techniques associated with survey research. Some of the techniques developed in the West are based on assumptions that may be invalid or impractical in Arab society. For example, survey research, which contributes to the transformation of Western society, is predicated on a belief that the individual is the most appropriate unit of analysis; thus the individual's attitudes or behavior patterns are surveyed. The only way to conduct survey research is to construct a questionnaire or interview schedule that will be administered to a number of individuals. This assumption has presented many challenges to survey researchers in the Arab world, however, and may not always be appropriate.

An alternative is to take the group as the unit of analysis in survey research, since in traditional or modernizing societies the decisionmaking unit may not be the individual. The individual may not initiate action. He or she may not be a free agent. In this respect, the difference between western and Arab societies is one of degree rather than of kind, but it is great enough to call into question the assumption that the individual is always the most appropriate unit of analysis. Alternatives can and should be considered, such as using a social network or some other kind of collectivity. An "ecological unit" might be a family, a formal social group or organization, a neighborhood, a market place, a tribe—some unit other than an individual. But we are victims of our own training, and we have not been trained to consider this possibility.

Concepts of sampling and a belief in the sacredness of sampling are things we internalize during our studies. Again, however, we assume that the individual is the ideal unit for research and that sampling should be directed toward the selection of a number of individuals. More generally, we attempt to respect the canons of various sampling techniques, ranging from random to cluster to stratified samples. We feel guilty if we have violated any of the meticulous procedures associated with the chosen sampling technique. We go to great lengths to justify any such violations, and we usually hold the idea that we are writing for and being judged by Western colleagues, even when we are writing in Arabic. In reality, we often find in conducting research that it is impossible to respect all the rituals of sampling.

Other issues relate to data processing and analysis. We often have a great appetite for collecting data. Every research organization in the Arab world that has carried out survey research has gathered mountains of data, but most have been able to analyze only a very small portion. We need to think about how the data collected can be exploited more fully. A related consideration is that analyses are often in the most elementary form—simple univariate tabulations and frequency distributions or, occasionally, some cross-tabulations and simple measures of association. Although fuller exploitation of data is needed in this area, I sometimes wonder about the wisdom of subjecting my data to more sophisticated statistical analysis, especially when I have doubts about using the individual as the unit of analysis. This is an area replete with doubt and cynicism.

An equally important problem is the publication and dissemination of research findings. At the NCSCR in Egypt, for example, a researcher is overwhelmed by the impressive quantity of research that has been done over the last twenty-five years. But the national center has not succeeded in disseminating the results of its studies to a wider audience, and thus researchers cannot take advantage of much of its work. The studies may be valuable, but we do not know much about any results or breakthroughs that may have come from the NCSCR's research. Even some of the studies that have been published appear late and are not in an easily accessible form, sometimes being just mimeographed reports. As a result, this great effort in survey research is hardly known in Egypt, to say nothing of the rest of the Arab world and beyond. This observation applies to most research centers in the Arab world, moreover; in fact, individuals have been more successful in disseminating the results of their studies than have most research institutions. Many individual scholars, despite limited energy and resources, have been able, because of flexibility and a commitment to the subject, to do a better job of publishing the results of their investigations.

Many of these problems and issues are central to the task of creating an indigenous social science, one that takes into account not only the legitimate universal preoccupations of social inquiry but also the specificity and uniqueness of the Arab world. Other problems result from different aspects of the quest for better and more useful knowledge about Arab society, and some of these are unique to survey research and some pertain to social research generally. All these problems can and should be discussed in forums like the Bellagio conference. We must reflect on these problems, take account of what has been accomplished, and decide where to go from here. This is not enough, however. In the final analysis, it is action that counts. Individual scholars and research institutions must become aware of these issues and must try to deal with them in actual research situations. They must innovate, experiment, and be creative, not only thinking about these problems but struggling to design programs of research that put their thoughts into action.

2

The Status of Survey Research
for Rural Development in the Sudan

M. O. El Sammani

Planning for rural development requires data at the macro and micro levels, to link the national goals of development to those of areas within the nation. Because rural development is a broad-based effort that aims toward economic advancement and an improvement in the well-being of rural communities, it must be founded on sound planning, which in turn draws from findings in both the physical and the social sciences. At the macro level, it is essential to have information that measures the needs and the progress so far attained by different regions of the country in order to determine existing regional disparities. Also, it is essential to have data on the natural and human resource potentials of different regions, to assess the existing capabilities for rural development programs. Such information enables agencies engaged in rural development work to determine priorities, to design and implement projects, and to allocate funds effectively. Many kinds of socioeconomic data and statistical information from national surveys are essential for rural (and other) development planning, including those pertaining to assessments of natural resources, population distribution and migration patterns, rural employment and income structure, and economic growth rates.

The Data Gap

Planning can be enhanced even more if adequate microlevel data can be obtained about groups, local communities, and individuals within areas where rural development programs are envisioned and implemented. Specially designed surveys are needed to fill the many gaps in national and regional data bases. Research is needed in many areas, including values and behavior patterns pertaining to work habits, childrearing practices, education, and health care. By examining the case of the Sudan, however, we can conclude that these kinds of data resources, descending from the national to the lower order planning space, are not readily available. For example, little study has taken place in the area of rural economies. Very few research projects have treated questions related to income, expenditure, consumption, savings, and investment in rural communities. Moreover, the few studies that have been done were carried out in the context of specific planning situations and do not provide a solid foundation for more general development efforts. The same is true for issues related to employment and rural-urban migration. The studies cited here and there do not add up to a concerted effort that yields systematic data on these topics.

The data gap becomes even more acute for questions related to social change and social planning. A basic shortcoming derives from the narrow way that many policymakers and executives choose to conceive and measure change and progress. Assessments of both are often provided only in terms of aggregate social and economic infrastructure. Advancement in education is measured by data on the number of schools provided, for example, rather than by gathering data about the quality of teaching or about student performance and the level of skill and knowledge attained. The same applies to health, water-supply, cooperatives, security, and community participation, areas in which an aggregate numerical figure is mistakenly assumed to be a valid and adequate indicator of achievement. Similar limitations pertain to economics. The volume of crop production attained at the end of the agricultural season or the amount of total income generated by the producers is often advertised as the only yardstick necessary for measuring progress.

This practice also leads to failure to investigate the impact of changing conditions and development projects on the life of the recipient population, an important consideration that can be addressed through survey research. This gap can be attributed partly to an absence of democratic processes and popular participation in the realization of development programs. Although decisionmakers often are not serious about opening a dialogue with those affected by development efforts, the performance of many programs would be enhanced greatly if mechanisms to provide feedback about the impact of such programs on the intended beneficiaries were developed.

This brief discussion points to several general shortcomings:

1. Incomplete geographical coverage, with data weaknesses most severe at the lower order tiers of the planning hierarchy.
2. Limited conceptualization, which narrows the intellectual parameters and practical value of survey activity and of data produced.
3. Inadequate development of time-series data, which are basic for sound analysis during both decisionmaking and program evaluation.
4. Inadequate integration of survey findings from different fields and failure to combine data produced by surveys with those resulting from other kinds of research, leading to explanations and applications which are incomplete and unduly restrictive.

5. Limited use in planning, since many agencies have an inadequate understanding of the potential value of survey research and of the way that survey data may be exploited.

Despite these gaps, survey research has played an important role in the planning of a number of development projects, and its value is gaining recognition every day. A close examination of successful cases shows that in most there was an appreciation of what social science, including survey research, can contribute to public policy formulation, implementation, and evaluation in the area of rural development.

In conclusion, rural development, having as its focus the improvement of the living conditions of the rural masses—which constitute 80 percent of the people of the Sudan—has to address many interrelated considerations. Some of them can best be studied through survey research. Also, although problems and shortcomings remain, survey research has sometimes been used effectively in rural development programs in the Sudan, for example, in the Jonglei Canal project.

The Jonglei Case

The Jonglei Canal project aims at conserving some of the water lost in the Sudd swamps of Bahr el Jebel. The proposed project has had a long history and has changed many times; it finally became a plan to dredge a 360-kilometer canal, extending from the tail of the swamps at Bor to the White Nile south of Malakal. The canal would convey an annual discharge of 4 milliard cubic meters of water, to be shared equally by the Sudan and Egypt. The project, in its present version, was initiated at the beginning of the 1970s.

The Executive Organ for the Development Projects in the Jonglei Canal Area was formed to look after the people affected by the project, as well as to monitor its future impact. To gather the information necessary to achieve these objectives, social and economic research was initiated. The task of conducting this research was entrusted to Sudanese agencies, which are more capable of understanding the current political situation and of conveying people's motivations and expectations than are foreign consulting firms. The research focused on three tribes inhabiting the area and directly affected by the canal: the Dinka, the Nuer, and the Shilluk. The goals of the research were to contribute to the formation of appropriate social and economic policies and to help the local people adjust to the conditions created by the canal and attain a better standard of living.

The selection of the team formed to carry out the necessary investigations was guided by the topics to be covered. The team was composed of three geographers, three social anthropologists, two sociologists, three statisticians, one agricultural economist, and two veterinarians. In addition, twenty-three interviewers were chosen from the local population on the basis of language ability.

To assemble such a team was a difficult task for several reasons. First, because the Executive Organ for the Development Projects in the Jonglei Canal Area was a temporary body it could not offer permanent employment. Those whose services were required by the organ were to join on a temporary basis, upon secondment from their permanent departments. This awkward situation did not help in getting the right people at the right time. Nobody was attracted to temporary employment, and secondment in many cases was difficult to obtain. Second, it would have been preferable to give priority for secondment to persons from the southern region, as a step toward full involvement of cadres from the region of the canal in the running of the project after the implementation phase. This approach was not feasible because of a shortage of trained personnel from the region, however, especially in the area of research. Third, many people were poorly prepared to work in the remote area. Apart from harsh conditions, the region was inaccessible for part of the year, and the political turmoil between the north and the south made many concerned about safety.

Another handicap was that the only available information about that part of the country came from work undertaken by the Jonglei Investigation Team in the late 1940s, published in the mid-1950s. This work had many shortcomings, since the emphasis was different and the techniques used were not adequate.

Despite these problems, measures were taken to assemble a research team. The support given to the executive organ by other agencies, in recognition of the role it could play in project planning and implementation, facilitated the recruitment of staff and the initiation of the research. Also, adequate budgets for the program permitted such incentives as salary increases and hardship allowances, which proved to be effective in attracting staff from the different agencies. Free accommodations during the field work was another inducement. Furthermore, a scheme for postgraduate training, worked out with international organizations cooperating in the project, offered an additional incentive. Finally, personal contacts were utilized; the heads of various government units were approached and convinced about the value of the project and the need for staff seconded from their agencies. Though individually selected, the staff members soon found themselves working as an integrated team. The clear objectives of the research and the training program greatly helped in consolidating the team.

The program of research was divided into two periods: field activities, with the team operating in the region, and data compilation, analysis, and report writing, mostly carried out in Khartoum. The first period began with presurvey work. The purpose of preliminary visits was to gain basic knowledge of the area, to define the scope of the field work, and to identify problems that might be encountered in conducting the research. In addition, existing facilities in the region were examined, and contacts were made with local government units that might have dealings with the research activity.

Following the presurvey visits, each member of the research team was asked to supply an outline for coverage of the topic under his or her area of specialization, as well as a tentative questionnaire for collecting data about this topic. Individual questionnaires were then integrated into one survey instrument, covering all topics to be investigated, which was taken to the field for pretesting. The pretest proved vital in pointing out shortcomings and in facilitating the precoding of questionnaire responses. After this, a refined survey instrument was taken to the field, where a seven-day training period for the interviewers was organized. Also, a field manual, in which the researchers provided information about the area, was prepared and presented to the interviewers.

Both individuals and groups were subsequently interviewed. Other research methods, including participant observation, were employed as well. Each team member was assigned to supervise the work of a group of interviewers, to check with them every evening concerning questionnaires they filled out during the day. This exercise was essential for minimizing error, and it greatly increased the reliability of the data collected.

In addition, each team member worked on the topic assigned to him throughout the survey period. In some cases, more than one researcher was assigned to the same topic, according to a set plan designed to ensure the integration of findings during the data collection stage. Evening discussions of daily results and problems were organized. Senior researchers visiting from Khartoum and experts from international agencies visiting the region often participated in these discussions.

Sampling procedures varied from one survey area to another. The techniques adopted in the Dinka case may be briefly mentioned for illustration. The traditional organization of Dinka society facilitated the selection of a number of heads of households to be interviewed. The Dinka population of the area was broken down into administrative subsections, represented by a total of eleven subchiefs. Under each were a number of headmen. The subchiefs were approached individually, and a list of the headmen under their jurisdiction was prepared; there were a total of 180 headmen. The 180 headmen were then interviewed to obtain a list of the family heads under each. A total of 1,300 household heads were identified in this manner, and this list constituted the Dinka population from which a random sample was then selected. This exercise was applied with some variation in all the survey areas, following as closely as possible the tribal organization of the local communities.

An important objective of the research team was to establish contact with the local people and to create a productive relationship between itself and the intended beneficiaries of the research project. This proved to be rewarding both during the survey and during the project's implementation phase. The contribution of both parties to the activities that evolved from this relationship was enhanced. The research team devised a number of approaches to build an atmosphere of cooperation with the local population. The team held meetings to introduce itself to the local communities and to gain an understanding of the latter's problems and expectations in relation to the canal project. Meetings were held with the court presidents of the different localities in the presence of various chiefs and subchiefs and with the formal leadership and dignitaries from each area. The people of the local villages attended many of these sessions as well. Local government officials, especially those belonging to the local tribe, were encouraged to participate in these meetings and were sometimes given a leading role in explaining issues related to the canal project and the research.

Contact with the local population was also facilitated by the choice of interviewers. Although these individuals were chosen primarily for their language skills, they also had to be from the area of the research project. Also, those whose families remained there were given preference whenever possible. Most interviewers were civil servants with secondary-school education, who normally worked as clerks, teachers, and nurses in the government departments at Malakal and Bor. By sharing the camp facilities with the other members of the research team and by participating in the team's day-to-day activities, the interviewers developed a close relationship with team members from outside the region that served as an important bridge to the local communities.

In meetings with local officials, it had been determined that visits between the research team and tribal leaders should be encouraged. Local dignitaries commonly visited the camp, and many fruitful discussions were carried out over a shared meal. The residences of tribal chiefs, and especially of the court president, were open to any team member who wished to discuss problems related to the research. Such contact was not limited to local leaders: In a remote area like Jonglei, the survey team had to be self-sufficient, not only in research materials but in food, fuel supplies, medicines, and the like, all of which had to be planned for in advance and catered from Khartoum. These facilities attracted the local people, and the team shared as much as it could with them. The presence of team members specialized in the care and raising of animals also attracted people from the region.

A related consideration was the team's provision of employment opportunities. The Jonglei area has a stagnant, subsistence economy. The team's presence during the dry season—December to June—provided employment in the localities where the research was conducted. The construction of the camp provided work for many, and others were hired to maintain the facilities and to run the camp on a day-to-day basis. There were also related economic contributions. During construction of the camp, building materials, such as wood and grass, were purchased locally; later, meat and milk and some other commodities were bought from the local inhabitants.

Another important service involved efforts by the research team to assist the local population in maintaining its water supply. During the dry season local communities depend on deep-bore wells, which often function poorly because of inadequate maintenance and irregular fuel supplies. During the period of its work, the research team assisted in repairing some of the wateryards and supplied the diesel fuel required for their operation. The research team also frequently used its vehicles to transport people traveling to and from the area. This service was particularly important since the region lacks regular transportation facilities, and trucks passing between the north and Juba rarely render any service to the local communities. Moreover, transportation assistance was occasionally provided to government departments, and many times the local police force was given use of a vehicle in an emergency. Service was also sometimes rendered by carrying relatives or goods for local officials.

On one occasion the team provided vital emergency relief for the local people. The Jonglei area is threatened by famine almost every year because it does not produce sufficient dura, the local staple. Though farmers raise two crops a year, the harvest is inadequate to meet the needs of most families. Furthermore, in some years dura is not available for purchase from local merchants. This kind of crisis situation occurred during the period of the research. On this occasion, the research team helped to alleviate the shortage by advancing its own funds to import dura, which it then transported in its own trucks and sold at market prices—services greatly appreciated by the local people.

The local communities derived much benefit from the presence of the research team, although these benefits were not all long term. The purpose of making these contributions was not only to gain support for the conduct of the research or even to compensate the local population for its hospitality and cooperation; it was also to lay some of the ground work for the next stage of development in the region. This practical link between the team's activities and local development was envisioned from the start. The team's presence made a direct contribution to improving local conditions and was a stimulus to further change. In addition, lessons the team learned through contact with the local population became a valuable part of the research findings and are the basis for many recommendations embodied in its reports.

Despite the care and effort of the research team, a number of problems were encountered while it conducted the research.

1. At the beginning some interviewees opposed the research because they feared the Jonglei Canal project would be disruptive and would benefit some more than others.
2. Long distances between households, coupled with the difficult terrain, made interviewing time consuming.
3. The frequent absence of the household head at the time of an interviewer's visit necessitated many extra trips.
4. The length of the questionnaire sometimes made respondents lose patience or concentration.

5. Some questions were misinterpreted by interviewers, resulting in unusable data.

6. The language barrier between the researchers and the respondents, which could only be bridged by the interviewers, prevented as full a measure of interaction as was desired.

In conclusion, the Jonglei case shows the valuable contribution that survey research can make in the field of rural development planning and implementation. But this contribution is very much related to a proper understanding of when and how such research should be carried out and of its limits and shortcomings. Such an understanding is not always present among the people at large or even among specialists in the field of rural development. The situation has recently improved somewhat because of an appreciation of what social science in general and survey research in particular can achieve. On the other hand, the status of social science is still below the expectations of its practitioners. In nearly all agencies running rural development programs, we see a leading role for the technical sciences and professions. The reason that the status of social scientists, with survey research as one of their tools, has not been upgraded and has not assumed a more prominent role is a subject that deserves attention; social scientists clearly have important contributions to make.

Editors' Note

Professor Sammani's presentation at Bellagio also included a short account of the role of survey research in a project to resettle Nubians affected by the High Dam at New Halfa in the early 1960s.

3

Issues of Sampling and Measurement in the World Bank Survey of the Saudi Labor Market

Naiem A. Sherbiny

Whether or not the World Bank has an opportunity to update the Saudi Labor Market Study (LMS) in Saudi Arabia or to carry out a similar study elsewhere, recording the experience of the research team is useful in guiding such efforts in the future. The team faced several issues of sampling and measurement at various stages of the study: prior to the field work, during the field work, and after the field work. Prior to the field work, the most significant issues were the frame and size of the sample. During the field work, the concern was obtaining sufficient representation of Saudis working in professional establishments. After the field work, the issue was the choice of appropriate variables to achieve two objectives: (1) to properly capture the indicators of fluidity and dynamics of the labor market and (2) to measure the relative contribution of a number of explanatory variables in determining the outcome of market mechanisms in three areas—income and wage determination, geographic mobility, and job mobility.

Frame and Size of the Sample

One of the main difficulties in planning a major survey study is the availability of an up-to-date sample frame. At the time of study preparation, census information was not available in a usable form (incidentally, this information is still unavailable). The only other data source was developed for the Ministry of Planning by the Cooper and Lybrand (C&L) macroeconomic study. Because of resources and time constraints, the study team used the C&L final sample as the frame for the private establishment sample. Aside from accessibility and convenience, the use of C&L sample as the LMS sample frame had other advantages, most important of which was that it included establishment-level data usable as a consistency check on the findings of the LMS. For that purpose a system of cross-matching between the two data sets was developed and integrated into the data filing system.

The initial study design gave scientific and general guidelines. Because of lack of information on the various details of the labor market, for example, on the proportion of Saudi workers in the various types of establishments, it was necessary to develop flexible adjustment rules. For example, contrary to expectations, it was found that limited numbers of Saudis were employed in private establishments. This information became apparent only after field work was well in progress. Scientifically, it was not possible to generate, or even guess, such information from the limited pretesting exercise. The fact that Saudis constitute a small minority among private establishment workers was itself a finding of the study. Accordingly, it was decided to supplement the sample of large establishments and to interview all Saudis up to a maximum of ten in every selected establishment. The added sample was selected scientifically with known probability.

The sample design and size allowed the following coverage:

- adequate representation of the sectoral classification of establishments and their technical and market characteristics
- by public/private breakdown of enterprises
- by the country's five regions
- by broad nationality identification of workers (Saudis and non-Saudis)

Given these constraints, a multistage stratified sample was developed that reflected the major characteristics of both supply and demand for labor. For the private establishment sample the C&L sample was divided by size (large and small) and by regions (five). An added classification to reflect the level of technology was also made. Within each category a specified number of establishments was selected randomly. In the case of public establishments, a list was prepared for each region. For each region, public establishments were classified into groups depending on the general level of technical skills required for operation, and a sample was selected accordingly. For each selected establishment, private or public, a comprehensive list of all workers was prepared and divided into Saudi and non-Saudi workers. A sample of workers was then selected within the broad nationality classification and stratified by levels of skills. Finally, an independent national sample of households stratified according to region and by urban and rural residence was developed. All heads of selected households and an additional adult male if available were interviewed. The final structure of the three samples is given in Table 3.1.

All the study elements at the various stages were documented: overall design, sampling, interviewing schedules, coding books, and computer

Table 3.1   Basic Sample Information

Item	Region					
	Central	Eastern	Western	Southern	Northern	All
Labor Demand						
Establishment/ managers	107	94	134	35	14	385
Labor Supply						
Workers: Saudis	283	318	329	64	56	1050
Non-Saudis	212	208	211	109	38	1002
Households: Saudis	186	163	221	150	152	867
Non-Saudis	38	103	60	31	40	272

analysis requests. A systematic reference procedure was developed and adopted throughout to link tabulation plans, computer output, coding books, and the original questionnaires. These procedures were necessary because the information collected in this study can serve as a basic socioeconomic data bank for planning purposes beyond the present immediate utilization.

The Dynamics of the Saudi Labor Market

Most members of the study team were close observers of the Saudi economy. They knew a priori that the rapid acceleration of economic growth could not have taken place without corresponding major repercussions on the labor market. The team sought to measure two aspects: the extent of fluidity in the labor market (present) and the prospects for business activity (future). The extent of fluidity of the market was conceptualized to have several indicators, the most important of which were duration of employment, availability of employment opportunities to entrants, the age of existing establishments, and job vacancies.

To a considerable degree, these indicators are closely related. The hypothesis underlying the introduction of such indicators was that for the labor market to be fluid, the following must hold: short duration of employment because of high labor turnover and/or constant creation of new jobs, numerous employment opportunities from which entrants could choose, young age of existing enterprises because of the recent formation of many, and the persistence, if not increase, of job vacancies. Significantly, the study's findings showed all of these indicators to hold, giving support to the appropriateness of their choice.

The other set of measures of the dynamism of the labor market pertains to the prospects for business activity, as perceived by managers in their expectations for sales growth. The underlying hypothesis here was that sales growth would continue in the future at the prevailing rate or accelerate even further. At the survey time, the average growth of the nonoil economy was about 15 percent per year. The results showed that a substantial number of the private firms (small and large) expected their growth during the following two years to be 15 percent or more: This expectation was held by 33 percent of the small firms and, significantly, 62 percent of the large firms.

With business anxieties rising during the 1980s because of significant slowdown in the growth of the Saudi economy, the labor market is likely to be less burgeoning than it was during the late 1970s. It would be quite useful to assess the dynamism of the labor market at present using the previous measures. The comparison of labor market conditions in the two periods would thus be based on firm grounds.

Income and Wage Determination

In traditional societies, age indicates experience in the labor market and is thus the main factor in determining wages. Education and training, as proxies for modernization, generally assume some weight in the wage determination process. Such weights depend on the extent of modernization itself. The hypothesis of the study was to introduce age, education, and training among other factors (occupation, nature of firm, region) to assess the extent to which each contributes to wage determination.

Using multiple classification analysis, which allows variables to enter the analysis in discrete groups or categories, researchers could test this hypothesis empirically. Age was accordingly classified into ten groups of five-year intervals, with the lower limit being "under twenty years old" and the upper limit being "sixty years and above." Education was entered in six categories: no schooling, and elementary, intermediate, secondary, university, and postgraduate schooling. Training was introduced in two categories: prejob and on-the-job. Occupation was introduced into six groups: professional/technical, administrative/managerial, clerical, sales personnel, service workers, and operative laborers and others. Firm affiliation was divided into three categories: public enterprise, private small business, and private large business. Workers location was classified according to the country's five regions. In some parts of the analysis the region variable had only two entries: the rapidly growing regions (east, west, and center) and the slowly growing regions (north and southwest).

The results (in addition to showing wage differentials by occupation, location, and nature of enterprise) unmistakably pointed up the central role of education and training in determining wage rates and family incomes. Although large-scale modernization is only a recent phenomenon in Saudi Arabia, the effects of education and skill formation were more important than age. In other words, the influence of modernization was shown to be stronger than the influence of tradition in determining wage rates in the Saudi labor market. Because of the increasing and more intensive modernization of Saudi Arabia during the last five years, education and training are expected to play an even more prominant role in wage determination than previously.

Geographic Mobility

When a static and geographically extended labor market is thrust into rapid modernization and large-scale socioeconomic development processes, it is customary to witness workers and households moving about significantly more than before: from one residence to another in the same town, from villages and towns to big cities in the same regions, or across regions. All such movements, termed *geographic mobility,* would be responses to new opportunities that provide better employment and higher earnings. Only the movement between regions is termed *interregional mobility.* All such movements are measured in terms first of changing residence, then of distances covered, during a defined time period.

Four questions, all relating to geographic mobility in Saudi Arabia, were raised in the study:

1. What is the extent of geographic mobility in general?
2. What is the extent of interregional mobility in particular?
3. What is the extent of future mobility?
4. What are the factors associated with such moves?

These same questions should be raised in the update to the survey.

The establishment sample showed that 16 percent of Saudi workers had changed residence in less than one year (1977/1978) and 28 percent during the three-year period 1976–1978. These figures are to be compared with 31 percent and 72 percent, respectively, for non-Saudi workers. The great majority of Saudis who changed residence did so within the same region, often within the same town. Only 20 percent of the Saudis who moved in less than one year—3 percent of the total Saudi labor—had crossed regions. This was one of the major findings of the 1978 survey. As it turned out, the mobility of the non-Saudis from the countries of origin to the particular Saudi regions of employment compensated for the limited interregional mobility of Saudi labor.

Determinants of such mobility were tested for fourteen variables and entered with their proper categories (e.g., age in ten categories, family income in seven, length of contract in five, education in six, and so on). The most significant of these turned out to be age, home ownership, and, to a lesser extent, education. In future work the same variables would be tested, plus ones not previously introduced. The objective is to build a comparative basis over time for a better understanding of the conditions that prompt Saudis to move from one place to another.

Job Mobility

When the development process is accelerated without serious constraints on capital availability, occupational and job mobility is an important indicator of the extent of labor adaptation to changing market conditions. This was one of the underlying hypotheses of the 1978 survey. Labor adaptation itself is usually a function not only of changing demand conditions but also of supply characteristics and the structure of the labor market. To establish a profile of job mobility, workers holding their first jobs were excluded (43 percent of Saudi workers). The coverage included workers who changed sectors of employment but remained in the same general occupations, workers who changed occupations, and workers who moved upward on the occupational ladder.

The results showed significant job mobility of Saudi labor in these categories. Furthermore, there was strong evidence of accelerated mobility from both the workers sample and the households sample. Saudi workers who changed jobs constituted 9 percent of the Saudi work force during 1974-1975, 19 percent during 1976-1977, and 20 percent in 1978. Determinants of job mobility were tested for fifteen variables, also entered with their proper categories, in a similar fashion to those involved in geographic mobility. The most significant of those were education and skill levels as stimulants and age and wages as deterrents.

A General Assessment

The outcomes of the labor market operation, whether in terms of wage determination, geographic mobility, or job mobility, resulted from common factors simultaneously impacting demand and supply of labor and the very process of their interaction. One additional outcome of the labor market, which should have been included in the econometric analysis (but was not), was skill formation. Skill formation is a fundamental process of adjustment of labor supply to the changing structure of labor demand. Any new or updated analysis should cover skill formation in a more systematic fashion.

Conceptually, a system of labor supply and demand underlies the operation of the labor market, and the research team has the responsibility to uncover such forces and measure the specific impact of individual variables. With the benefit of hindsight, it it now clear that the processes of wage determination, geographic mobility, job mobility, and skill formation are interdependent and are themselves determined simultaneously by the operation of several behavioral factors. Careful measurement of such factors is crucial to the success of the survey. One important test of the reliability of data was the extent of "robustness" of the results of employing different model forms (full model; reduced model) throughout the analysis; that is, when the short model forms were used, the initially significant variables remained unchanged in sign or size of coefficient(s).

The thrust of the study was geared to finding regional differences in the phenomena analyzed. At the time of the survey (summer 1978), however, the structure of the economy was somewhat thin (i.e., in stratifying the economy by sectors and regions, some of the cells in such matrix contained insufficient observations). This was particularly true in the northern and southwestern regions. Much has changed since, and the previously near-empty cells have filled up reasonably satisfactorily during the last five years. The hypothesis of virtually independent regional labor markets could not adequately be tested with the previous data base. An update should provide richer regional analysis.

Because of the expressed policy orientation of the survey, the analysis presented by the World Bank was necessarily limited to policy issues. However, the data base generated could be used to explore other issues, especially those of theoretical importance, which would expand the frontiers of application of survey research in the Arab countries. Such areas include the informal sector and the process of job information. Although the latter is presently at the core of a new bank project for the United Arab Emirates, no analysis was done on the informal sector, either for Saudi Arabia or elsewhere. This is a peculiar gap, especially as the study showed that one out of every three working Saudis was informally employed (working for relative or self-employed). The data base contains detailed information on the characteristics of the informally employed, their regional distribution, sectoral activities, skill levels, income attainment, preferences, attitudes, future plans, and so on. Such information can provide a basis for a systematic analysis of one of the least known segments of the Saudi labor market.

Finally, it is useful to derive the lessons of experience, especially for sampling and measurement issues, from the 1978 survey. The first such lesson is the necessity of having a reliable sample frame. In most countries in which census data are not so confidentially treated, the population census offers a valuable sample frame to survey the labor market. In Saudi Arabia, a convenient frame must be sought because the population census is now dated. So much change has occurred in the Saudi society since 1974 that that year's census is of little value for a labor market update.

The second lesson is the necessity to articulate and insist on having the required time to carry out the survey successfully. A practical way is to divide the project into clear-cut segments, each with a realistic schedule. Some segments are by definition sequential with others and thus either they cannot be lumped together or the required time cannot be arbitrarily shortened. Most surveys of the LMS type take a minimum of two years from start to finish. With considerable strain, the LMS took twenty months, from February 1978 to September 1979. Even for an update, the twenty-month estimate should not be violated; otherwise, the quality of the work may seriously suffer.

The third lesson is the uncompromising need to document carefully the various stages of the study from overall design, sampling, interviewing schedules, and coding books to computer analysis requests—so that every step is traceable. Such a procedure assures reviewers that sufficient care and attention were given to the survey to produce reliably representative results.

4

The Question of Measurement in Survey Research in the Arab World

Huda Zurayk

The question of measurement is at the essence of survey research, and to my mind it accompanies the process of investigation from the very beginning, when an idea is born, to the very end with the statement of the conclusions. Survey research can be defined as a method for collecting information, within a theoretical framework, from a sample of subjects who vary with respect to attitudes or behavior, and for systematically analyzing the collected data in order to draw conclusions about patterns and relationships that can be generalized to the population of subjects under consideration. The questions of measurement arise in all the stages of a survey research project: Is the measurement representative in the sample design and implementation? Is it valid and reliable in the design of the measuring instrument and in data collection? Is it adequate for estimating and testing hypotheses (i.e., measuring levels and relationships) in data analysis and for inferring conclusions?

I would like, therefore, to give a wider scope to my remarks on measurement issues in the application of survey research to the study of Arab society than I give to questions related directly to the measurement instrument, although still providing due consideration to the instrument as an important component of the measurement process. I will not here consider the implications of the processes of sampling and interviewing, since other chapters are devoted to these issues.

Conceptualization and Definition

An initial requirement for the correct application of the measurement process in survey research is that the entity to be measured is properly conceptualized and defined. Generally stated, the concern in applying survey research to the study of Arab society is to describe or test relationships between social science constructs. A key to the success of such application is that the relationships to be studied are derived from a well-developed theoretical framework, that the constructs to be measured have clear theoretical definitions, and that theory is relevant to the society under study. Such a comprehensive theoretical conceptualization defines and gives context and focus to the problem under study—a first prerequisite to efficient and accurate measurement.

In my experience in the application of survey research in the Arab region, I have observed that not enough consideration has been given to the development of theoretical models of social reality and dynamics applicable to Arab society. In fact, models derived in the West are often utilized without due investigation of their applicability in the study of Arab society. Prominent among the many factors that contribute to this tendency are the following three.

1. The West is far ahead of the Arab world in theory construction and cumulation of evidence, so that researchers naturally seek to learn from the vast body of literature produced in the Western world.
2. The process of conceptualization and theory construction requires the researcher to devote absolutely his or her time and thought to the project. Most researchers living in the region are overloaded with teaching and service activities and live under conditions that make a continuous devoted thinking process almost impossible.
3. The process of conceptualization also requires that the researcher interact with others working on the same problem, personally and through the literature. Unfortunately, the communication networks for researchers in the region are not well developed and are currently being obstructed by the increasing tendency toward isolation within countries of the region.

An example of how failure to build a proper theoretical framework leads to improper measurement can be seen in the measurement procedure currently used to assess the work of Arab women and men. In analyzing economic activity in Arab society, researchers applied the definition developed in the industrialized West without due consideration to the special characteristics of work and to attitudes toward work in Arab society. In the industrialized West work is mostly organized as paid labor for one contracted job; in our society, particularly in the large agriculture sector, a lot of family participation is involved in work and it is not compensated directly. Moreover, individuals frequently hold secondary jobs.

The result of utilizing unrealistic definitions of the concept of work in the Arab region is that national statistics are producing drastic underestimates of the work contribution of women and of many men in our society. There is thus need for a more realistic conceptualization of what constitutes economic activity in Arab society and what is influencing such activity. Only then can we develop measures that reflect the reality of work contributions by individuals and the determinants of such contributions.

The absence of a relevant theoretical foundation, illustrated in this example, is a problem that appears in most areas of research in the social sciences in our region.

Questionnaire

One of the most important problems of the application of survey research in the Arab world is that the attention of researchers is too quickly drawn to the questionnaire as the tangible expression of their research concern. This tendency leads to two major problems in questionnaire construction.

First, it further hinders the process of conceptualization discussed in the preceding section and leads to a lengthy and inefficient questionnaire that includes all possible variables that may have some relation to the topic being investigated. Of course, the proper procedure is for the questionnaire to follow the completion of the development of the theoretical framework, as proper theorizing delineates the relevant constructs for the problem under study. Only then can the questionnaire be an efficient measurement tool.

Second, to develop a questionnaire often leads to adopting inadequate operational measures of theoretical concepts. This deficiency occurs either through the utilization of measures that have been developed elsewhere, without due consideration to their validity in reflecting the construct being measured in Arab society (sometimes the whole questionnaire is taken from a similar study conducted in a different society) or through the utilization of measures devised by the researcher without proper testing.

Not enough attention appears to be given in the region to methodological research concerned with developing valid measures for theoretical concepts. For example, Frederick Shorter developed a measure of the social class of an individual, using Syrian census data, that took into account the characteristics of the family within which the individual lives. Researchers customarily define the social class of an adult by level of education, occupation, income, or a combination of these three variables. Shorter adopted education as the construct reflecting social class. Whether this is the correct definition of social class for Arab society is not the question here; rather the question is, supposing this is the proper definition, how can we best operationalize the measure of education in this context.

Shorter pointed out that for many adults in the Arab region, particularly for women, educational level may not reflect the social class in which they live. In his words, "perhaps the family as a whole includes members whose education, occupation, or economic activities place the family within an upper class cycle of relationships." He, therefore, proposed to represent for every adult person a class score that is the mean score of the educational attainment level of all adult individuals who live in the same household.

Although this may not be the best measure of social class for an adult individual in the region, it certainly is more accurate than measures relying on the individual's characteristics alone. The purpose of this example is to illustrate the function of methodological research in achieving measures that validly represent theoretical constructs in Arab society. There is strong need for such research, particularly in sensitive areas such as the measurement of opinions and attitudes.

Quality Control Procedures

The other important aspect in questionnaire construction is the insurance of reliability through proper quality control procedures. (I will not discuss the interviewing process since other chapters are devoted to that issue.) Two procedures are essential for quality control: pilot testing and training for interviewers.

Pilot testing of the questionnaire does not appear to be carried out with adequate thoroughness in many survey research projects in the Arab region. In the words of Catherine Marsh,

> questionnaire design is a very complex task in interpersonal communication, especially if it is designed to stand up to being handled via a third party, namely, an interviewer who did not herself frame the question. It means that before a fixed form for the question can be settled on, piloting various versions of the question and depth interviewing of respondents and interviewers about what they thought the question meant absolutely must occur.

Because of the context of questionnaires in Arabic, in which different colloquial dialects could exist even within a given country and for which the very richness of expressions can be a source of ambiguity, the need for pilot testing becomes even stronger for survey research in the Arab region.

Training sessions and written instructions are procedures probably undertaken automatically by most researchers in the region. However, the quality of such procedures is very important because they wield a strong influence on the accuracy of the data, and there is great room for improvement in these procedures for survey research in the region. To illustrate this point I will again use an example from the measurement process of the work contribution of women. This example is particularly valuable because it involves a situation in which written instructions included biases in regard to the society rather than procedures to neutralize them. The example comes from the coding instructions for interviewers in the CAPMAS (Central Agency for Public Mobilization and Statistics) labor force survey in Egypt.

In defining individuals that should be considered economically active the manual refers to the labor of children as follows: "Since the pattern of labour in Egypt is characterized by the participation of children between six and eleven years of age, particularly in agricultural activities in rural areas, the labour force should include the children who undertake such work with the consideration that those who do not should not be indicated as unemployed even if they are not students." No similar statement is made for women. Whatever income-generating work contribution a woman makes in agriculture is considered part of her household duties. In describing categories of inactivity, a student is defined as the full-time student who has not undertaken the minimum amount of work required by the definition of work in the survey, namely, fifteen hours during the week of study. The housewife, on the other hand, is defined as the female who is involved full time with household activities and does not have a job. No mention (similar to that for the student) is made of the woman who is working at home or in the informal market, in income-generating activities for more than fifteen hours per week. In fact an evaluation study undertaken by CAPMAS, in which an in-depth reinterview was undertaken of families who entered the labor force survey of 1982, revealed many such working women who had not been counted in the survey. Fortunately, CAPMAS is evaluating its procedures, and improved training will be undertaken this year. The accuracy of measuring the work contribution of women, within current definitions of economic activity, will certainly improve as a result of better quality control measures.

Data Analysis

Data analysis issues have important implications for survey research efforts to properly present and accurately test the dynamic interrelationships of social science constructs in Arab society. In undertaking an investigation, very little thought is given a priori to the analysis procedures, which are usually considered only after the data have been collected. Giving due consideration to the possible analysis techniques and to the assumptions they impose can often lead to a better design of the instrument and to a better data collection strategy. The input of the statistician can be most rewarding in this area and should be sought before, rather than after, the data have been collected.

Although computers have greatly aided the process of analysis, because of the ease with which package programs can be used, they are often applied without understanding the implications of the procedures or the correct interpretations of the output. Again the participation of the statistician can provide a useful dialogue leading to an interpretation of the results that meets both methodological and substantive considerations.

Despite a tremendous advance in quantitative techniques for analysis in the social sciences, they do not appear to be utilized extensively in survey research in the region. In fact expertise in such techniques as factor analysis, path analysis, and the application of multiple regression to qualitative data is not forthcoming even among statisticians, who are classically trained in analysis techniques more appropriate to the physical sciences. There is need for more exposure among researchers, especially the statisticians, to techniques of modeling and of multivariate analysis especially applicable to the social sciences.

Statement of Conclusions

The implications of the measurement process continue into this stage because at this point inference needs to be qualified by the nature of the measurement process. In defining concepts, in operationalizing their measures, in constructing questions, and in analyzing the results, re-searchers are forced to make decisions and restrictions that affect the conclusions of the study. However, they often reach the end of a project and make generalizations while forgetting the implications for the results of the study of the painful decisions they made at every stage of the measurement process.

In summary, I have attempted to point out the most prominent features of the measurement process that affect the application of survey research in the Arab region. Most of these problems can be solved by a more thorough design of all components of the survey research method: theory construction, definition of concepts, operationalization, pilot testing, training of interviewers, sample design, and finally plan of analysis. Although this attention to design is the responsibility of individual researchers, at present the pressure that they continuously face for writing proposals and publishing often forces many to move too rapidly through the design phase of the study. Universities, research institutes, and funding agencies can assist researchers by providing the time, the funding, and the opportunity for interaction with other researchers that will enable them to develop fully the theoretical and methodological foundations of their projects.

References

Bohrnstedt, G. W., ed., "Social Science Methodology: The Past Twenty-Five Years," *American Behavioral Scientist* 23, no. 6 (1980):775–924.

Marsh, C., "Problems with Surveys: Method or Epistemology?" *Sociology* 13 (1979):293–305.

Shorter, F. C., "Inequality and Development as Seen Through the Population Census—Damascus 1976," Regional Paper of the Population Council, 1978.

Zurayk, H. C., "The Measurement of Women's Economic Participation: Report of a Study Group," Regional Paper of the Population Council, 1979.

5

Challenges and Rewards of Survey Research in the Arab World: Problems of Sensitivity in a Study of Political Socialization

Michael W. Suleiman

This essay deals with selected aspects of a continuing program of research devoted to learning about political socialization among school children in the Arab world. Particular attention is paid to problems arising from the potential sensitivity of the research, in connection with the need both to obtain permission to conduct the investigation and thereafter to secure cooperation while carrying out the research. Systematic survey research is not the only method of data collection that I have employed in my study. For example, I conducted personal, openended interviews in the 1960s in Lebanon, Syria, Jordan, Egypt, and Iraq and among the Palestinian diaspora. In addition, my research on political socialization among Arab school children has required some structured and systematic interviews, in which a questionnaire was administered to a sample of respondents. In the present report I focus principally on this latter dimension of my investigations, as the problems associated with survey research tend to be of a different nature.

Because of the size of the Arab world, I have obviously found it necessary to limit my research to specific countries. Thus, I started in Egypt in 1972-1973. Because of financial and time restrictions, as well as Egyptian concerns with national security, only certain aspects of the project could be successfully researched. The original design envisioned three objectives: (1) a thorough investigation and delineation of the basic attitudes toward society and politics as presented in primary school primers; (2) an assessment of the relationship between the content of these primers and the attitudes and beliefs of school children; and (3) a determination of whether or not there is any significant relationship between the attitudes inculcated in the young at school and the attitudes

of the adult population as represented by three sets of authority figures—
elementary school teachers, textbook writers, and public officials responsible for elementary education. As will be seen from the following
discussion, I have had to make some compromises and to abandon some
lines of research, which is not unusual (Ward 1964, p. 53), but have
succeeded beyond my expectations in other areas (for example, in
expanding the sample in Morocco and Sudan to include junior high
and high school students).

Permits

In the year preceding the October war, Egyptians were quite justifiably
concerned about security, including foreign intelligence gathering. This
concern, as well as their frustration at the apparent lack of U.S. interest
in or movement toward a peaceful settlement that would ensure Israeli
withdrawal from the territories occupied in 1967, led the Egyptian
authorities to issue a blanket cancellation of new research permits for
Americans in summer 1972. As I was already in Egypt (with my family),
under an American Research Center in Egypt (ARCE) grant—and the
only fellow to have arrived—I felt financially vulnerable and insecure.
However, I had two points in my favor: I knew a lot of academics and
members of the intellectual community, and I was often viewed as both
an American and an Arab, one committed to better Arab-U.S. understanding and improved U.S. media coverage of the Middle East. Thus,
through contacts and referrals to the ministries of education and foreign
affairs, I was assured that I could stay and finish the project. Shortly
thereafter, through U.S.-Egyptian negotiations, the cancellation order
was withdrawn and the other U.S. grantees began to arrive. As it turned
out, the temporary crisis and my appeal to high officials made it easier
for me to get the permit to do my survey of elementary school children
in Cairo. The permit was secured through the Ministry of Education
rather than the Statistics and Mobilization Office, which in those days
seldom authorized such surveys, even for Egyptians.

When in 1978 I applied for a Fulbright grant to continue my political
socialization research, I had to decide which Arab country would welcome
or at least permit the research. I chose Jordan because it would provide
me with an opportunity to compare Palestinians and Jordanians. However,
despite my selection as a fellow, no response came from the U.S. cultural
attaché in Jordan even as late as mid-April 1979. I then discovered that
the American Embassy had not even submitted the proposal to the
Jordanian government because it allegedly dealt with a sensitive topic.
Since any Arab country would have been a satisfactory research site, the
proposal was suggested to several others, including Morocco, Tunisia,
North Yemen, and Sudan. In the meantime, taking advantage of my
presence in the Middle East to attend a conference, I stopped in Jordan
to check on my proposal. After I assured the U.S. cultural attaché that

I would be able to get a research permit, he agreed to present the proposal to the Jordanian government after I secured the permit. I agreed to the condition, but family matters eventually made us decide to stay in the United States. Within a few months, other responses were received. Through a friend who was helping establish the Yemeni Center for Research and Studies, I was advised to change some of the wording and drop some questions to make the proposal more likely to be approved in Yemen. Around November, however, permits were received from Morocco and Sudan.

Because of these delays, I was unable to finish all aspects of the research, even if complete cooperation was assured. The problem of securing permits resurfaced in 1983-1984 when I requested to complete the project, particularly focusing on interviews with teachers in Morocco. Since the previous permit had no specific date for concluding the project, the U.S. cultural office in Rabat was assured by the Moroccan Foreign Ministry (but not in writing) that there would be no problem. Because immediate decisions had to be made about schooling for the children, university leave, and so on, the Moroccans were pressed to give a written response, and, simultaneously, the proposal was forwarded to Tunisia on the assumption that the research climate in that country was freer than it would be in most parts of the Arab world (Raccagni 1972, p. 30), as reflected in the amount and quality of research (including survey research) done there in the past (Palmer et al., pp. 306–369; Sack 1972; Smith 1973; Rodolosi 1973; Taylor 1974). On the basis of verbal approvals from the foreign minitsry, I was advised to proceed to Morocco to begin my research. There were serious delays in securing the written permit, despite several official memos and numerous visits to the education and interior ministries. Eventually, the U.S. ambassador personally approached the Moroccan authorities to make a decision, which, happily, was positive.

Shortly thereafter, I was advised that a written approval was received from the Tunisian government. As required (Clancy-Smith 1984, p. 34), when I arrived in Tunisia I was attached to a Tunisian sponsoring institution, the National Institute of Educational Sciences (NIES). Since I arrived in the summer, some government offices were working with reduced staff or were completely shut down for several weeks. Because schools were not in session, not until October were serious efforts initiated to review the questionnaire to determine whether changes or deletions were necessary before an authorization was issued to visit schools. Here I will detail the questions and issues deemed sensitive. The following questions were deleted in the first round:

1. Is it easy to change any of the laws in Tunisia? Yes, No, DK (Don't Know).
2. Are all laws just? Yes, No, DK.

3. What the government does will take place no matter what people do. It is like the weather; there is nothing people can do about it. Yes, No, DK.

4. My family's opinions and ideas are not significant so far as the government is concerned. Correct, not correct, DK.

5. How far do you agree that effort rather than success is what is important? Fully agree, Agree somewhat, Disagree fully.

After further discussions and additional minor changes, I met with three NIES officials, and we went through the remaining questions very thoroughly. Examples of the suggested (and accepted) changes were

1. *Original:* If you were not Tunisian, what other country would you rather belong to and why?

New: After Tunisia, on which other countries do educational curricula focus?

2. *Original:* Which of the following characteristics is the *most important* for the head of state to have? (Choose only one.) He must be (a) very smart, (b) very honest, (c) able to deal with all sectors of society, (d) courageous, (e) democratic (non-despotic).

New: In general, what qualities should a head of state have?

3. *Original:* Name the three most famous Tunisians.

New: Name the three most famous personalities in Tunisia whether in the fields of politics, literature, culture, sports, etc.

4. *Original:* If you have knowledge of the following personalities, write a little something about each: Husni Mubarak, Ayatollah Khomeini, etc.

New: Do you have any information about the following personalities? Write it down: Husni Mubarak, Ayatollah Khomeini, etc.

In these examples, the incorporated changes were not viewed to be merely cosmetic; rather, the new wording was intended to lessen any potential sensitivity and perhaps generate somewhat different data. For example, there was concern as to what school children viewed as the most important quality in the president, even though all listed alternatives were good ones. In another question, which asked the students to name the prime minister in office, concern was expressed that some students might not know the name.

Once the questionnaire was in a form acceptable to NIES, its staff helped me draw a fairly representative sample, taking into consideration geographical, economic, and social factors. NIES then typed the questionnaire in Arabic on stencils, and it was ready to run off about 1,500 copies (and 500 short forms for teachers). However, an expected authorization from the Ministry of National Education did not arrive. The ministry claimed NIES could proceed without such authorization, but the latter refused. When the matter was placed before the minister himself, he denied permission. However, after further high-level discussions and a call to the prime minister's office, I was told that I could proceed with some minor changes to a couple of (unspecified) questions (clearly intended as a face-saving device). In a meeting with the minister of national education the next day, however, the public affairs and cultural officers from the U.S. embassy were told that, "under the present circumstances," there was no way the government could authorize administering questionnaires in schools. The circumstances concerned president Habib Bourguiba's serious illness in early November 1984 and the difficult economic conditions, the strikes, and the threatened strikes in and out of schools. These produced, according to many observers, a deep-seated sense of insecurity at the highest echelons of government (Ware 1985).

Conducting the Research

The research plan throughout the various parts of the project has been multifaceted, including both survey and content analysis data in addition to informal interviews and library research. The only sensitive area proved to be the surveys, meaning that other research was carried out without delays, hassles, or interruptions. I will, therefore, focus on the survey research.

Because of the atmosphere in Egypt in spring 1973, foreign researchers (especially Americans) were nervous to be seen with Egyptian officials when conducting interviews or gathering data. I was very pleased to receive the permit to visit schools in Cairo, but I was also concerned that at any time the permit would be withdrawn or the administered questionnaires seized. Consequently, I literally stayed up most of the night coding the data (about 400 in total), with the help of my wife, in case the questionnaires were later seized. Also, to administer a good-sized sample, I enlisted the aid of the classroom teachers from the schools where the survey was being conducted. Later, however, I found out that, despite my strict instructions about individual student responses, the students in a couple of classes supplied identical answers to all questions—which meant that these were useless and had to be discarded.

In 1980, a fortuitous set of circumstances facilitated my research and produced excellent results. My Palestinian background worked to my advantage, as did my Arabic language facility, in discussions with some Moroccan officials in the Ministry of Education who were embarrassed that their French was better than their native Arabic. The questionnaire was approved in my presence after a quick reading and a remark that "Morocco is more democratic (i.e., open) than Algeria. This would never be approved in Algeria!" At the time, I was pleased that regional rivalry helped facilitate my research and thought little about the validity of that comment. I discovered later that Morocco and Sudan were more open to research than were other Arab countries (see, for instance, Zartman 1970; Ibrahim 1980). Tunisian colleagues and officials at the NIES found it very hard to believe that I could conduct the survey in Morocco and Sudan, but especially in Morocco.

After receiving the Foreign and Interior Ministry approvals as well as the Education Ministry authorization, I had to get the approval of each subdistrict of the Ministry of Education that I planned to visit. Each required a written application and a copy of the questionnaire. Then, with the aid of their school supervisors, I selected appropriate schools with a proper mix of social class and urban-rural and male-female composition. Sometimes the target schools were named; at other times I was given information, advice, and a list of the schools in the district to visit as I saw fit.

Because so many approvals were required and as a result of the structured nature of the Education Ministry, no major problems were anticipated, but one did develop. As I was administering the questionnaire in one of the Marrakesh schools, the principal suddenly walked into the classroom and instructed the students to stop writing and to pass the questionnaires to his assistant. He then invited me to his office to lecture me about how disappointed he was that I would trick him into doing something illegal (unapproved). He had called the Ministry of Education subdistrict, he said, and it in turn had called Rabat and found that no one had approved a questionnaire that contained questions like the following: Are all laws just? What is a political party and what functions does it perform? Is what goes on in the government all in the public interest?

As we got into his car to drive toward the subdistrict office, I let him know how disappointed and hurt I was by his actions and suspicions, and I assured him that he would soon find out that he made a big mistake. He then realized that he could be in serious trouble and, almost in tears, begged me to consider his precarious situation.

At the subdistrict, the regional director told me that he was told that no copy of the questionnaire was provided to the Ministry of Education in Rabat. I then gave him the name and telephone number of the responsible official and invited him to call him in my presence. By then, he judged that it was time to solve the problem amicably and yet try to save face. He, therefore, proceeded to tell me how much is at stake for the school principal—that if any information from the survey reflected badly on his school, his career would be over and he could suffer in other ways. He then suggested that I eliminate some questions (i.e., to make it look like they had a point) and that the principal apologize to me. He would then offer the full cooperation of his office to help administer the questionnaire in any school in his district, including the one in which the incident had occurred. I decided it was a good compromise and asked which of sixty-seven questions he objected to. Three questions (almost randomly selected) were then crossed out, and I returned to my interrupted survey—after an apology from the principal. In total, I administered the questionnaire to about 1,400 students in Rabat/Sale, Casablanca, and Marrakesh.

In 1983-1984, I conducted over fifty in-depth interviews with elementary school principals in Morocco and administered a structured questionnaire to 563 teachers in forty-two schools in Rabat/Sale, Casablanca, Meknes/Toubkal, and Marrakesh. Only after the January 1984 riots (mainly initiated by students and teachers at elementary and secondary schools) did I encounter resistance to carrying out my survey; the Ministry of Education was reluctant to authorize research in the areas most affected by the riots. Also, in Marrakesh, two principals said they would cooperate but that I should start the survey in other schools and then return to them. Another principal, also in the Marrakesh area, said she would have preferred one question to read: "Which of the following characteristics is the most important for *a* (instead of *the*) head of state to have?" But she did not resist or object.

In Sudan, as others have noted (Bechtold 1973; Hale and Hale 1975), the research climate has been relatively permissive compared to that in other Arab countries. However, because of the problem in the south, I had to present persuasive arguments to the deputy minister of education to get the letter authorizing my research there. The main problems I faced were ones relating to the climate, lack of cross-country transportation, and disease (cholera and other epidemics). But I was able to secure the assistance of friends and new acquaintances who volunteered their cooperation in the administration of the questionnaire (about 1,700 students) in the Khartoum and Juba regions.

Summary and Conclusions

Conducting survey research in the Arab world is possible, especially on topics acceptable to or approved by the governments in office. Other issues are usually termed sensitive (they are seen as likely to cause embarrassment or some harm to the authorities). The authorities often refuse to allow such research, claiming that it constitutes a threat to the security of the state. In other words, they equate their political survival with state security—a situation not entirely unique to them, as we have seen in Western democracies, especially at the time of the Vietnam War and the Watergate scandal. Frequently, their main concern is internal, not external. They are not, strictly speaking, opposed to research as such but to any potential embarrassing or harmful consequences. Thus, to conduct individual interviews, even among adults and even concerning state foreign policy and security issues, is often feasible and perhaps tolerated, in part because the authorities are unable to stop it but also because they do not see it as threatening to their positions.

Survey research is a completely different story. In the case of school socialization, the survey instrument itself—the questionnaire—is feared because it is likely to introduce new ideas to the students and teachers involved. This is perhaps why some questions, including the following one about democracy, were viewed as sensitive by some Tunisian officials. "What is democracy? For each of the [six] following definitions, indicate Yes, No or DK.: (1) A system of government in which the people govern

. . . (5) A system of government in which people criticize the government without problems. . . ."

There is often suspicion and mistrust of outside researchers. Apart from the sensitivities described, the individuals being interviewed or the research population as a group often have legitimate concerns. In my Moroccan survey, individual teachers were anxious for fear that their names would be associated with some views provided in the questionnaire. Also, principals worried that the teachers' views might reflect badly on the school, for example, by being too radical or critical of the regime. They also worried, as one principal put it, in case it became known that many of his students did not know the name of the prime minister.

Despite the problems and the frustrations, however, the rewards are great. In fact, if the research is carried out properly and under the right circumstances, the governments concerned realize and willingly admit its value. I was pleasantly surprised to receive a letter from the Moroccan Ministry of Education long after I provided them with a brief report and left the country. The letter praised my research effort, wished me well on future research, requested copies of future writings on the subject, and generally expressed the government official's good will.

References

Bechtold, P. K. (1973), "Research Facilities in the Sudan," *MESA Bulletin* 7:2, 23–31.

Clancy-Smith, J. (1984), "Research Facilities in Tunisia—Part II," *MESA Bulletin* 18:1, 31–34.

Hale, G. A., and S. Hale (1975), "Research Facilities in the Sudan: Addendum," *MESA Bulletin* 9:2, 30–35.

Ibrahim, S. E. (1980), *Ittijahat al-ra'iy al-'amm al-'Arabi nahwa mas'alat al-wahda (Arab Public Opinion and the Question of [Arab] Unity)*, Center for Arab Unity Studies, Beirut.

Palmer, M., et al. (1982), *Survey Research in the Arab World: An Analytical Index*, Middle East and North African Studies Press, Outwell, England.

Raccagni, M., and J. Simmons (1972), "Research Facilities in Tunisia," *MESA Bulletin* 6:1, 30–36.

Rodolosi, R. A. (1973), "A Study of the Development and Role of Secondary Schools in the New Independent Republic of Tunisia," unpublished Ed.D. dissertation, Wayne State University, Detroit.

Sack, R. (1972), "Education and Modernization in Tunisia: A Study on the Relationship Between Education and Other Variables and Attitudinal Modernity," unpublished Ph.D. dissertation, Stanford University, Stanford, Calif.

Smith, S. L. (1973), "Nation-Building in Tunisia: The Impact of Education and Socialization," unpublished Ph.D. dissertation, Louisiana State University, New Orleans.

Taylor, E. C., Jr., (1974), "Education and Nation-Building: A Behavioral Analysis of the Political Socialization of Tunisian Lycee Students," Unpublished Ph.D. dissertation, University of Michigan, Ann Arbor.

Ward, R. E., ed. (1964), *Studying Politics Abroad*, Little, Brown, Boston.

Ware, L. B. (1985), "The Role of the Tunisian Military in the Post-Bourguiba Era," *Middle East Journal* 39:1, 27–47.

Zartman, I. W. (1970), "Research Facilities in Algeria," *MESA Bulletin* 4:1, 42–50.

Zghal, A., and H. Karoui (1973), "Decolonization and Social Science Research: The Case of Tunisia," *MESA Bulletin* 7:3, 11–27.

6

Some Political and Cultural Considerations Bearing on Survey Research in the Arab World

Iliya Harik

It is no surprise that survey research appeared first in countries with a democratic system of government. In a democracy, more than in any other system, public opinion carries considerable political weight; hence it is much sought after by public officers, elected and appointed alike. For the appointed, it is important to have feedback regarding policy and policy implementation; for the elected, it is a matter of political survival. Initiative for gathering information comes thus from the very nature of the political system. At this level, survey research becomes a matter of business; the demand for information generates business agencies ready to provide the merchandise, hence polling centers.

Survey Research and the Political System

The principle of linkage between the political system and information holds true for academic circles as well. Only under conditions of political freedom can one inquire about how people feel and think about policy and public servants. Under such conditions, inquiry of all kinds flourishes. Academics interested in reaching generalizations about political behavior and attitudes apply their ingenuity to develop techniques for eliciting information from the public. Democracy by itself, however, does not necessarily lead to the discovery of survey research. This form of academic inquiry is the product of developments in political thought in the West and in the United States, under the influence of the Chicago school, and Merriam in particular. Emphasis on politics as a form of activity and on the individual citizen as the unit of analysis and action led research to focus on individual attitudes and behavior. Psychology and sociology preceded political science in eliciting information from individuals about attitudes and behavior and provided political science with the techniques necessary for survey research. In short, survey research, a relatively recent phenomenon, is made possible under conditions of freedom and is inspired by developments in political thought and the social sciences.

In Third World countries, interest in survey research has been the product of dissemination of information and technology from advanced nations to the less advanced. It has no indigenous cultural or technological basis in the new lands where it has been adopted. The Arab world is one such recipient culture. But has the Arab world been a hospitable recipient of survey research as we know it? The extent and depth of survey research in the Arab world are still very limited, and in large measure they are the product of research initiated and conducted by foreigners (Lerner in the Levant, Ashford in Morocco, and Berger in Egypt, on the pioneering side). Many expatriates and foreign-educated academics have been conducting research in Arab countries, and many also are writing their results in Arabic (witness S. Ibrahim). Yet on balance, the total product is meager. Why is that?

Obviously, the first answer is that the history of modern education in the social sciences in this region is very recent, and therefore the movement may be considered to be in its incipient form and not likely to develop rapidly. This explanation, however, should not be exaggerated. Reasons beyond time militate against the development of survey research in the Arab world. The most important is that the political climate for this type of research does not exist. Aside from Lebanon, whose political system currently lies in ruins, there is not a single democratic system of government in the Arab world. Thus neither the freedom to exercise one's knowledge exists, nor does the desire among people in power to elicit such information. On the contrary, the influentials have shown a desire to curtail such tendencies among scholars. Moreover, since most scholars are also employees of the state, they are particularly dependent on its good will for permission to exercise their expertise and interests and to obtain the funds necessary for such research. The Arab world, with few exceptions, has no private institutions that provide support for scholarly work, and therefore funding comes mainly from official sources. This situation imposes additional constraints on scholars who wish to conduct research. Authoritarianism complicates the picture further in that the free flow of information is viewed as inimical to the political interests of national leaders. Thus even if research is permitted, its publication is by no means certain.

This does not mean that research is completely blocked in Arab countries. The kind of research and the degree of authoritarianism affect what happens in academia. Research is discouraged in political fields of inquiry or related subjects; restrictions are not as stringent in certain areas of sociology, economics, and even psychology. A number of political regimes in the Arab world are more open than others (e.g., Egypt, Kuwait, Tunisia, and Morocco). No official restrictions have ever been imposed on research in Lebanon, the major problem there being a scarcity of scholarship and funding. One can identify research done in the area of politics, of both survey and field nature, though it is not excessive and is often conducted under the label of sociology or rural development or some other euphemism. For example, most research about politics in Tunisia is conducted under the label of sociology, whereas political science sections at universities are almost entirely legalistic. This applies to most North African countries.

Motivated by nationalistic interest, the Arab Unity Center, located in Beirut, recently sponsored a study of political attitudes among the citizens of Arab states from the Maghreb and the Mashreq. Conducted under the leadership of Saad Eddin Ibrahim, the study is a unique piece of work: It is sponsored by a private scholarly agency and applied in a large number of countries with varying degrees of authoritarianism, and it is explicitly political. Perhaps the fact that the study was concerned not with the attitudes of citizens toward their own leaders and government but with general cultural-political attitudes made this study possible. Still, only nine out of twenty Arab states allowed the research to be conducted. Politically sensitive governments prevented the research designers from including questions of a nationally political nature. As Ibrahim put it, "This research experience has shown that the Arab political environment is extremely hostile to scientific field research and deeply suspicious of the motives of serious and objective inquiry when it does not emanate from within itself or one of its trusted agencies."

Foreign Involvement in the Arab Research Effort

Foreign researchers are mainly American and have received greater cooperation from Arab governments than have Arab citizens themselves, perhaps because of the expectation that research results would not be disseminated in the country itself and that they would be published in a foreign language, anyway. When it started in the early 1950s, foreigners conducting research were limited to Ph.D. candidates responding to the surge in the study of foreign countries in U.S. universities after World War II. This was also prompted by the change in orientation of political scientists from legalistic to sociological and psychological approaches and by the realization of the importance of comparative findings for scholarship. The fact that the United States government encouraged studies of foreign countries for reasons of national interest made available abundant funds for such research. Private foundations, following the official lead, committed generous sums for this purpose. Thus in many ways, the 1950s and 1960s were the golden era of comparative research in the United States.

The 1970s was a period of decline, the result of prolonged recession and disillusionment with foreign involvement on the part of Americans after Vietnam. The retrenchment and drying up of funds for research were not limited to official sources: private organizations followed suit. The change is noted by jokes in the 1960s related to the various rates peasants charged for master's degree interviews and those for Ph.D. degree interviews. In the 1970s, the mood in academia was expressed by a scholar declaring that he or she was dressed up and ready but had no place to go.

The results of most research conducted by foreigners and expatriates never reached the native people in their own language, though they were made available in English. I, for one, never heard a complaint from officials who gave me permission to do research or from local scholars regarding the results of my research. When I returned with copies of my book, it was received with amusement and politeness and put on shelves of uninterested bureaucrats. In Egypt, one of very few developing countries where my book was known, it was used by faculty at the American University, and though it was known to some faculty in the national universities, it was never used. This is in a way instructive, because Egypt has the most advanced research and scholarly community in the Arab world.

Foreign involvement and particularly U.S. involvement in research in the Arab world did not die down or decline for long; it returned in the late 1970s in a new form: as part of the massive aid effort extended by the U.S. government to Egypt. I do not know, however, of any other Arab country in which U.S. research interests have been revived except in Egypt. Minor efforts have started to be made in northern Yemen and Tunisia recently to encourage Americans to conduct research, and U.S. institutions have been set up with governmental support in these countries. The research effort launched by USAID in Egypt was carried out by the joint efforts of Egyptian scholars, U.S. scholars, and U.S. consultant houses. It involved a wide range of fields ranging from local government and rural development to urban water projects. It was, on the whole, oriented toward particular projects of a practical nature and therefore took the form of reports. These reports were made available in most cases for review by whomever happened to ask for them, but USAID itself made no effort to disseminate the product.

This effort went unhampered until recently and in particular until spring 1982, when an article in protest against this free foreign reign in the research domain of the country appeared. The weekly magazine, *al Ahram al Iqtisadi,* which published the article, followed up with a series of articles, some attacking USAID research and others defending it. These articles are instructive in the way they reflect the variety of attitudes by Egyptians regarding research in their country, ranging from the chauvinistic and unenlightened to the very learned and instructive. While I have no extensive sources of information on the impact of the campaign, I know from personal experience that it has had an inhibiting effect on USAID and has triggered such defensiveness of the part of Egyptian officials that foreign academic institutions in Egypt have suffered as a result.

The episode with USAID may not be the most serious encounter with foreign officially directed research. A rather disturbing new development has emerged in the United States that might put most U.S.-directed research in the Third World in jeopardy. The Department of Education, which for years provided funding for U.S. universities to teach foreign languages, is in danger of being dismantled and funds for it cut off. On the other hand, enormous sums of federal funds have been put into the Department of Defense and are at the disposal of the intelligence section in that department. A rather strong push is being made now by officials from the Defense Department to entice university faculty and centers to accept the funds they generously offer for research in other parts of the world. This new tendency in the disposal of official funds for research does not seem to disturb specialists in European studies and in Soviet or East European studies. The tradition in these areas has been an open linkage between officially supported research and security matters.

However, in Third World countries sensitivities run high and the national feeling, unlike in Western Europe, does not identify its security with that of the United States. Thus center directors who have to do with Third World countries are concerned about the possible effect all this will have on the continued viability of academic research in developing countries. Many center directors have refused to accept funds or associate themselves with the Defense Department's effort. Their concern is that there is no possible check on individual scholars accepting such funds and traveling to developing countries for research. Once one American academician is identified as a recipient of intelligence funds, a shadow would be cast on most others, since little can be done to distinguish between clandestine research and honest scholarly research. This storm is in the formative stage and will soon, I expect, blow forcefully on the research field. We can only brace ourselves for the worst and hope for the best.

Survey Research and the Cultural System

I will now return to the domestic arena and try to identify some of the cultural (unofficial) biases against research in the Arab world. In many quarters, one encounters objections to survey research by Arab scholars who question the validity of the techniques or the concepts employed. These objections come mostly from those who are not educated in Western countries or have little education in the social sciences in general. The most common argument is that survey techniques are products of Western cultures and do not apply to Arab culture. One such argument was made by a reviewer of Ibrahim's book. Ibrahim's response was succinct and to the point and, I hope, will put this matter to rest. He pointed out that instruments of science have no nationality and only confused minds would think otherwise.

Another argument of the same nature is that social science concepts developed in the West are inapplicable to Arab culture. Here the case is not so clear cut. We are familiar, for instance, with the long-standing debate regarding the concept of social class and whether or not it applies to Third World societies. Similarly, one can raise questions regarding such concepts as anomie or alienation. Where is the source of confusion? To answer this question, we may have to underline the difference between analytical thought and applied science. The social sciences are based on the principles of consistency of deductive thinking and the truth of empirically derived information. Violation of the deductive or inductive methods cannot be justified in Timbuktu any more than in Paris. There is no geographic home for the laws that govern rational thinking and empirical inquiry.

To properly utilize these methods, it is necessary to conceptualize, to rise to a level of abstraction. When one proposes a hypothesis that the accuracy of information is directly related to the number of intermediaries through which it goes, one is conceptualizing and also making an observation about the real world that may or may not be true. The way we find out if it is true or not is through a proper empirical inquiry. First, one has to observe something about the factual world. Thus if a scholar observes symptoms of group anxiety in a very mobile and industrial setting, then goes to a village in Tunisia at a time of drought and identifies peasants' concerns about drought with anomie observed in a different setting, he is simply confused. This by no means makes concepts such as anomie, or conceptualization in general, a pattern of thinking applicable to some cultures but not to others. The fact that some scholars confuse and misrepresent the phenomena they examine does not reflect on the adequacy of social science concepts. The tendency of Western and Western-educated scholars to flippantly compare unrelated manifestations of behavior in two different settings and cultures makes survey researchers and others subject to a charge of misapplied cultural thinking. This may indeed happen in one society and one culture and does not occur only in cross-cultural contexts.

Other cultural biases or conditons have to be carefully considered in Third World countries. In Arab countries, for instance, the researchers may have to establish a relationship of trust with the subjects before asking them personal questions. They are not dealing with an open society where the activity of research is understood and where interviews could be secured by a simple explanation; the level of suspicion and distrust is higher. A subject may naturally inquire why a stranger asks personal questions, what is behind it, what it may this lead to, can the questioner be trusted, and what is in it for the subject.

The survey researcher may step on a very slippery cultural slope. Asked to answer questions by a stranger, an Arab may be distrustful but compelled by cultural norms to show friendliness to strangers and hospitality. He or she may well oblige but not offer honest answers. In

Arab culture this does not constitute dishonesty; it is rather a cultural pattern of behavior known as "face." A person may ask an Arab friend for something or just mention the need for something, and the Arab would readily offer assistance, knowing full well that he could not deliver. To do otherwise would be in violation of the pleasantries associated with sociability. Face is a very important phenomenon in Arab culture. If a person takes a walk with an Arab and moves toward a narrow door, the Arab will make room for the friend or companion to move in first; he will indeed insist that the companion go in first out of politeness. If these two persons the next day drive separate automobiles on the city streets and do not know who is behind the steering wheel of the other car, the reverse will follow. The hassle becomes not who should oblige but who should get the better of the other. They will have no eye-to-eye contact and exchange no pleasantries. Field researchers are sometimes in the same situation: If they just present themselves to a person, introduce themselves, and tell the person that they want to ask questions for some reason, they may not be rebuffed but they also may not receive the right answers.

Another phenomenon is the effect of status, which is noticeable among poor people. If an educated person presents himself or herself to them, they may not deny a request because of the aura of power that they attribute to the effendi. As a result they may produce answers that they imagine to be what the effendi would like to hear.

These two cultural phenomena can be circumvented. It may require some expense, but it has to be done. First, a researcher must establish more than fleeting contact with the subject. Several visits and skillful effort to present the case clearly and to dispel any fears or suspicions are in order. If, on the other hand, a researcher is dealing with a small group such as the inhabitants of a city quarter or a village, a reasonably long stay in the community is advisable, and visits to the notables and not-so-notable members of the community are necessary. I feel most satisfied with the field approach by which the scholar lives in the community before conducting a fomal survey and becomes familiar with the community, its problems, leaders, conflicts, friendships, political predilections, and the like.

Pros and Cons of Foreign-Directed Research

Let me now summarize some of the pro and con arguments gleaned from the articles in *al Ahram al-Iqtisadi* regarding foreign conducted research, beginning with a word about the context of the journal articles. Obviously the editorial board of the journal is inclined toward the conspiracy theory by allocating more space and the most prominent space to the most extreme writer over a long period of time. It should also be noted that the critical campaign was not directed against USAID-initiated research only but also included all foreign-directed or -conducted research, the American University of Cairo included. Third, many writers do not trust the government to be a good judge of the national interest in research. Finally, though the following account reflects the basic views, it is not exhaustive, especially in that the writer missed a number of the early issues discussing the controversial subject.

The various views expressed may be presented on a continuum starting from the most extreme to the moderate to the opposed. Those who express the most extreme views maintain that foreign-directed research represents imperialistic interests, that it is inimical to Egyptian national interests, and that it is conspiratorial. They suspect the motivations of the foreign agents conducting research, attribute undisclosed purposes to them, and feel that the information collected will be used against Egypt. Thus they maintain that research by foreigners renders a disservice to national interests and is harmful to national security. Those Egyptians who cooperate in the enterprise are either traitors or dupes. This category of writers includes those who maintain that research conducted by foreigners represents an assault on Egyptian culture and should not be tolerated. One writer went so far as to insist that sending Egyptian students to study abroad is a form of assault on the Egyptian culture since study abroad has the tendency to change the norms and values of these students.

Although moderate critics do not share the conspiracy theory, they maintain that research is political and that information flow should be carefully scrutinized by Egyptian national authorities and subjected to Egyptian direction. Joint U.S.-Egyptian projects tend to allocate Egyptians to a subordinate position, reflecting a general dependency relationship that is no longer tolerable. These writers also suspect that the foreign party, or even worse the funding agency, interferes in the construction of questionnaires and the theoretical perspective of the inquirers. They advocate the elevation of the Egyptian party in the joint research projects to an equal if not dominant position. They would like to see the end of the so-called patronizing attitude of foreign donors or participants. They accuse the Egyptian side (the government) of having abdicated its role in carrying out national research and of having created a research vacuum that is being filled by foreigners.

Those opposed to the criticism campaign present a set of defensive arguments: that national interest or security is not impaired by foreign research since it has to be approved by the government, that there are no secret clauses or objectives, and that all research procedures and products are made public. They argue that Egyptian scholars on joint projects have been slighted, but they are either naive people who could easily be duped or people who were insulted by having their national integrity questioned. They point out that some research is done by foreign participants upon the request of Egyptian universities or government. They make distinctions among various foreign researchers and do not accept the allegation that all foreign researchers work for intelligence agencies. They tend to ridicule the notion that information in this day and age could be restricted and bottled up inside national borders. Finally, they warn that the negative attitude shown by the critical writers may lead to restrictions on the freedom of research, not only for foreigners, but for Egyptians as well.

PART TWO

Issues of Relevance, Methodology, and Cumulativeness

7

The Relevance of Survey Research in Arab Society

Barbara Lethem Ibrahim

The greater part of this book is devoted to discussion of ways in which survey methods can be applied more effectively in the Arab world. The prior question of why one has chosen to study a given topic through the lens of survey techniques is the subject of this chapter. Unless the researcher is absolutely clear about the relationship among the study's purpose, the necessary data, and the methods suitable for data generation, no amount of technical advice will ensure the desired outcome. Good social science research results when the methods of data gathering flow from the nature of the subject under investigation. In this chapter I will argue that the range of social questions appropriate for survey treatment may be narrower than current practice has indicated; at the same time, there are new and creative applications of survey methods that have not yet been fully explored in the Arab world.

The issue of relevance will be treated in terms of appropriateness—the fit between topic, data requirements, and method. The discussion necessarily leaves aside broader questions about whether a given research topic is worthy of investigation. Such issues are raised in other chapters in this book—in discussions of ethical considerations and of the ways that Western paradigms have tended to determine the content of survey studies in the Arab world.

In keeping with the spirit of discussions at the Bellagio conference, relevance issues are framed here in terms of a series of questions that researchers need to pose at the outset of their work on any new project. Conference participants agreed that failure to ask and answer the following questions at the design stage often resulted in the failure of a study to reach its intended goals, even when subsequent data gathering stages were well executed. Who is the intended audience for the study findings and how will the results be used? What is the scope and depth of information needed to address the research problem? What is the appropriate sampling unit to target?

Although these questions are general and apply equally to national-level statistical surveys and case studies in a single community, they are often ignored: Either the method is selected first and this determines the kind of data generated ("We should conduct a survey before launching the development project"), or the questions are incompletely raised and methodology decisions are based on such considerations as audience, without taking into account cost effectiveness or the real information needs involved. In the latter case, donor agencies as well as government bodies have sometimes been guilty of encouraging costly surveys when other methods would have produced equivalent or superior results (Chambers 1983).

The following sections address each of the questions in turn, drawing on the experiences and insights of Bellagio conference participants to point toward the optimal strategic use of survey techniques for the advancement of Arab social science.

Who Is the Audience?

A research undertaking typically involves at least three parties: those sponsoring the study, those carrying it out, and those who will ultimately become "consumers" of its results. Assuming that most readers of this book fall into the middle category—practitioners and students of the research process—the other two categories may be considered as the audience. The members of the audience are often people whose orientations and interests diverge from those of social scientists. A closer examination of the requirements of the audience for a prospective study may be crucial to its ultimate success. All too often, however, researchers have in mind a different audience for results than do the study's sponsors, and this divergence can lead to inappropriate decisions about the study design.

At Bellagio participants from around the region identified the groups that have made steadily increasing demands for survey data: the growing number of Arab social science research centers, commercial interests, governmental agencies, military institutions, and the international donor organizations involved in promoting development. To gain some idea of the volume of survey research these demands have generated, Monte Palmer and his colleagues compiled a bibliography of published survey studies for the Arab region up to 1982. Three hundred and sixty-one studies were cited, excluding the annual statistical surveys conducted by national census bureaus. In a forthcoming bibliography for Egypt alone, the authors found more than 150 separate survey studies over a twenty-year period (El Safty et al. 1984). Judging from these inventories and from the identifiable research that remains unpublished, it may be safe to estimate that at least 100 new surveys are carried out in the Arab world each year.

In the midst of this burgeoning volume of survey activity, social scientists in the region rarely have time to reflect on the needs and characteristics of their research audience. The Bellagio conference provided an opportunity for a distinguished group of survey practitioners to ask, "Survey knowledge for whom?" In so doing they identified some important unresolved issues and problems and were able to offer practical suggestions for narrowing the gap between sponsors, practitioners, and consumers of survey research.

In Western societies where survey methods first emerged, two primary audiences stimulated the development of this technique: (1) the social science community itself, committed to scientific examination of social phenomena to advance understanding and to predict human behavior and (2) commercial firms, which required detailed information about consumer attitudes and behavior to plan market strategies in a competitive economic environment. Politicians and government agencies could be added to this list of audiences in the West. Each used survey techniques developed by indigenous researchers to address local research problems, whether theoretical or applied.

A different situation has emerged as survey research was introduced in the Arab world. Foreign researchers conducted the earliest studies in the region, typically directing their findings back to the Western social science community. Many Arab social scientists trained abroad have continued this scholarly tradition. Over time, and because of the expense involved in large-scale surveying, Arab governments have gradually emerged as the major local sponsors of survey research in their respective countries.

The data requirements of government agencies usually derive from the necessity of deciding how to employ scarce resources to further development objectives. These eminently practical needs can be well served by good survey studies. Problems arise, however, when social scientists misperceive this audience and produce studies more suitable to their academic peers. Because applied social research continues to hold an important place in Arab society and to influence the course of development in all its dimensions, closer attention is needed to the interplay of objectives that motivate governmental sponsors, on one hand, and social science researchers, on the other.

The case of applied research in Arab countries commissioned directly by government officials or indirectly through donor agencies is illustrative. Usually these sponsors want easily interpreted data, presented in a concise format, to answer a set of practical questions about a target population. For example, what are the health practices affecting infant mortality in the countryside? What is the effect of labor migration on wage rates in the construction industry? Typically, the answers are needed immediately (or yesterday), so that this audience is not persuaded by the elegance of sophisticated methodologies if their application will require months or years to produce a finished research monograph.

Although the cabinet minister or other agency chief who ultimately must approve study requests may be fluent in several languages, more typically a middle-level technical person will in fact utilize the study results. At this level it is rare to find persons who are comfortable working with documents unless they are in Arabic. Also, the tremendous workload of most of these civil servants makes it a near certainty that they will not read in detail any report of more than ten or twenty pages.

How do the needs of this audience mesh with the needs and characteristics of those who produce social surveys? Faced with exponential growth in the demand for information, sponsoring agencies have relied heavily on the resources of Arab universities to carry out needed social science research. This relationship gives rise to a special set of circumstances, some of which are conducive to excellent studies and some of which may lead to gaps between study objectives as viewed by sponsors and by researchers.

Academic professors, many of whom have been trained in the West, are typically commissioned to supervise a needed study. These individuals work under several constraints. Because they have multiple demands on their time they must remain close to the city in which their university is based. In approaching a research problem, faculty members may favor the sophisticated techniques learned during their graduate training; however, these methods often require expenditures that exceed the means of most professors in the region engaged in independent research. Research requested by the government or a donor agency is accompanied by a level of funding that makes application of these techniques possible. Furthermore, faculty members and their students naturally hope to publish the results of their work in places where it will be accessible to other social scientists, in book form and in academic journals. Those with Western training often are more comfortable writing in English or French than in Arabic.

Given these factors, it becomes easy to see why the audience for the writings of a university-based social scientist may be far removed from the world of the civil servant or development officer who originally commissioned the study. Not surprisingly his or her sense of a preferred audience will influence the choice of method for conducting research. In many cases in which a survey strategy was inappropriately applied to a research problem, the underlying reason has been that a survey was judged to produce the sort of quantified data and potential for statistical analysis favored by an academic audience.

The result is all too often a bulky research monograph full of charts and tables, which sits unread among a pile of other reports on the official's shelf. The information needed for the official's work may in fact be contained within the study. In this case, the form of presentation of results, not the method, is mainly at fault—a problem that could be corrected relatively easily. In other cases, the usefulness of the information itself as generated by a survey design must be questioned. Sometimes the user has well-focused data needs: a profile of one population group, the distribution of public services, or a reading of individuals' attitudes toward a given program. In these instances, information needs may be well served by a survey. If, on the other hand, the user wants to understand changing behavior patterns and the key influences are not yet known, or the subject is one that has not previously been systematically studied, a survey may be premature. Especially when a little understood microlevel social process is the focus of study, sample surveys are likely to be less effecive than selective in-depth interviews or other intensive field methods. As a general rule, when the study's aim is to enter a new research area—and ask "What's going on here?"—it is probably too soon for surveying.

Policymakers are only one of several groups in the Arab region that routinely turn to social scientists for their information needs. Instead of attempting to discuss in detail all these actors and their specific data requirements, I will offer a thumbnail sketch of each, with suggested guidelines for selecting research strategies consonant with its general orientation and need (see Table 7.1).

Table 7.1 offers suggestions for better definition of the intended audience for study findings and a guide to the choice of an appropriate methodology. The table's format is a general typology that identifies a range of potential users of research findings in the Arab region. Although it may not apply to every country and field of study, it is presented as a rough guide for those embarking on field research projects. The table draws on conference discussions both at Bellagio and at a previous seminar on field data collection held in Beirut in 1974 (See Roling in Kearl (ed.) 1976).

In practice, more than one group is often the intended audience for a given study. As previously mentioned, the funding source or sponsor of a project may be different from the consumer of its findings. As the Bellagio discussions made clear, a policy-planning audience and an academic audience can be accommodated simultaneously and effectively. The keys to success are early explication of the requirements of both and some creativity in designing research that serves multiple purposes without compromising standards.

When more than one group is expected to make use of survey findings, researchers can take steps to enhance the effectiveness of their prospective study design. First, agreement should be reached about the primary audience to be addressed. Here the word *primary* may mean most important, or it may denote the group with most pressing need for the study findings. Policymakers and program implementers generally have the most urgent requirements for quick results. Target populations may in fact have a more pressing need for information, but because their needs are rarely articulated, they are usually perceived to be a patient audience.

Survey researchers can address the need for timely findings, even on projects in which lengthy data processing and analysis will be required for the final report. Several techniques have been developed in Third World settings for providing quick results from the field. A family of

TABLE 7.1
Guide to target audience and methodology

Target Audience	Implications for Methodology
Policymakers: need data on national trends, sensitive indicators of change, problem diagnostics, indicators to provide feed back on policy measures.	Surveys useful when statistical verification needed and if (1) relevant variables are known, (2) target population is well defined, and (3) findings needed for planning can be produced in a timely way. In other cases, a preliminary expedition to map the subject using selective interviewing and observation may be appropriate.
Project Implementers: need area baseline data, profiles of target beneficiaries, tested action strategies, feasibility, monitoring, and evaluation studies. (This category includes project supervisors as well as sponsoring program officers.)	Case studies, community network analysis, participant observation may yield most useful data. Surveys, to be effective, should be narrowly focused, rapidly executed, and reported in terms of problem-solving information. Groups, rather than individuals, or households, workgroups, and organizations may be most relevant as sampling units
Research Colleagues in Same Field: need to know state-of-the-art theoretical and methodological approaches, look for hypothesis tests. (This category is often the most salient for researchers.)	Best method will be that which advances the level of knowledge or understanding in a given field. Important considerations may be potential collaboration, replication, secondary analysis from existing data sets.
Researchers in Other Fields: need jargon-free studies with findings relevant to their work and clear explanations of the rationale behind research strategies in other disciplines. (This is a neglected but increasingly important audience.)	This will usually be a secondary audience for research findings. Useful to draw in members of this audience as advisers to the study to encourage collaboration and to sustain interest in results.
Communication/Dissemination Agents: need information about target populations to pursue public education or opinion-molding objectives.	Useful: knowledge, attitude, and practice (KAP) surveys, marketing surveys, opinion polls, panel designs to measure change over time.

TABLE 7.1, *cont.*

Target Audience	Implications for Methodology
Target Groups Themselves (The research subjects): (1) Individually: need concrete information to improve current practices in health, nutrition, livelihoods, etc.	Surveys may be of little direct benefit. Useful: results of experimental interventions and demonstration projects, case studies, evaluations of alternative practices. Illiteracy may limit access to written reports.
(2) Collectively: need information to aid in organizing for change (data on local power channels, legal processes, lobbying tactics, access to resources).	Useful: network analyses of power relations, participatory research where the involvement of community members in data gathering becomes an avenue of mobilization.
Students: need teaching materials written at their level of understanding based on conditions in their own society. Need ample discussion of the problems encountered in the research process, not just the polished final product.	Useful: reports that include multiple methods used to address the same problem. These will illustrate for students how the form of data gathering can sometimes influence the direction of findings.
The Literate Public: need information and analysis that is free of jargon and technical terms but which conveys the strengths of a scientific approach to public issues. Rarely the primary audience for a study, but one that deserves consideration by social scientists in the region.	No implications for methodology. Useful: presentation of findings in low-cost paperback books, clear and simple tables of statistics; important to stress how conclusions derive from systematic data-collection, not ideological positions or traditional wisdom.

these methods, which are well tested and documented, are known as Rapid Rural Appraisal (RRA) (See Barnett 1979; Rhoades 1982). These methods often draw in members of the population to be studied as key informants, as leaders of group interviews, or as coinvestigators alongside social scientists. (Chambers 1983).

The basic tenets of RRA could be applied in a variety of settings and substantive fields. With forethought such techniques could be incorporated as the initial phase of a broader research project. Production of an interim report that concisely summarized the initial findings would meet the user's need for timely data, as well as provide the basis for midcourse adjustments in field work as it continued. Upon the completion of the research, a detailed final report of findings would serve to reinforce or suggest revision of the first-round results. If this report is highly technical, a summary should be prepared, based on those aspects of the findings relevant to accurate interpretation of the earlier report. With advance planning, this kind of staged survey design could be achieved without adding greatly to the overall costs or time required by a standard sample survey.

Recent advances in data entry technology make it possible to have relatively inexpensive portable machines in the field while surveying is under way. Coding, entry, and cleaning of data can be managed simultaneously with each day's caseload of interviews. This means that basic statistical manipulations of a subsample can be done prior to covering the entire sample. Creative use of this capacity might also be a way of producing timely feedback for the audience and perhaps "buying time" for a more rigorous subsequent analysis. In such cases, the research director would be called upon to make a careful judgment as to the degree of generalization justified from the preliminary findings.

To summarize, the Arab world has a continued need for the analytic tools of survey research, both to advance general understanding of societies in transition and to inform the policies and programs of national development. Social scientists can improve the quality of their contribution in both areas, by consciously seeking to address the data requirements of their audience. In addition, they can continue to innovate and adapt standard approaches to survey data collection to reflect practical contingencies and to serve the multiple needs of survey sponsors and survey users in the region.

What Scope and Depth of Information Are Needed to Address a Research Problem?

The necessary scope and depth of information are central issues to any research undertaking, but the relative importance of determining these at the outset of a project varies with the research strategy. With field methods such as participant observation it is relatively easy to make midcourse adjustments in the variables under scrutiny, the type and number of informants, and even the language and format of data gathering. Unproductive lines of inquiry can be abandoned entirely based on early findings, provided that the field observer has allotted sufficient time for this sort of reorientation. Survey methods, on the other hand, enforce a higher degree of prior planning to successfully achieve their objectives. Not only must the sample population be identified and question wording determined; the survey researcher should also have every step of the analysis of the data clearly in mind before moving into the field. This requirement for prior planning can be an advantage of survey approaches to the extent that it encourages logic and efficiency of effort. At the same time, mistakes made in judging data requirements in advance will be costly.

A familiar paradox of survey research is that more data are usually collected than will ever be effectively utilized; yet in the analysis stage, too often the information needed on a key variable is incomplete. A good deal of waste and oversight can be avoided in survey studies if researchers plan their data needs ahead in some detail. One implication is that in situations in which the researcher does not know from the outset what variables are central to his or her analysis of a social phenomenon or what level of detail is necessary to adequately answer the research questions, a survey method is almost always premature. Other techniques of observation or selective in-depth interviewing can more effectively deal with the prior need to identify important relationships among variables. When that point is reached, the researcher will be able to design a survey with greater confidence. The survey characteristics—scientific sampling, generalizability of findings, ease of replication—can then be exploited to good advantage for testing the relationships uncovered by prior studies.

The Novelty of Surveys

Besides these general considerations, which apply wherever social research is carried out, some issues of data relevance take on special importance in Third World settings and particularly in the Arab region. They derive from aspects of the social environment and the constraints these pose for conducting sample surveys.

Most Arab peoples are unfamiliar with social science research aims and methods, though a growing number of communities, such as Lebanese university students, may in fact be overstudied. The novelty of collecting data for scientific purposes requires that researchers pay special attention to the act itself. Interviewing is an interaction setting, with all the accompanying implications for possible manipulation or misunderstanding of behavior. Cynthia Nelson argued at Bellagio that regardless of chosen methodology, social researchers should see themselves as entering into a dialogue with their subjects. This approach requires taking the field experience as a source of data itself and remaining alert to the perceptions and concerns of respondents.

These perceptions may take unexpected forms. An anthropologist studying health practices in a Yemeni village discovered that some of her informants had concluded that she must be approaching senility, despite a youthful appearance. Their evidence: She had to record everything said to her in a notebook in order not to forget it. Likewise, survey takers who are the first to show an interest in people's attitudes or problems can easily arouse expectations among respondents that cannot realistically be fulfilled. This poses an ethical dilemma as well as problems of data reliability. Beyond acknowledging as clearly as possible the likely consequences to the community of a study, the researcher needs to be on guard for deliberate distortions of information by those who hope to benefit in some way.

Researcher/Respondent Relations

Whenever studies are undertaken to plan social intervention, the opportunities for researcher/respondent misunderstanding are increased by the high stakes that respondents may perceive. These are cases in which survey data have the potential to materially benefit or damage a community. Suspicion, unfamiliarity with research methods, and lack of independent sources of knowledge can all combine to seriously distort the information a respondent offers. Usually the problems could have been anticipated and countered in designing the field techniques and by giving careful training to interviewers.

When a district of inner-city Cairo was slated for demolition and its residents were to be relocated elsewhere, an area survey was conducted. Interviewers, who were poorly prepared for their task, canvassed households to determine the number of occupants and the presence of commercial shop space in the district. Local residents, fearful of losing their homes and businesses, tried to second guess the aims of the survey takers. Many who had unlicenced shops or stalls did not report them, fearing confiscation. Later, when shops were allocated in the new area, these respondents were unable to claim space. Similarly, relatives who lived crowded six and eight into a single-room dwelling in the old district reported smaller families broken into nuclear units, hoping to qualify for more than one apartment. In the end, few additional housing units were assigned. So by reporting small families these households actually qualified for fewer rooms than they would have if they had given accurate figures to the survey takers.

Many members of the populations interviewed have had previous negative experience with people who collect information. Until recently, their only contact with survey takers was likely to have been connected with tax collection, military conscription, or other forms of arbitrary intervention by a distant authority. In defense, people became wary of any stranger seeking information and reluctant to cooperate fully if they did not know the ultimate uses of the data being sought. Their resultant secretiveness is based less on cultural norms than on concrete experience;

it represents their logical attempt to protect themselves, their families, and their community from perceived external threat.

On balance, some elements of Arab culture familiar to every local researcher actually encourage rapport and cooperation with the inquiring stranger. Showing courtesy and hospitality to visitors is a cornerstone of traditional Arab society. Indeed the norms of generosity to visitors, particularly in the home, are so thoroughly taught from childhood that adults feel compelled to respond to a guest's request, even when it requires inconvenience or discomfort. Often this impulse to accommodate a stranger is coupled with an unrestrained curiosity toward visitors— their origins, reasons for coming, and opinions about the community they have entered. Researchers can and should build on these positive elements to create an atmosphere of trust in the encounters of data collection.

The challenge is greatest in large-scale household survey projects, in which contact with respondents is typically brief. Often a researcher cannot prepare a community in advance of the interviews. In effect, researchers have only one opportunity—at the outset of administering the questionnaire—to establish trust and persuade the respondent to answer frankly and completely. The situation is somewhat better when respondents are not geographically dispersed. A sampling design that draws respondents from a limited number of work settings or organizations, for example, enables the research team to establish its identity through officials or key individuals whose endorsement is respected. Nevertheless, survey methods in general allow a minimum of prior interaction to establish trust and ensure full cooperation.

Problems of respondent trust and strategies to overcome them are more fully discussed in other chapters. The implication for concern with the appropriateness of data collection methods is twofold: Of primary importance, when the topic of a study requires asking questions of a highly personal or sensitive nature, is that the field methods will enable researcher and subject to develop an adequate level of trust. If detailed and accurate data on income, for example, are essential to the aims of a study, most researchers in Arab countries have found that single-round surveys do not produce reliable findings. Similarly, subjects such as premarital sexual behavior, attitudes toward the ruling elite, and ethnic discrimination probably are too sensitive to be addressed through survey techniques.

Subject Sensitivity

A second consideration is that the degree of sensitivity of a given topic may vary from society to society and within subgroups of a single community. For example, valid data on voting behavior will be difficult to get via questionnaires in places where nonvoting is highly sanctioned. Some occupation groups within Egypt would be proud to report that they work at several jobs to augment their incomes; other groups, like government workers, cannot freely admit to secondary jobs even though the practice is widespread because it is in violation of the law for civil servants. In such cases, survey responses are unlikely to provide adequate information or comparable data across subgroups.

The sensitivity of a particular research question is subject to possible change during the course of data collection. Although this problem is more difficult to anticipate in the design of research, it is one that social scientists face repeatedly in the region.

Arab societies are generally characterized by highly centralized authority structures. Therefore pronouncements from a person in authority will send disproportionately large ripple effects down through the hierarchy. The author experienced sudden politicization of a formerly neutral survey item during field work in Egyptian public sector factories. The offending question was a standard item used to scale individual modernity: "Can a person be truly good without having any religious beliefs?"

Midway through the interviewing of production workers a national leader condemned atheistic elements in society during a televised speech. From that day forward, workers became visibly uncomfortable when asked the religion question, fearing that it might be an indirect way of testing their own religious convictions. Although the item itself had to be discarded, one could argue that the incident was itself revealing as data; it showed that this group within Egyptian society does display attributes of modernity, if that term is defined to include awareness of the issues of contemporary political concern to the nation's leaders.

To establish that a given topic is amenable to study using survey techniques, the researcher should list all the necessary data items and anticipate the level of accuracy, detail, and completeness that can be tolerated during analysis. Trade-offs are inevitable in this process of weighing benefits and liabilities.

When the aim of the study is to test a hypothesis involving identified variables within a defined population, then a probability sample and survey questionnaire may well be the optimal method. In these cases, a researcher is challenged to solve the problem of sensitive topics by developing creative question items and training interviewers to use skill and tact in the field.

Wherever possible, multiple strategies should be employed. For example, if a survey is expected to produce inadequate data on incomes, the study might be expanded to include intensive reinterviewing of a selected subsample of cases. This approach would serve two aims: gauging the extent of misreporting in the larger sample and providing more accurate income data based on additional interviewing. Proxy indicators can also be employed; in the case of income these might be based on observation of household furnishings, food consumption, or ownership of particular items such as a car or a refrigerator.

Shared Conceptual Categories

Even when respondents are predisposed to cooperate with survey takers and the subject matter is amenable to an interview format, data requirements may be undermined by subtle but important differences in how researchers and their subjects think about the world and how they verbalize their perceptions. In survey research this issue is of primary significance because of the extent to which the questionnaire superimposes categories of response onto social phenomena. The degree of structure provided in survey items will vary from minimal ("What are your views on breastfeeding?") to extensive ("During the last 24 hours, how many times did you nurse your infant?"). But in all cases, survey items depend for their effectiveness on shared understanding of the terms they employ.

The standard procedures to improve convergence of meaning in questionnaires include the use of native informants in constructing items, pretesting, and the inclusion of multiple probes to improve reliability of responses. However, a more generic aspect of the problem, which is frequently overlooked, has to do with the cognitive processses by which people recall past events and attempt to quantify their recollections.

Ability to recall past events depends on conceptual categories that filter those experiences. Relevant categories may differ for researchers and for their subjects. A question that is worded "How many times during the past month did you . . . ?" assumes that a month is a meaningful unit for a respondent. It also assumes that by asking "how many times" a similar process of estimation will be used by everyone. Demographers are familiar with the clustering phenomena in any distribution of reported ages in a population. More people report being thirty, thirty-five, and forty, than report being thirty-one, forty-three, or forty-nine. Even in societies in which nearly everyone knows his or her birth year and in which birthdays are marked each year, individuals still tend to round their age to the nearest five-year interval even though survey takers have assumed—and would prefer—the greater accuracy of a one-year interval.

In Arab societies, the issue of how people estimate quantities or arrive at averages has not been studied in detail. Survey questions are designed on the assumption of shared categories, and only rarely does independent evidence emerge to caste doubt on the quality of findings that these questions generate. Especially when a sample population covers individuals with a wide range of educational or economic backgrounds, the likelihood is great that there will be disparity in how events are recalled and how information is quantified.

In deciding whether prospective survey questions directed to Arab populations will give the degree of data accuracy required, one needs to ask, What are the meaningful conceptual categories in everyday use? How can questions be designed to correspond to common language patterns and to avoid confusing or meaningless categories?

Conceptions of time are a good illustration of this process. Researchers in Muslim societies have found that the prayer intervals are useful daily time markers, especially for rural groups. Because this category is a familiar unit of time in common use already, incorporating it in a survey results in more accurate time estimates than asking questions in terms of number of hours. Similarly, intervals between Fridays, the lunar months, and the planting/harvesting seasons have proved to be effective units for asking about longer time spans.

In urban settings, the salience of clock time may be replacing prayer intervals for more educated respondents. Even in cities, however, a researcher needs to test categories of data collection against common practices and thought patterns. The most appropriate interval for requesting information about household expenditures, for example, may be the unit corresponding to one pay period. If a worker is paid daily or weekly, it may be difficult for him or her to aggregate expenditures into a month. In this instance it would be helpful to stage the question in two parts: "How often are you paid at your work?" and "How much do you usually spend on food during one [the mentioned interval]?"

As a general rule, survey items will stand greater chance of tapping the information sought when single item questions are avoided. These provide no chance for interviewer or respondent to check whether mutual understanding on questions has been reached. Whenever possible, probe questions or alternative versions of the same question should be included. For example, in labor force surveys researchers commonly ask only one item about a person's economic status on a particular day of the previous month. For those with full-time formal jobs, this format poses little difficulty; but for individuals whose work is seasonal, irregular, or part of the informal sector, the framing of the question encourages them to answer "no activity." Since developing economies contain large proportions of nonformal workers, considerable underestimation often results.

Of greater concern in this particular case, the subgroups in Arab society most likely to be underenumerated—women, landless laborers, rural to urban migrants, and child workers—are precisely the disadvantaged groups whose economic status needs to be more fully understood. Two participants at the Bellagio conference have worked to develop improved survey techniques for determining economic activity rates in Arab countries (see Zurayk 1979; B. Ibrahim 1983).

The preceding discussion addresses the mechanics of questionnaire design to illustrate the importance of specifying data needs in advance. When making the decision whether or not to employ a survey method, a researcher wants to ask not just whether the topics are amenable to survey treatment but also whether the strengths of the survey technique in enabling quantification of variables are appropriate for the population under study. When surveys ask for recollected behavior, especially if respondents will be required to estimate quantities of time, events, expenditures, and so on, it must be demonstrated that the appropriate categories and question formats can be developed.

The progress on this front by social scientists conducting surveys in Arab countries ranges from excellent to poor, as it does elsewhere. At the Bellagio conference concern was targeted to the uncritical application of concepts and measures that have been developed outside the region. This widely observed tendency weakens the quality of survey findings. It also absolves researchers from active intellectual grappling with the issues of Arab traditions and current social transformation. Saad Ibrahim spoke for many at the conference when he predicted that if the objective of an indigenous Arab social science ever emerges, it will probably not consist of a novel paradigm or even new theoretical formulations; rather, Arab social science will build on a set of concepts and constructs that authentically reflect social realities within the region.

What Unit of Analysis Is Appropriate?

One remaining issue confronts the researcher who is assessing the scope of his or her information needs to select the best method of data collection: Which social unit will be most appropriate as the locus of analysis? For a given research problem is it more logical to sample workgroups, neighborhoods, married couples, or individuals? At what level does the social interaction occur that has the greatest impact on the topic to be investigated? As central as these questions obviously are, a great deal of field research is undertaken that, out of convention or convenience, focuses on the individual.

An illustration of inappropriate sampling of individuals comes from early survey research in the family planning field. Saad Gadalla described at Bellagio the misleading conclusions on contraceptive use and fertility intentions derived from surveys of wives in rural Egypt. Somewhat better results were obtained when survey data from samples of husbands were included in the analysis. But truly effective prediction of contraceptive acceptance and reproductive behavior required focusing on the interaction of couples as social units. Recent applied research in Egypt has adapted surveying techniques to analyze decisionmaking processes among samples of couples.

In a similar way, research on agricultural innovation has evolved away from a focus on farmers and an earlier reliance on surveys of individuals' attitudes and behavior. Researchers have come to see that changes in farming practices are embedded in a network of relations within rural households and between these households and other actors—landlords, irrigation authorities, market agents. Farming systems research often makes effective use of surveys, but typically the unit of analysis is the rural household. Decisions about investment, division of labor, and time use are examined as household processes. This approach requires collecting information from wives and children, as well as adult males, and analyzing interactions among these role positions.

Figure 7.1   Selection of Appropriate Sampling Units

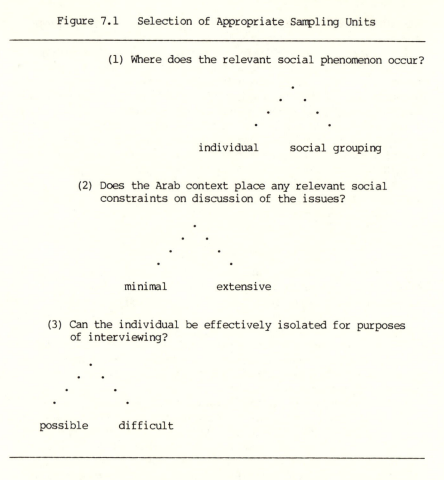

(1) Where does the relevant social phenomenon occur?

individual   social grouping

(2) Does the Arab context place any relevant social
    constraints on discussion of the issues?

minimal   extensive

(3) Can the individual be effectively isolated for purposes
    of interviewing?

possible   difficult

The subject of appropriate sampling units received considerable attention at Bellagio. The issue of appropriateness or fit between survey methods and sampling units emerged with at least three distinct dimensions (see Figure 7.1). A three-stage series of questions arises as a researcher thinks about the design of a field study. Each question takes on special considerations depending on the group within Arab society that is to be studied.

Where Does the Social Phenomenon Occur?

The first and most basic question concerns the nature of the research topic and its relation to existing social configurations. When researchers have given explicit attention to the nature of the social phenomenon they wish to explain, then the logical level to target for analysis will often be clear. In ambiguous cases, a researcher might ask, "At what level does the influence on behavior occur that is central to my topic?" Sherif Kanana, in his conference presentation, suggested a related approach, by recommending that for any research question a researcher might ask, "What is the relevant decisionmaking unit?" Some of the potentially important social groups in Arab societies are *osra* or *ayla* (family), *bayt* (household), *shilla* (friendship clique), *magmuaa* (workgroup that interacts closely), or *hiy* (neighborhood).

For which topics are individuals more likely to be appropriate as sampling units? Studies of political beliefs, voting behavior, the links between education and occupational attainment, the needs of working women—a wide range of subjects has been effectively treated by sampling individuals. An exhaustive list is not possible, nor would it be useful. Each study imposes its own unique analytic requirements that proscribe any sort of formulistic answers.

Studies of opinion, for example, might seem to be a case in which individual behavior is clearly at issue and therefore individuals are the relevant sampling unit. And in practice this approach has often proved effective, when researchers were primarily interested in the distribution of opinions among a population or in knowing what other individual characteristics are associated with the holding of various opinions. In other cases, the object of research may be to understand processes of opinion change or to determine how a certain set of opinions came to be held. In this case it is not clear that a sample of individuals will yield the most relevant information. A research design that examines networks of communication and influence in a community, for example, might be more appropriate.

Having considered these issues and determined whether the research subject should logically be addressed at the level of individuals, two other questions remain concerning the influence of a specifically Arab societal context on aspects of individual autonomy. Figure 7.1 divides these factors into theoretical considerations (level 2) and logistical considerations (level 3) in data collection.

What Are the Social Constraints Imposed?

At the second level a researcher is asking, given a focus on individual behavior, what are the special conditions imposed by Arab social contexts on examining that behavior? Framed another way, can a researcher assume that processes such as opinion formation or opinion articulation are similar for Arab respondents and for their more widely studied Western counterparts? If the answer is yes, then social scientists are justified in replicating opinion surveys across cultures, with modifications only at the level of translation of question items. If, however, societies differ in the nature and degree of social constraints brought to bear on supposedly private aspects of individual life, then a new consideration is introduced.

The Arab world is constituted largely of social settings in which group solidarity is a central feature of the individual's perception of his or her place in the world. Self-esteem, social status, and in some cases even survival may rest on how well a person integrates personal attitudes or inclinations into larger group interests. The implication is not that individual autonomy is nonexistent, nor is it that individuals cannot assert divergent views or singular behavior—they can and often do in every part of Arab society. Rather, reseachers need to remain sensitive to the fact that Arab respondents are far more likely to identify themselves consciously in relation to important social groups, such as kin, than are their Western counterparts.

One implication of these associations may be that asking an isolated individual to give his or her opinion, attitude, or prediction of the future can cause confusion and discomfort, especially if the subject is an unfamiliar one. Most people will have a personal viewpoint, but it is one that has been formed through processes of group consensus and very likely by taking a reading of the views of other significant people. Arabs often feel more comfortable reporting, "This is what we think," than giving an individual viewpoint.

In contrast, the survey method achieved prominence in Western societies partly because of an ideological climate that stressed the individual and autonomous individual rights. Among these were the right to express opinions and to participate in the democratic selection of rulers. To be able to choose intelligently among candidates, individuals were expected to weigh political issues and form discrete opinions. In an attempt to gauge shifts in public thinking, conceived as the aggregate of individual opinions, survey techniques were refined and standardized. They soon became a familiar fixture of public life in Europe and the United States. Today in the United States, polltaking is such a pervasive aspect of the political scene that some analysts believe survey results have begun to influence election outcomes, not merely reflect voter preferences. At a minimum, most Americans recognize the survey process as a normal if bothersome method of information gathering, and they take for granted having opinions of their own to express for pollsters.

In the Arab world, opinion surveys have been introduced into a vastly different political and cultural environment. For the most part local social scientists have not examined critically the assumptions of opinion research, either conceptually or in terms of practical application. The Bellagio conference afforded an opportunity to begin that critique, and various chapters of this book elaborate on aspects of the problem.

The present concern is with the expression of individual opinions in a survey context. Researchers need to ask whether the individuals they plan to sample are in fact likely to hold a crystalized orientation toward the opinion items to be asked. Having determined that articulated opinions probably exist, then it is equally important to know whether respondents will be likely to verbalize them to interviewers. Both are questions tied closely to the social constraints on individuals in Arab society. As previously discussed, individuals may hold vague or well-defined orientations toward a subject, depending on how salient it is as a topic of concern in their social milieu. It would seem improper to many Arabs to take an opinion on some unfamiliar subject without first consulting others.

An example is the modernity scale item previously discussed: "Can a person be truly good without having any religion?" When confronted with this question, urban factory workers in Egypt often asked to have the question explained. Religious affiliation is so central a feature of one's identity that most respondents could barely imagine an absence of religious belief. Many answered with hesitation, a few with conviction, but the question obviously aroused concern, for several respondents returned to the interviewer at a later time to discuss their answers. In each case, the person had consulted with friends or family or respected persons with religious training to seek validation for the answer they had given. Those whose original response was out of step with the consensus among people they later consulted felt dissonance. Some asked if their answer could be changed. (This occurred before the intrusion of political events, after which respondents became reluctant to discuss the subject at all.)

This experience pointed up for the survey researcher how explicitly social the opinion formation process can be. Since there is no society in which opinions are derived in complete isolation, the case in Arab societies is probably best seen as one of greater degree and overtness of social influence. One implication is that when topics are unfamiliar or lack salience for the respondents, individual level surveying may not be an effective research strategy.

Even when discrete and variable opinions are held among a sample group, other forms of social constraint may inhibit individuals from stating them. This is another aspect of the problem often overlooked by survey researchers in Arab societies. Expressing conformity to group norms and collective beliefs generally brings higher reward to the individual than would be the case in Western contexts. It therefore becomes habitual to express an acceptable set of opinions when asked. The greater the felt significance of the topic under discussion the higher will be the likelihood of eliciting conforming views.

The relationship between stated opinions and other forms of behavior deserves more focused attention from Arab social scientists. In those rare studies that address this issue, there is a suggestion that the relationship is relatively weak, especially for topics involving religion, political allegiance, or beliefs about proper sex roles. The penalties for expressed deviance may be almost as high as for behavioral deviance, a fact that will constrain people's responses to survey opinion items.

The author's research experiences suggest that the issue goes beyond one of sensitive topics. In addition, Arab culture encourages the use of language and verbal statements in strategic ways. Much has been written about the power of language among Arabic-speaking peoples, including the belief that to have stated something confers a tangible sense of reality to it. In some traditional communities this takes the form of a conviction that spoken words have the power to influence events. Thus Egyptians will report on another's illness, however serious, as a form of "tiredness" rather than sickness. Similarly, spoken expressions of envy are thought to have the power to bring misfortune to the one who is envied.

In more general terms, people often utilize verbal statements to establish a sense of concreteness or reality, whether in regard to themselves or to aspects of their environment. Researchers need to become more aware of the ways in which this aspect of verbal behavior affects what is said in interview settings. For example, the author's survey of factory workers was concerned with the experience of women who had entered the nontraditional sphere of factory production work in Cairo. One aim of the study was to examine the relationship between women's factory work and their orientations toward marriage, economic roles, and political involvement. Several survey items asked about opinions regarding power relations in marriage. On one item there was virtually no variation in responses: All women answered affirmatively to the question, "Do you think it is a husband's right to keep his wife from working if he disapproves?" Similarly, nearly all the women, whether married or not, gave the opinion that a woman should stay at home if her husband's salary is sufficient for the needs of the family.

Independent from the survey, observations were made of the same sample of women at the workplace and in their homes. It soon became apparent that over half of the married women faced moderate to strong opposition from husbands regarding their employment. Women whose husbands earned well continued to work over repeated objections. Clearly, the relation between stated opinion and personal choices was not straightforward for this group.

Because the study employed multiple data gathering strategies these anomalies could be examined in more depth. What emerged was a picture of the special tactics developed by women who had stepped outside the traditional expectations by taking up factory work. To reestablish their conformity to accepted norms, it became important to emphasize verbally adherence to the shared beliefs of the wider community. Ironically, but perhaps significantly, many of these workers were more adamant in stating their traditional views than were their neighbors who were housewives. The latter presumably had less felt need for social validation. When a discrepancy between workers' opinions and their day-to-day behavior was pointed out, most women employed a rationale that enabled them to see their own situation as unique or exceptional. Still, they affirmed those general opinions that showed them not to be deviant from accepted norms for women in their society.

To conclude this discussion by saying that opinion surveys are invalid and therefore inappropriate in Arab contexts would be too extreme.

Well-conceived surveys based on opinion questions have made significant contributions to social science understanding in the Arab world. These studies have succeeded to the degree that they have reformulated opinion measures to reflect social realities among the study population. Responses to opinion items on a survey need to be treated explicitly as verbal behavior and examined in that light. Research that aims to predict other forms of behavior from opinions will be on stronger ground if no assumptions about correlation are made a priori and if other forms of independent data can be marshaled to support and interpret survey responses. More studies are needed that explicitly address the methodology of individual opinion research and seek to refine its techniques in Arab settings.

Can Individuals be Effectively Isolated?

A final set of questions confront the researcher in deciding whether the individual is the most appropriate unit of analysis in a planned survey study. Having decided on theoretical and cultural grounds that the subject is best addressed by sampling individuals, there are still purely logistical considerations. This is the third level diagramed in Figure 7.1. Will it be possible in the interview setting to isolate individuals from their social environment sufficiently to obtain unbiased responses? In many (but not all) Western settings this question need not arise. Where privacy is an accepted value, it is relatively easy to obtain data from each subject with a minimum of outside interference. Interviews conducted at home can usually be arranged in a room away from intrusions. Employers often are willing to cooperate with survey takers by providing a place apart where workers can be interviewed.

Rarely are these conditions present in Arab contexts. In fact, it is unusual and often perceived as undesirable to find individuals alone in any setting. Homes are crowded and rooms have multiple uses so that it is difficult to isolate an individual for an interview. The visit of a stranger to a home or workplace is the subject of great curiosity. Neighbors and onlookers are likely to invite themselves to observe the proceedings. Of greater concern for survey researchers, those present during an interview will not feel inhibited from contributing opinions and often will answer questions for the respondent. This is especially the case when the respondent is younger, less educated or of lower status than an observer. When interviewing wives in the presence of their husbands, for example, this is a commonly reported problem.

Several research tactics have been developed to address the difficulty of isolating individual respondents. Household surveys can be scheduled for a time during the day when respondents are least engaged by their social networks. Wives may be interviewed during the hours when husbands are most likely to be away at work. In planning such strategies, however, it will be important to consider what other kinds of biases may inadvertently be introduced. In the case of labor force surveys conducted during daytime working hours, housewives with few economic activities tend to be overrepresented because households in which women are employed are more likely to be empty during the day and to fall out of the sample.

Some researchers in the Arab world, having found it nearly impossible to achieve the ideal of private interviews, have turned this liability into a positive aspect of their research designs. Two examples were presented at the Bellagio conference. Rita Giacoman found in her community health studies near Ramallah that interviews were of necessity conducted in the presence of a crowd of onlookers. Field workers used this as an opportunity to record how health and sanitation were discussed among families and neighborhood groups. From these discussions promising individuals were identified and trained to become part of the research team. The research thus took on a participatory aspect that is rare in standard survey research.

Saad Ibrahim reported on the experience of a research team examining religious militancy in Egypt. Leaders of militant organizations were interviewed while serving prison sentences, following conviction for violent assault against government installations. As originally designed, the study intent was to interview individual leaders from high- and middle-range positions in the hierarchy of two religious movements. In practice this proved unworkable. Interviews had to be conducted in cramped rooms with several inmates present. More significant, respondents themselves refused to cooperate unless they could reply collectively.

For the researchers, it was a novel situation to find subjects imposing their own conditions on the research team. On reflection the researchers realized that similar less-than-ideal conditions are imposed de facto on nearly every survey study conducted in the region. They determined to rethink the research design, basing it on group interviewing, and to build on the strengths this approach would afford them. Examining the dynamics of interaction during interviews became a valuable source of data in itself. The unit of analysis for findings was leadership groups rather than individuals.

In summary, the data requirements of any proposed study need to be carefully assessed in terms of the special constraints on research in Arab societies. Judicious decisions about the suitability of survey methods rest on at least four prior considerations: (1) the degree of sensitivity of the research topic, (2) the extent to which relevant variables have already been identified, (3) the availability of suitable conceptual categories and reliable means to capture data through questionnaire items, and (4) the appropriateness of focusing on individuals as the unit of analysis and the likelihood that individual level data can be effectively obtained through interviewing.

Conclusion

In this chapter the author has argued that survey methodology can be a potent research strategy for addressing significant issues in contemporary Arab society. However, to fulfill this promise and to deliver truly relevant data and analysis, greater attention should be paid by survey practitioners to questions of appropriate fit between method, subject, and aims in any given study. As way of summarizing these issues, there is one final aspect of the survey approach that may be examined for its relations to the relevance questions this chapter poses.

Critics of survey methodology have argued that the one-time, "snapshot" character of survey data limits its usefulness when societies are undergoing rapid change. Single-round surveys, as the argument goes, fail to reflect processes of social transformation over time. Although multiround surveys address some of these concerns, they can be costly and often require a level of administrative continuity that is difficult to achieve. Experience in the region suggests that it is possible to design creative applications of single-round surveys that take account of change as an inevitable feature of the research environment.

In Amman, Jordan, the Urban Development Department (UDD) of the municipality needed information about infant health and sanitation practices in squatter neighborhoods prior to launching a physical upgrading project. UDD researchers conducted a household sample survey to obtain baseline health data from mothers of small children. (Tekce and Shorter 1984; Population Council 1982). The study was designed with two primary goals. First, results of the survey would provide the project's engineers and planners with indictors of the quality of life before upgrading. After water lines and sewers were installed, it would be possible to resurvey the same population to learn what health impact, if any, was achieved by physical upgrading.

But a second important goal of this survey did not depend for its usefulness on conducting a follow-up round. Researchers wanted to know what range of behaviors regarding health and sanitation existed in the community and how knowledge about disease prevention was distributed among various types of households. The survey results told them which types of families already followed practices that reduced infant illness and death. By utilizing this information, it was possible to plan for the involvement of community residents in upgrading activities. Decisions about optimal locations for water lines, toilets, and kitchens were informed by the survey data about everyday practices within households.

This example illustrates a fundamental point about survey relevance and the problem of shifting realities over time. One can never assume that social change will stand still after a survey is taken. Rather, those aspects of change that have an important effect on the subject of the study should be made explicit. Wherever possible, resurveying a second time should be encouraged to avoid the possibly biased conclusions of the single survey snapshot. Other techniques for dealing with the problems of change over time are suggested in Chapter 10, which concerns cumulativeness in survey research. The relationship of external events and processes of change to survey goals, if fully confronted at the planning stages, can render surveys a potent intellectual and applied research tool.

In the Amman health survey, researchers' knowledge of the point in the change process at which to step in with data collection allowed them to make effective use of the method. Baseline surveys prior to a planned social intervention, when done with care, have become a valuable source of applied data. At the same time, they provide rich information about patterns of social life in the Arab world, which are in many cases fragile and subject to rapid transformation.

In a similar way, survey researchers from a wide range of disciplines are seeking more effective ways to refine and adapt their research tools to the realities of the Arab region. The remaining chapters of this book examine some of the specific areas in which progress has been achieved. They also suggest issues that remain problematic and therefore will constitute the challenges to a new generation of social scientists in the Arab world.

References

Barnett, Andrew, 1979. "Rapid Rural Appraisal: A personal view of the first IDS workshop." Paper for the second workshop on Rapid Rural Appraisal, Institute of Development Studies, University of Sussex, Brighton; 4–7 December.

Chambers, Robert. 1983. Rural Development. *Putting the Last First.* London: Longman Group Limited.

El Safty, Madiha, et al. forthcoming. *An Analytic Index of Survey Research in Egypt.* Cairo: Cario papers in Social Science, AUC Press.

Holt, Robert T. and Turner, John E. 1970. *The Methodology of Comparative Research.* New York: Free Press.

Ibrahim, Barbara. 1980. *Social Change and the Industrial Experience: The Case of Female Factory Workers in Urban Egypt,* dissertation, Dept. of Sociology, Indiana University, Bloomington, Ind.

———. 1983. "Strategies of Urban Labor Force Measurement," in Richard Lobban, ed., *Urban Research in the 80's.* Cairo: Cairo Papers in Social Science, AUC Press, 6:46–54.

Ibrahim, Saad Eddin. 1980. "Anatomy of Egypt's Militant Islamic Groups," *International Journal of Middle East Studies* 12:423–453.

Kearl, Bryant, ed., 1976. *Field Data Collection in the Social Sciences: Experiences in Africa and the Middle East.* New York: Agricultural Development Council.

Palmer, Monte, et al. 1982. *Survey Research in the Arab World: An Analytical Index.* London: Menas Press.

Population Council. 1982. *Baseline Health and Population Assessment for the Upgrading Areas of Amman.* Giza, Egypt: Population Council Regional Papers.

Rhoades, Robert E., 1982. *The Art of the Informal Agricultural Survey,* Social Science Department Training Document 1982—2, International Potato Center, Aptdo. 5969, Lima, Peru; March.

Sammani, Mohamed. 1983. "The Status of Survey Research for Rural Development in the Sudan." Paper presented at the Bellagio Conference on Survey Research in the Arab world.

Tekce, B., and F. Shorter. 1984. Determinants of Child Mortality: A Study of Squatter Settlements in Jordan. *Population and Development Review*, vol. 10, supplement.

Zurayk, Huda. 1979. *Measurement of Female Economic Activity: Report of a Study Group*. Giza, Egypt: Population Council Regional Papers Series.

8

The Conceptualization and Design of Survey Instruments for Use in the Arab World

Monte Palmer

Survey research, as the preceding chapters have elaborated, is a technique in which questionnaires and interviews are used to gather information on the attitudes, values, opinions, and behavior of large groups of individuals. Survey research as a tool in the United States and Western Europe has benefited from the relative openness of Western political systems and the existence of social or cultural norms that facilitate the sharing of personal information on a wide variety of issues. The challenge of conducting survey research in the Arab world centers on the fact that the political systems of the Middle East are rarely open and that the predominant norms of the region do not facilitate what many Middle Easterns might describe as the frivolous discussion of personal affairs. In the very private, family-oriented Arab culture most people believe that personal and family affairs are best kept within the family. Individuals are wary of the unknown uses to which their revelations may be put, particularly in regard to politics, income, sex, and religion, the favorite topics of Western survey researchers. The challenge of designing questionnaires for use in the Arab Middle East, then, centers on designing a research instrument that will be effective in gathering the information desired without offending either the political authorities or the sensibilities of the populations surveyed. This is not an easy task.

In reviewing the special considerations of questionnaire design in the Middle East, the discussion will follow the logical steps involved in designing a questionnaire for use in any corner of the world, noting at each juncture those adjustments or choices imposed upon survey researchers by the special circumstances of Arab society. In some instances, it will be possible to suggest how those obstacles characteristic of the Middle East can be overcome or avoided. Usually, however, the discussion will focus on the choices or trade-offs that survey researchers in the

Middle East will be forced to make. In some instances, the choices may involve avoiding sensitive subjects for the sake of increasing the reliability of information gathered in less sensitive areas. In other cases, the choices will involve choosing between minimally reliable data for a large population on one hand or significantly better data for a smaller population on the other. There is no simple answer to these and related choices other than to note that unreliable data are of little use to anyone and can only result in erroneous and misleading conclusions. How reliable the data must be, within minimally accepted limits, is a question that must be answered by the individual researcher.

The major topics to be discussed in this chapter include (1) the selection and definition of concepts and variables; (2) the dangers of imposing Western concepts upon Arab societies; (3) the difficulty of perceiving all the concepts that might be relevant for the analysis of human behavior in the Middle East; (4) the extreme sensitivity of many research topics in the Arab world; (5) the development of questionnaire items and multi-item scales; (6) the advantages and disadvantages of replicating Western questionnaire items in the Middle East; (7) special problems of questionnaire construction and validity in the region, including the advantages and disadvantages of unobtrusive (indirect) measures; (8) the distinction between measuring attitudes versus behavior; (9) response formats; (10) questionnaire size; (11) questionnaire language; and (12) difficulties of pretesting survey instruments in the Arab world.

It should be noted that the chapter is directed equally to Western and to Middle Eastern audiences. Western scholars often experience difficulty in conducting research in the Middle East because they fail to take adequate time (perhaps years) to understand the region properly. Middle Eastern researchers often experience difficulty in conducting research in the Middle East because they tend to assume that they understand their region far better than they do.

The information provided in this chapter is based largely on materials presented at the Conference on Survey Research in the Arab World held in Bellagio, Italy, in June 1983. The chapter also relies on the author's personal and sometimes painful experience gained by participating in some fifteen survey research projects conducted in various states of the Arab world, including Morocco, Egypt, Saudi Arabia, Lebanon, and the Sudan.

Selecting and Defining Concepts and Variables

The initial step in any survey research project is to specify the concepts (topics) to be investigated. The participants in the Bellagio conference, being social scientists, were primarily concerned with the use of survey research to study such concepts as political participation, alienation, nationalism, socialization, social class, feminism, birth control, religiosity, and modernity, to mention but a few. Educators and psychologists, by contrast, might be more interested in utilizing surveys in the measurement of such concepts as motivation, learning, and personality. Economists and public administrators, in turn, would tend to use surveys to investigate the concepts of innovation, risk taking, or market appeal.

Once a researcher has selected the concepts to be studied by a particular survey research project, the next logical step is to place the concepts in a testable framework. At the simplest level, for example, a researcher might specify that the object of his or her research project is to measure levels of religiosity in Egypt. Or, the researchers might wish to express their research topic as a simple descriptive hypothesis such as "The people of Egypt are religious." By transforming a goal of simply measuring levels of religiosity in Egypt into the hypothesis that "Egyptians are religious," the researcher acquires the added burden of specifying the basis for accepting or rejecting the hypothesis. How much religiosity must the researcher find before accepting the hypothesis that "Egyptians are religious"? In most instances the researcher will want to go beyond simple descriptive hypotheses and will develop inferential or explanatory hypotheses. For example, one might hypothesize that the level of religiosity in Egypt decreases with education.

When concepts are used in hypotheses or explanatory statements, they are often referred to as variables. In the case of the hypothesis that religiosity decreases with education, religiosity is the dependent variable and education in the independent variable. Religiosity is referred to as the dependent variable because it is the central focus of the hypothesis. Education is referred to as the independent variable because it is hypothesized that education influences the level of religiosity. The level of religiosity is thus hypothesized to "depend" upon the level of education.

By specifying a set of hypotheses at the beginning of a survey research project the researcher is providing the project with rigor and precision. The researcher is specifying (1) the central concept(s) of the study, (2) the concepts believed to influence the central concept, and (3) the criterion for accepting or rejecting the hypothesis. In the case of the religiosity hypothesis, the researcher is asking how much religiosity is present and the extent to which education influences the level of religiosity. The researcher is also accepting the rigor of specifying in advance the extent to which increased education must influence religiosity before accepting the hypothesis that education is inversely related to religiosity.

In addition to increasing the rigor of a research project, hypothesis formation and testing form an important step in building theory and in comparing human behavior in one culture to that in another. If religiosity is found to vary (be influenced) by education levels in Egypt, for example, a researcher might wish to test the same hypothesis in Jordan, Libya, or other Middle Eastern states. If studies in Jordan and Libya also support the hypothesis that religiosity decreases as education increases, it might then be possible to theorize that religiosity decreases as education increases throughout the Arab world. The validity of this theory could then be tested in an increasing variety of circumstances in the Arab world in order to provide an ever clearer picture of just when and how education influences religiosity. The hypothesis could also be tested in Latin America, Asia, or North America to examine the extent to which the influence of education upon religiosity is common to all human societies. The generation and testing of hypothesis, then, are essential to the development of serial theories, which in turn enable social scientists to predict and explain human behavior in the Arab world or in any other region.

Although hypothesis testing is central to scientific rigor and theory building, the clarity or precision of a hypothesis or a theory is limited by the clarity and precision of its component concepts. If the concepts are not clear, the hypothesis is not clear. How, for example, can one discuss the influence of education upon religiosity without a clear, precise definition of both education and religiosity?

Once the hypotheses of a survey project have been specified, each concept in the study must be provided with both a conceptual and an operational definition. A conceptual definition is a verbal definition designed to communicate what the researcher means by the concept. Religiosity, for example, means different things to different people. The same is true of virtually all social science concepts, including political participation, power, democracy, and alienation. An operational definition, by contrast, refers to the specific technique for measuring a concept. In the context of survey research, concepts are operationalized by a specific set of questionnaire items.

The conceptual definitions must be as precise as possible, for conceptual definitions provide the guidelines for constructing the empirical (operational) definition of the concept that will be represented by one or more questionnaire items. If the conceptual definitions provided for the concepts used in the study are vague and imprecise, the researchers will find it difficult to generate precise questionnaire items that provide clear measures of the concepts in question. A clear specification of the conceptual definition of the variables is even more crucial when questionnaire items are being generated by a cross-national research team, for all members of the team must agree on exactly what they are attempting to measure. To understand the magnitude of this problem, one need only consider the inherent vagueness of such central social science concepts as power, social class, modernization, participation, culture, efficacy, empathy, or personality. If members of cross-national research teams do not share a common understanding of the conceptual properties of their major concepts, they will be unable to agree on the proper measures for those concepts. Projects that begin with imprecise conceptual definitions will produce only frustration and disappointment for their sponsors. They will also do a profound disservice to the field of Middle Eastern studies by compounding the quantity of unreliable data already available to scholars in the region. More damning is the fact that such data will be presented in the name of science, tempting scholars unfamiliar with the frailties of survey research to inflate its credibility.

As might be anticipated from this discussion, the special problems of designing questionnaires for use in the Middle East begin at the conceptual level. Three points must be considered: Have all the relevant concepts been included in the research design's conceptualization? Are all the concepts specified for measurement actually present among the populations being surveyed? Is it feasible to include all the specified or desirable variables in the questionnaire?

Imposing Western Concepts on Arab Societies

To give the discussion of conceptual problems a specific Middle Eastern focus, these questions will be illustrated by reference to a survey of Egyptian bureaucrats recently conducted by the Al Ahram Center for Political and Strategic Studies, portions of which have been replicated in Saudi Arabia and the Sudan.[1] The general purpose of the study was to examine the constraints on the ability of the bureaucracies of Egypt, the Sudan, and Saudi Arabia to play a dynamic role in the economic development of their respective states. The dependent variables (concepts) included innovation, achievement motivation, job satisfaction, incentive values, professionalism, regard for the public, risk taking, and acceptance of responsibility. The independent or explanatory variables included age, sex, marital status, social class, recruitment patterns, modernity, religiosity, ideology, information sources, and external social and economic pressures.

The first conceptual problem faced by the research team was the observation that all the concepts initially included in the project were generated by U.S. or European studies of development and bureaucracy. As such, all the original concepts represented behavior patterns or phenomena observed or conceptualized by scholars with a Western frame of reference. This aspect in itself is not inappropriate as long as one does not assume that Middle Eastern bureaucrats perceive their world with precisely the same frame of reference as Western bureaucrats and that the concepts being measured, if they do exist in Middle Eastern culture, shape the behavior of Middle Eastern respondents in the same way that they do in the West.

For example, unlike less precise variables, age has a clear empirical referent (everyone knows what you are talking about) and it can be measured by a single specific questionnaire item. Thus age presumably poses no problem in the conceptualization stage of the research. Interpreting the relevance of age to bureaucratic performance, however, may be less simple. Age, in Middle Eastern societies, is venerated: Older individuals in the Middle East receive far more respect, especially for their knowledge and wisdom, than they do in the United States. To make matters more complex, intervals of age may be of different weight in the Middle East than in the United States. In the United States it is common to speak of individuals as being in their thirties or forties as if every member of a generation was worthy of relatively equal deference. In Arab societies, by contrast, a common proverb stipulates "one day older, one year wiser." What this suggests is that interpretations of precisely how the concept of age influences the bureaucratic process may differ markedly between the United States and the Middle East. Similar complexities arise from the concept of family. The word *family,* in the United States, is generally understood to refer to the nuclear family. In the Middle East, however, the simple word *family* could refer to a variety of social structures including the nuclear family, the clan (extended family), or the tribe.

If complexities can arise from simple and explicit concepts such as age and family, it is not difficult to imagine the conceptual and measurement problems that arise with complex and emotionally laden concepts such as social class. Social class, in the view of many Western philosophers and social scientists, is an outgrowth of the industrial revolution. As such, the term generally implies two conditions: (1) social stratification based upon occupational roles in a capitalist-dominated industrial society and (2) class consciousness or class solidarity.[2] The dominant classes are the proletariat and the industrial capitalists. Some Western social scientists, less concerned with class consciousness, have simply equated social class with occupation and income. Implicit in this categorization, at least in the United States, is the assumption that social status is accorded primarily on the basis of wealth and that all occupational roles falling within a particular income range are of relatively equal social status.

It could well be argued that Western concepts of social class are inappropriate if not misleading for the analysis of Middle Eastern societies. To begin with, none of the Muslim countries of the Middle East is predominantly industrial, nor are the ruling classes in the region dominated by industrial capitalists. Thus the two major elements in many Western concepts of social class—the proletariat and the industrial capitalists—are marginal elements in virtually all Middle Eastern societies.[3] This is not to suggest that Middle Eastern societies are not stratified; however, the lines of stratification are both different and more complex than those in the West. The complexity and uniqueness of Middle Eastern stratification patterns result from the fact that traditional patterns in the region have been overlaid by a veneer of Westernization resulting from colonialism, economic development, and other forces of social change.

To understand this complexity it must be noted that classical stratification patterns in the Middle East tended to evolve around two dimensions: (1) tribal and family hierarchies in primarily tribal regions and (2) land distribution patterns in the predominantly agrarian areas.[4] In many instances, status systems based upon tribal and land considerations were blurred by religious movements, such as the Wahhabis in Saudi Arabia, the Senussi in Libya, and the Alawites in Morocco. In each instance, the leaders of the religious movements became leading members of the ruling elite and, in some instances, the dominant elite itself. Religious leaders and mystics, of course, have historically been revered in the East, though in ways that would defy a neat class designation. Moreover, in many parts of the Middle East the commercial classes— an important element in Western social classes—were often dominated by foreigners and were frequently judged to be outside of society. Horizontal stratification patterns (social class) were also blurred by the intensity of vertical stratification groups (tribes, ethnic groups, religious groups), identification with which generally precluded class consciousness. Individuals perceived themselves as members of a tribe or an extended family or of a religious group, not as a member of a rural proletariat. On top of this traditional pattern of social stratification, the colonial experience and limited industrialization imposed a veneer of Western social classes, the depth or penetration of which is truly difficult to gauge.

To further complicate the picture, class distinctions in the Middle East have been altered by two additional forces. In states such as Libya, Iraq, and South Yemen, socialist political leaders have attempted to transform their traditional tribal societies, characterized by tribal or feudal stratification patterns, into classless modern societies. These attempts have not been particularly successful; yet they have clearly altered existing social alignments. Whatever the altered class alignments may be, they do not conform to classical Western notions of social class. In the oil-producing states of the Gulf region, the magnitude of oil revenues has transformed many members of society into prosperous consumers living on income that has accrued to them largely by accident.[5] This wealth has been used to hire laborers from Egypt, Yemen, and other less prosperous Arab states to provide services at all levels. How, then, does one conceptualize stratification patterns in Saudi Arabia and the oil states of the Arab Gulf? Moreover, in what class do the Eygptians and Yemenis working in Saudi Arabia fall when they return, far richer, to their homelands?

This discussion of social class, though excessively simplified, accentuates several important points in designing questionnaires for use in the Middle East. First, measures of social class based simply on occupation, income, or education are wholly inadequate to measure the richness of social stratification patterns in the Middle East. Also, Western definitions of social class involving a sense of class consciousness or class loyalty are even more inappropriate. Moreover, if Western measures of social class are used (imposed) in Middle Eastern questionnaires, they run the very real risk of creating fictional classes that have no basis in reality. Such a procedure, then, results only in self-deception. Second, if one judges social stratification patterns in the Middle East to be worthy of measurement (as opposed to verbal or conceptual debate) a tremendous block of questonnaire items, not to mention a considerable amount of imagination and experimentation, must be devoted to developing valid measures of all facets of the stratification problem. Adequate measures of social stratification could consume most of the questionnaire, an unacceptable condition for projects using social class as one of several concepts to be investigated by the survey.

It is not easy to solve the problem of transferring concepts developed in one culture into a second culture with a radically different history. In the case of social class, some researchers have experimented with simply asking the respondents which social class they belonged to. This procedure, though valued in the West as a means measuring perceived class identification, may require Middle Easterners to respond to a question that may have little or nothing to do with their frame of reference. To make matters worse, if Middle Eastern respondents are requested to indicate if they belong to the upper, upper-middle, middle, lower-middle, or lower class, experience shows that they will respond by checking one of the categories provided whether they think in class terms or not. If they do not understand the parameters of each choice, the results are misleading because the researcher and the respondent are operating on different mental wavelengths.

The solution to the social class problem adopted by the Al Ahram project was to include a battery of questions relating to income, occupation, and education without making any assumptions about a presumed link between these parameters, on one hand, and social class, on the other. By using this approach the researchers did not attempt to measure social class as a specific concept, choosing instead to limit their analysis to the individual and collective influence of income, occupation, and education upon various forms of bureaucratic behavior. Thus they helped to clarify their results as well as to make it easier to compare their results with parallel findings from the Middle East and elsewhere. If complex concepts such as social class can be reduced into clearly specified components such as income, education, or occupation, they should always be simplified.

Social class is merely one example of a complex Western concept that may be dangerous to impose upon Middle Eastern societies. Western concepts of democracy, morality, equality, efficiency, objectivity, and secularism, to mention only a few, all possess a culturally determined framework in the minds of Western-oriented researchers. If such concepts are to be included in Middle Eastern questionnaires, researchers must make every effort to measure behavior patterns that exist in the empirical reality of the Middle East.

The Problem of Unperceived Concepts

We turn now to the problem of whether researchers know enough about human behavior in the Middle East to include all the relevant concepts in their research design. David McCelland, for example, explained economic development in the West on the basis of a cultural concept—achievement motivation—that he found to be present in the West but not (or less) present in many of the less-developed areas of the Third World, including the Middle East.[6] If such a major motivational concept is present in the West but not the East, does it not also stand to reason that cultural or psychological concepts are present in the Middle East that are unperceived or poorly understood by Western researchers? The less researchers are aware of such indigenous concepts the less able they are to accurately delineate the forces shaping the behavior of Middle Eastern populations. Even more problematic is the fact that their poor understanding of causal relationships in the Middle East may lead Western researchers or Western-trained researchers to explain Middle Eastern behavior in terms of those concepts that they do understand. This is a particularly severe problem because of the present state of Middle Eastern studies: Information on human behavior and human motivation in the Middle East is extremely limited, and scholars have a tendency to overemphasize data that appear to possess an empirical foundation, regardless of their validity.

The problem of the unperceived concept is a particularly perplexing one for the Western researcher because it seems to suggest that only Middle Easterners can understand the Middle East. This assertion can be rejected, perhaps, on the ground that all human behavior is subject to discovery with adequate preparation and sensitivity. The requirement that researchers be adequately familiar with the populations they are studying, however, cannot be overemphasized. The most satisfactory solution to this problem is for Western researchers to work in very close cooperation with social scientists from the particular country in which they are attempting to conduct their research.

The problem of the unknown variable and similar problems relating to research conducted by nonmembers of the target group being studied does not merely confront Western social scientists working in the Middle East. How well do the urban scholars of Cairo, Damascus, or Beirut really understand their rural brethren? Does the mere fact of being Arab mean that Christian Arabs intuitively understand Moslem Arabs or vice versa. Are Egyptians on the same wavelength as Saudi Arabians or Iraqis? Or, for that matter, do older Arab scholars really share the same values and life experiences as newer generations of Arab youth? After all, the social, economic, and political changes in the Middle East over the past thirty years have been truly staggering. Again, it is essential for survey researchers to work in close cooperation with individuals from the target population in the design of their research instruments. Simply being an Arab does not automatically make one an expert on the behavior, attitudes, and emotions of Arabs everywhere. Indeed, Arab researchers must fight the temptation to assume that they understand all Arabs in order to prevent being lulled into a false sense of complacency in the design of their research projects.

The problem of the unperceived concept also relates to a persistent theme raised at the Bellagio conference—the contention that the Western paradigm (approach) of social research is inappropriate for the Arab world and that it is incumbent upon Arab social scientists to develop a uniquely Arab paradigm. The issue of an Arab paradigm is much broader than that of the unperceived concept because it questions not only the ability of Western scholars to understand the Middle East well enough to include the right concepts in their research designs, but, more important, the ability of the Western scientific method to discover and chart human behavior in the Middle East. At the heart of the issue is the fundamental question, Is science applicable the world over, or is there one scientific method for the West and another for the East? Arab participants at the conference were sharply divided on the answers to these questions.

Topic Sensitivity

A third major problem involved in selecting concepts for questionnaires used in the Middle East is sensitivity. If topics included in the study are judged to be inappropriate by local authorities, those authorities probably will not allow the questionnaire to be administered. At the very least, the sensitive portions of the questionnaire will have to be deleted, thereby wasting space that could have been used for less sensitive items. Virtually all survey research projects in the Middle East must be approved by at least one set of authorities, and such approval is made on the basis of final rather than preliminary questionnaires. As other papers presented at the Bellagio conference have pointed out, questionnaires make political and institutional authorities nervous. Their gut response will likely be to kill the project rather than to request its designers to revise and resubmit it.

The inclusion of sensitive topics in a questionnaire may also set off alarms in the minds of the respondents, who may be uncomfortable with the survey/interview process to begin with. Respondents will not provide valid answers to questionnaire items that infringe upon privacy, make them look bad, or leave them vulnerable to perceived social or political pressures. In regard to the last point, the problem is not what the researchers think the respondents should perceive as harmful, but what the respondents actually do perceive as harmful. The best result that can be expected from the inclusion of excessively sensitive topics is that the respondent will ignore them and answer the remaining questions; the second best result is that respondents will terminate the questionnaire at that point, having provided valid responses up to the point. The least desirable outcome is that respondents will falsify their responses to the sensitive items, thereby providing the researcher with partially invalid information. Particularly problematic in this regard is ascertaining whether respondents falsified only the sensitive questions or whether they falsified all questions following the sensitive questions. Once respondents have been forced to falsify their responses by what they consider to be threatening questions, it is unlikely that they will approach the questionnaire with the same degree of sincerity or openness that they did before encountering the sensitive items. Because of the clear possibility of inaccurate responses, researchers attempting to measure sensitive concepts must be particularly stringent in assessing the reliability of their data. They may even wish to develop special reliability scales for inclusion in the questionnaire. Psychological inventories, for example, regularly contain scales designed to ascertain if respondents are falsifying their responses.[7]

A third penalty of including sensitive variables in a survey is the likelihood that such an approach will poison the waters for future research. For example, some years ago incoming students at the University of Tehran were required to complete a questionnaire designed to measure their sexual behavior. As a consequence of the uproar it caused, the university was closed for three months and the possibilities for further survey research at the university were closed for some time.[8]

The solution to the sensitivity problem is simple. Researchers should avoid sensitive topics whenever possible. Under no circumstances should sensitive concepts be added to a questionnaire out of random curiosity or because they might prove interesting. Even simple solutions, unfortunately, are not simple in the Middle East. Virtually all topics are sensitive to one Middle Eastern population or another: The list of such topics is headed by politics, sex, religion, and income—often the primary topics of survey research in the West.

The first step in solving the sensitivity problem is to ascertain the sensitivity levels of each of the populations to be sampled and to exclude topics judged to be excessively sensitive either to that particular population or to the relevant authorities. The question of whether to include or delete a topic is one of the most crucial choices that has to be made by survey researchers in the Middle East. Eliminating a sensitive concept may eliminate a crucial dimension of the study, thereby limiting the utility of the study; alternately, inclusion of a sensitive concept may restrict the study to Western-oriented populations, thereby limiting the applicability or generalizability of the results. The decision to include or not to include sensitive concepts must be made with consummate care only after extensive consultation with local experts. If a sensitive concept is used in a questionnaire, its sensitivity or potential damage can be mitigated by the use of unobtrusive measures and by tactics of item placement.

The most reliable procedure for avoiding the problems involved in the selection and operationalization of variables is the formation of a panel of experts intimately familiar with both the populations to be sampled and the theoretical importance of the concepts to be measured. The greater the panel members' understanding of the purpose of the project, the greater will be their ability to evaluate the appropriateness of Western concepts to the goals of the research project, suggest strategies for adapting or recasting Western concepts in a Middle Eastern context, suggest uniquely Middle Eastern concepts for inclusion in the study that may have been overlooked by non–Middle Eastern researchers, evaluate the sensitivity of the concepts to be included in the study, recommend whether the theoretical importance of a particular concept is worth the risk of its inclusion in the study, advise on the use of direct or unobtrusive measures, and assist in the drafting and evaluations of questionnaire items to be used in the research instrument. The panel can also be invaluable in judging the contextual reliability of the results of the project, as well as in interpreting the results. In this regard, gathering the data is only half the challenge of conducting survey research in the Middle East; interpreting the results is the other half. Results that seem illogical or unreliable to Western researchers may become eminently logical when seen through the lens of Middle Eastern perceptions. The opposite, of course, is equally true.

Generating Questions and Constructing Multi-Item Scales

Once the concepts to be included in the questionnaire have been identified and carefully defined, the next logical step in the design process is to generate questions that will provide valid and reliable measures for each specific concept to be included in the study. Only after the questionnaire items have been selected and evaluated is it necessary to worry about the order of their inclusion in the questionnaire. It should also be noted that each specific concept included in the questionnaire is preferably measured (operationalized) by a scale or index consisting of several questionnaire items rather than by a single item.

Using multi-item scales rather than single questionnaire items to measure specific concepts serves a number of ends. The use of multiple items to measure a concept ensures that assessments of that concept are unlikely to involve inaccuracies resulting from the poor phrasing of a single questionnaire item or other random influences that might influence the results of any single item. Such random or unexpected effects are particularly likely in areas such as the Middle East, in which many populations are being surveyed for the first time and may not be familiar with either survey procedures or the content of the survey. Also, invalid responses are more likely to be visible in the context of a cluster of uniform-scale items than they are among numerous single item concepts, each of which attempts to measure a different theme. Moreover, by using multiple-scale items, questions that yield poor results can be dropped without sacrificing the concept entirely.

The use of scales rather than single items to measure the concepts included in the questionnaire also increases the validity of the questionnaire. The more items a researcher uses to measure a particular concept, the greater the likelihood that all dimensions of that concept will be tapped and that the heart of the concept will be the primary force in shaping the combined scale score. Use of a single questionnaire item to measure a variable presents the very real risk of measuring only one dimension of a variable and equating that dimension with the totality of the broader concept. In the earlier example of the difficulty of measuring social class in the Middle East, for example, attempts to use a single item such as income or occupation to measure the complexity of the social class in the Middle East clearly could only lead to inaccurate results and misleading interpretations.

The importance of scales in the construction of questionnaires for use in the Middle East raises the difficult question of the number of questionnaire items required to constitute a satisfactory scale. Answers to this question are best found in methodology texts.[9] As a rule of thumb, the more complex the variable under consideration or the more central that variable is to the overall goals of the research project, the greater will be the number of questionnaire items that should be used in its operationalization. Again, given the uncertainties that accompany survey research in the Middle East, it is better to err on the side of having too many items in a single scale than too few. It is difficult to imagine an adequate scale of less than five items for use in the Middle East, a figure that some scholars would find excessively low.[10]

Without entering into the complexities of scale construction, it must be noted that questionnaire items that appear to measure a single concept in the eyes of the researcher may, in effect, be measuring two or more distinct concepts in the eyes of the respondents. This point can be illustrated by a recent attempt to measure fatalism in the Middle East. The fatalism scale consisted of six items, three of which were built around the Islamic belief "that everything is in the hands of God" and three of which stressed the role of human volition in determining the course of the individual's future but made no mention of God. The panel of consultants agreed that all six items were unidimensional (all measured the same thing) based upon their content (unidimensionality being a key requirement of any scale). When the results of the project were factor analysed, however, researchers found that responses to questions containing a direct reference to God were answered differently than the fatalism questions that did not mention God. The researchers were thus left with a three-item scale that measured one concept, presumably fatalism, and a second three-variable scale that measured either religiosity or the fact that few of the respondents were willing to state that things were not in the hands of God. As it is difficult to prejudge how individuals in the Middle East will interpret questionnaire items, regardless of their apparent clarity to the research team, it is essential that a sufficient number of items be included in all scales to ensure that adequate measures of each specific concept will be available to create a unidimensional scale for use in analysis. This precaution is important because some items from the original scale as conceived before application of the questionnaire may be found to be extraneous to the scale by factor analysis, Guttman scales, or other scaling statistical techniques that come into play after the data have been gathered.

Designing Questionnaire Items: New Scales or Old?

There are two ways to generate questions for inclusion in a survey instrument: borrowing items used in other survey projects or generating new items tailored to the specific needs of the project. Both techniques have advantages and disadvantages. Scales on virtually every topic of interest to survey researchers can be found in published compilations such as Shaw and Wright's *Scales for the Measure of Attitudes*.[11] Copies of questionnaires can also be obtained by writing to the authors of published research involving the use of survey questionnaires. An extensive list of survey research in the Middle East published in Western books and journals is provided in Palmer et al., *Survey Research in the Arab World: An Analytical Index*.[12] A review of some three hundred Egyptian survey research projects may be found in Safty, Palmer, and Kennedy's *An Index of Survey Research in Egypt*.[13]

One obvious advantage of borrowing sales from existing studies is that it is easier to borrow scales than to construct new scales from scratch. Borrowed scales presumably have been judged to be valid indicators of one specific concept among at least one specific population (though not all populations).

A far more important reason for using established scales is that they provide a basis for comparing results among different populations in the Middle East or elsewhere. By replicating and extending scales across diverse populations, a much sounder basis is laid for cross-cultural comparison and theory building than would be laid if each researcher defined and operationalized his or her variables in a unique, ideosyncratic manner. This is not to say that such results cannot be compared; rather the quality of such comparisons would be of much higher order if identical scales were used. The problem of cumulativeness and theory building was one of the major topics discussed at the Bellagio conference and is discussed at length by Mark Tessler in Chapters 10 and 11.

Yet another advantage of using existing scales is that norms may exist for evaluating the content and reliability of the new data. If similar items administered to similar populations result is dissimilar results, the validity of one of the studies may be in question. The more norms (a systematic record of prior results) for various scales that can be established for use in the Middle East, the more effective such norms will become as a guide for evaluating the reliability of future projects.

Because a scale is included in a compendium of scales or has been the subject of scholarly articles offers no guarantee that the scales were designed with care or that they were validated. In compiling the *Analytical*

Index of Survey Research in the Middle East, for example, the authors originally intended to include extensive data on reliability and validity for each of the projects reviewed. Less than 5 percent of articles surveyed in the *Index,* unfortunately, contained information relating to reliability or validity. Utilizing borrowed scales in the absense of information on their reliability and validity may create more problems than it solves.

A second serious problem of borrowed scales is that they may be culture bound. Many Western scales contain localized expressions such as "political hack" or "red tape," which may not have an easy and explicit translation in Arabic or other Middle Eastern languages. Similarly, psychological instruments may contain specific references to U.S. figures or uniquely U.S. problems.[14] Great care must thus be taken in adapting foreign scales to the Middle East, for even slight changes in the meaning of questions can alter scoring patterns. The greater the number of cultural adaptations that have to be made to render a scale valid for use in the Middle East, the less desirable borrowing scales becomes. Altering the position of a scale from one questionnaire to another may influence its performance; if a scale appears near the front of the questionnaire in the original project it should appear near the front of the questionnaire in follow-up or parallel questionnaires. As modifications increase, comparability decreases.

The problem of transfering scales from one culture to another may also involve far more than adjusting questionnaire items to meet the circumstances of the new culture. In some instances, the meaning or interpretation of questionnaire items, regardless of the similarity of their wording, may differ radically from one culture to another. Many surveys of voting behavior in the United States, for example, attempt to measure political efficacy by asking respondents if they understand how their political system works. Individuals who respond positively are judged to be efficacious and to be positively involved in their political system. When Nedelcovyich and Palmer replicated the U.S. efficacy scale among a sample of Moroccan university students, they found that the students possessed extremely high levels of political efficacy, a finding that came as a complete surprise.[15]

In discussing the meaning of these findings with Moroccan students and scholars, however, it readily became apparent that the U.S. efficacy questions, in the Moroccan context, were measuring alienation. When U.S. respondents express an understanding of their political system, they are judged to efficacious. That is to say, in the U.S. context it is assumed that individuals who have taken the time to understand their political system believe that voting and other political acts enable them in some small way to influence their political system. Understanding the political system is thus interpreted as positive support for the political system. The Moroccan students who indicated an understanding of their political system, as later analysis revealed, were expressing the view that they understood the corrupt and dictatorial nature of their political system and that they were not deceived by its democratic facade. Identical questions were thus measuring diametrically opposed attitudes. Similar problems of transferring questions and scales from one culture to another may also occur in transfering scales within the Middle East. The diverse cultures that constitute the mosaic of the Middle East are as renowned for their diversity as they are for their similarities.

The fewer established questionnaire items and scales that are judged to be appropriate for inclusion in a new questionnaire, the more time and effort researchers must expend in the construction of their own items. This expenditure should not be taken lightly, for the procedures required to generate and validate questionnaire items in the Middle East are lengthy. The main advantage of using new questions is the researcher's ability to tailor the questionnaire items to the specific needs of the population(s) being surveyed and to ensure quality control over all phases of the research project. By generating new questionnaire items, one seeks to increase the reliability and validity of the data obtained by the survey. The cost of generating new questionnaire items is that gains in reliability and validity are offset by losses in comparability and theory building.

Before undertaking the construction of new scales, it is essential to estimate just how big the increases in reliability and validity generated by the new scales will be and whether such increases warrant decreases in comparability. A hundred surveys, each utilizing an ideosyncratic questionnaire, probably do less to further our understanding of Middle Eastern society than twenty-five studies that are readily comparable over time and across the myriad population segments that constitute the region. Even in cases in which the specific needs of the population demand new items or in which existing items are inappropriate, it is preferable to use established items to the greatest extent possible, limiting the use of new items to create specialized scales to match a specific need. Such scales would then be incorporated within the general framework of existing questionnaires, allowing researchers to meet the specific needs of their population in regard to specific scales while retaining a capacity for comparability in regard to the remaining questionnaire items.

To recapitulate briefly, then, construction of the questionnaire should begin by a delineation of the variables to be included in the study. Once the concepts to be measured have been specified, scales will be borrowed or created to measure each specific concept. Only after determining the questionnaire items (scales) to be used for measuring each specific concept is it necessary to worry about the arrangement and structure of the questionnaire items within the body of the questionnaire. By using scales as building blocks in questionnaire construction it is possible to derive maximum benefit from the use of established questionnaire items while still allowing flexibility in tailoring questionnaires to meet the specific needs of the research project or the specific needs of population.

Although using established scales to the greatest extent possible has obvious advantages, the special requirements of survey research in the

Middle East urge experimentation and creativity in the construction of survey instruments. Western social science concepts may not be fully appropriate for use in the Middle East, and various dimensions of Middle Eastern behavior may fall beyond the frame of reference of many Western social theories. Finally, many topics routinely included in Western questionnaires may be highly sensitive in the Middle East. Scholars conducting survey research in that region must exercise imagination and creativity in designing scales for inclusion in their questionnaires if they are to overcome these problems and reveal the full richness of Middle Eastern society. Without such creativity, social research in the region could stagnate as a result of excessively rigid attempts to impose a Western frame of reference. It is essential to build upon Western-oriented social research without being restricted by it.

The apparent contradiction between the need for replication and the need for experimentation is far less great than it would appear at first glance. Experimentation in the construction of questionnaires for use in the Middle East should be done on a concept-by-concept basis, not on the basis of total questionnaires. Thus experimental scales must be a careful blend of the new and the old.

Generating Valid Questionnaire Items

Given the difficulty of applying Western concepts to the Middle East, not to mention the sensitivity of Middle Eastern populations and authorities to what Western researchers consider routine questions, it is essential that questionnaire items be generated and evaluated by a panel of experts familiar with both the theoretical content of the research project and the populations in question. Whenever possible, members of the target population should be represented on the panel. The same panel that was involved in selecting the concepts for inclusion in the study should also participate in the generation of questions. Once the members of the panel have reached a consensus on the definitions of the concepts to be included in the study, each member of the panel should prepare five to ten questions for each specific concept that he or she feels would provide both a valid measure of that concept and a measure that would mitigate the sensitivities of the relevant populations and authorities.

For a seven-member panel, a pool of from fifty to seventy-five questionnaire items would be generated for each concept. Each member of the panel would then receive a listing of the pool of questions for each concept and would be requested to evaluate each on the basis of such points as validity, reliability, objectivity, clarity, and simplicity. Evaluations would be done independently to ensure the greatest degree of objectivity. Once the evaluations had been made by each member of the panel independently, they would be discussed by the panel as a collective unit.

Validity, in the context of formulating questions, refers to the simple question "how do you know you are measuring what you think you are measuring?" Does each question specifically address the concept under consideration, or does the question allow a variety of interpretations? The difficulty of assessing validity, of course, is that members of the panel are being asked to assess how members of the target population are going to interpret the question. The less familiar they are with the target population or the fewer the members of the target population that are involved in the formulation and evaluation of questionnaire items, the less effective panel members will be in judging the content validity of the items. Researchers who think they can judge the validity of their questionnaire items without extensive consultation with individuals intimately familiar with the target population are deluding themselves.

Validity also refers to the ability to generate questions that will receive honest answers. Questionnaire items that systematically force respondents to falsify their answers are not valid. Excessively sensitive questions may not receive honest answers, particularly if they are presented in a direct and explicit manner. Assessing reliability forces researchers to choose between direct (explicit) and unobtrusive (indirect) measures for their concepts. An obtrusive measure of religiosity, for example, would simply ask respondents how religious they were or how frequently they went to the mosque. An unobtrusive measure of religiosity might take the form of asking respondents what type of programs they preferred on the television or radio and what newspapers they read and what sections of the newspapers they preferred. Individuals who listed religious programs and media sources would then be judged to be more religious than those who omitted religious choices. A measure of religiosity could also be constructed by adding the number of times the respondents listed religious preferences as well as by whether they listed religious programming as their first, second, or third choice.

Similarly, sensitive areas such as political participation could be directly assessed by asking the respondents to indicate the number of times they voted or participated in strikes or riots. Alternately, respondents might be asked whether "most people" voted or participated in strikes. In the later instance, respondents would not be placed in the position of incriminating themselves. The underlying assumption of the "most people" format is that individuals who participate in riots will be more likely to answer in the affirmative than nonparticipants. This assumption may or may not be valid. The choice between direct and unobtrusive measures is often a choice between valid and reliable information on one hand and clarity on the other.[16] In some instances the best solution may be a balance between reliability and clarity. Such determinations must be carefully weighed by members of the research team.

Precisely because of their lack of specificity, unobtrusive items tend to undermeasure the behavior in question. The use of media preferences to measure religiosity, for example, suffers from the fact that many religious people—perhaps the most religious people in the case of religious extremists—may be avid followers of political events. Accordingly, they might score higher on politics than on religiosity when, in fact, the opposite was the case. Similarly, Nasr and Palmer, in experiments in which Lebanese students were asked if "most people" participated in student strikes, found their questionnaires annotated with comments that the respondents could not speak for most people, but that they themselves had participated in student strikes and that they personally were proud of the fact.[17] Numerous respondents also added that they believed the questionnaire was sponsored by the Central Intelligence Agency (CIA) and that they wanted the CIA to know how they felt. Direct measures are far superior to indirect measures but only to the extent that they are valid.

The choice between direct and unobtrusive measures is unfortunately more complex than a mere choice between precision and validity. The validity of questionnaire items is also influenced by their directness. The more unobtrusive the question, the less confident researchers can be that the question is measuring what they think it is measuring. The reason for this is that the more frequently indirect questionnaire items are used to measure a sensitive concept, the greater the likelihood becomes that assumptions will have to be made about the link between the unobtrusive indicators and the behavior in question. In using media habits to measure religiosity, for example, it must be assumed that religious people follow religion in the mass media and that nonreligious people do not. Although this assumption might seem reasonable in the United States, it would be far less valid in the Middle East, a region in which religion permeates most aspects of social and political life. In the years prior to the downfall of the shah of Iran, for example, religious programming in Iran was full of potential clues concerning the plans and likely moves of the Ayatola Khomeini and his supporters. Religious programming was thus a matter of intense interest to broad segments of the Iranian population, regardless of the intensity of their religious feelings. Similarly, the Egyptian government has allowed religious extremists implicated in attempts to overthrow the government to debate religious issues with Egypt's mainline religious leaders on national television. The debates, though religious programming, are reputed to be of great interest to all segments of the population, their popularity generated as much by the political and intellectual appeal of the debates and curiosity about them as by their religious content.

The use of media preferences as an unobtrusive or secondary measure of religiosity, though desirable in terms of the respondents' willingness to comment openly and honestly on their media habits, may be of questionable validity. Moreover, as an unobtrusive indicator of religiosity, media preference suffers from a lack of stability across time. General interest in religious programming would be far more intense during periods of religious activism than during periods of relative passivity by religious leaders. Media preferences as a measure similarly suffers from a lack of consistency across countries within the Middle East, for the salience of religion to political activity varies dramatically from one Middle Eastern country to another. The quantity of media space devoted to religious programming also varies markedly among Middle Eastern countries. In Saudi Arabia, for example, religious programming is so widespread that anyone attuned to the media is bound to get some religious programming, if only by default. Finally, many Arabs listen to religious programs because of their historical or nationalistic rather than their religious content. Arab history and Arab nationalism are inextricably tied to Islamic history. The great historical feats and conquests of the Arabs are also the historical feats and conquests of Islam, for they occurred in a time period and cultural context in which the conceptual division between church and state so prominent in the mind-set of U.S. scholars was either nonexistent or of minimal consequence in the Middle East.

Stressing the validity problems inherent in the use of media habits as an unobtrusive indicator of religiosity is not intended to suggest that media habits are a widely accepted measure of religiosity but merely to indicate the complexities of interpreting measures that, on the surface, appear to be clear and unambiguous. It could well be, of course, that media habits provide a better indicator of politics than religion, a supposition that would have to be evaluated on its own merits.

If simple and apparently explicit unobtrusive measures such as media habits can be subject to such an array of interpretations and validity problems, it is not difficult to imagine the validity problems that occur as unobtrusive measures become increasingly indirect. In a recent experiment, for example, Al Nimir, Palmer, and Thompson utilized Arab proverbs to measure modernization values among a sample of Saudi Arabians.[18] They anticipated that by utilizing time-tested proverbs, the respondents would reveal their core values without realizing the goal of the questionnaire. They believed that proverbs, familiar and low in sensitivity, would promote honest responses, overcome reluctance to the questionnaire, and generate a high level of respondent interest in the questionnaire.

Lured by the prospect of overcoming the formidable validity and reliability problems associated with survey research in the Middle East, a large panel of Arab students at Florida State University set to work gathering all the Arab proverbs familiar to the Arab community in Tallahassee. The search also included books of proverbs used to interpret Arab society and culture, such as Hamady's *The Temperment and Character of the Arabs*.[19] Finally, the project incorporated proverbs used to good effect by Khalil Nakib to measure the values of bureaucrats in Lebanon and by Omar Fathaly to measure core values in Libya.[20] Nakib and Fathaly had each incorporated a limited number of proverbs in a questionnaire dominated by standard questionnaire items. In both instances, responses to the proverb items had been judged superior to parallel items presented in a direct format.

Once an extensive list of several hundred proverbs had been gathered, the panel of Arab students was requested to match each proverb with that category of traditional/modern behavior that they felt it best measured. At this stage the experiment hit its first snag, for the dimensions of modernization to be operationalized by means of the proverbs had been selected from a variety of learned studies on the topic of modernization, most of which had been defined and operationalized in diverse, ideosyncratic ways and some of which had never been operationalized at all. It was not fully possible, accordingly, to give precise conceptual definitions to each of the categories into which the proverbs were being sorted. Nor was it entirely clear that all members of the panel, some of whom were not social scientists, shared the highly developed sociological imaginations of the principle investigators. The project thus endeavored to utilize unobtrusive measures to measure imprecise concepts.

Despite these problems, the panel agreed with more or less unanimity that well over a hundred of the proverbs from the original pool matched one of the specified conceptual categories. The proverbs, originally organized by categories, were then scrambled to preclude the clustering by subject matter, and the questionnaire was pretested in Saudi Arabia among a sample of some one hundred Saudi nationals.

The results of the experiment overwhelmingly sustained the assumption that the use of proverbs could dramatically reduce the resistance to questionnaires frequently encountered in conducting survey research in the Middle East. Resistance to the questionnaire was virtually nil, as were nonresponses. No indicators of response bias or related problems of "truth in answering" appeared, and respondent interest in the questionnaire was so intense that many respondents requested copies of the questionnaires to show their friends.

If the questionnaire acceptability problems associated with the proverbs were nil so, alas, was the validity of the responses. A factor analysis of response patterns produced virtually a zero relationship between the original categorization of the proverbs by the panel and categorization of the proverbs reflected in the response patterns of the sample. Moreover, later consultation with panel members designed to aid with the interpretation of the results merely demonstrated that a majority of the proverbs could, in fact, fit a number of conceptual categories. In its efforts to make the proverbs fit one category, the panel had neglected to evaluate the complexity of the proverbs, most of which turned out to be multidimensional. Many varied in interpretation from one population segment to another. Later consultation with an anthropologist specializing in Arab proverbs revealed other deficiencies. Arab proverbs, it turned out, are a complex cultural phenomenon, the meaning of which may be determined as much by tone and structure of the proverb as by its actual content. To achieve valid responses from the use of proverbs as unobtrusive measures, a researcher would need an intimate familiarity with both Arab proverbs and the specific populations being sampled.

The experience with both examples of unobtrusive measures—media habits and the proverbs—suggests a number of cautionary points that must be considered in selecting such measures for use in the Middle East. First, unobtrusive measures are generally less valid than obtrusive measures. This lower validity results from the ease with which the erroneous interpretation of the items can be made by both the respondents and the researcher. This means that unobtrusive measures (1) should be avoided in measuring concepts that are themselves difficult to operationalize, (2) should only be employed to measure the most sensitive variables, and (3) should be as specific as possible and should be rigorously tested to ensure that they are unidimensional.

Second, unobtrusive measures are often more culture bound than specific questionnaire items. As such they should be avoided in cross-cultural research, including research that crosses national boundaries or that compares cultural groups within the same nation. Finally, it is very important in constructing unobtrusive measures for use in the Middle East not to underestimate the intelligence of the respondents. Answering a questionnaire in the Middle East is likely to be a new and challenging event for most respondents. It will also involve a modicum of risk. Accordingly, Middle Eastern respondents may scrutinize questionnaire items with greater intensity than do their Western counterparts. Simple-minded efforts at deception will do more to discredit the questionnaire and undermine the validity of its results than straight-forward questions that put the subject in the open and that provide the opportunity to avoid objectionable items. Truly sensitive topics are difficult to disguise and should be avoided unless extensive pretesting indicates that they are acceptable to the populations in question. Moreover, the tasks of pretesting and adjusting unobtrusive items are much more arduous and time consuming than that of pretesting direct questions. This fact is especially important in conducting survey research in the Middle East, as opportunities for extensive pretesting may be precluded by timing and political circumstances.

Another consideration in the panel's evaluation of the suitability of potential questionnaire items is their neutrality. Although biased questions should be avoided in all survey instruments, regardless of location, strenuous efforts must be made to ensure the neutrality of questionnaire items used in the Middle East in as much as many respondents, being unfamiliar with questionnaires, will be searching each question for clues to the proper answer. Many participants at the Bellagio conference noted that respondents in the Middle East tend to be very polite and accommodating. Frequently they try to please researchers (or get the researchers off their back) by providing the answers they believe the researchers want to receive. Such behavior is particularly common among rural and lower status populations, populations long accustomed to providing deferential if superficial agreement to the demands of individuals in authority positions. Under such circumstances, even minor nuances in the content of the question could reduce the validity of the items by shaping response patterns. Again, perceptions of what would or would not be considered shaping must be viewed from the perspective of the target populations. Western researchers, in particular, may find it difficult to appreciate the frame of reference that Middle Eastern respondents bring to their understanding and assessment of questionnaire items.

An additional criterion for the evaluation of questionnaire items is their applicability over time and space. The more references in questionnaire items to local items or recent events, the more their utility will be restricted to a specific population at a specific point in time. In designing questionnaire items then, a researcher must be constantly aware of the trade-offs between the advantages of greater specificity on one hand and greater breadth on the other. Questions of broad applicability offer the opportunity for replication on a longitudinal and cross-sectional basis and should be given preference over narrow-range questions to the extent consistent with the objectives of the project.

Finally, questionnaire items must be evaluated on the basis of such factors as clarity, unidimensionality, and simplicity. Content or face validity tends to be the basic guarantee of the validity of most survey instruments. It is certainly the only validity check available prior to the administration of the questionnaire. The more the content of questionnaire items is self-evident and unambiguous to members of the panel and to pretested subjects, the greater the likelihood becomes that its meaning will be self-evident and unambiguous to members of the target population. Content validity, in turn, is heightened by simple, explicit questionnaire items that possess a single empirical referent. Long, involved questions invite confusion and misunderstanding.

Behavior vs. Attitudes

Related to virtually all the considerations in the formulation and evaluation of questionnaire items is the choice between measuring attitudes and measuring behavior. In the measurement of attitudes a researcher is attempting to gauge psychological predispositions likely to influence behavior. The measurement of behavior, by contrast, refers to specific actions by the respondent at some previous point in time. In measuring attitudes, the researcher is often attempting to predict future behavior on the basis of psychological predispositions; in measuring behavior, he or she is probably attempting to assess future behavior on the basis of past behavior. In either case, the link between what is being measured and future behavior will be far from perfect and is likely to be tenuous. Past behavior does not always indicate future behavior, nor does the existence of attitudes guarantee that individuals will act on the basis of those attitudes. Attitudes and behavior are two distinct entities. Attitudes may or may not shape behavior, depending upon the circumstances. Although this universal phenomenon is clearly not unique to the Middle East, its applicability to that area does require special consideration.

In terms of hard principles, the first observation is that behavior possesses a clear empirical referent (a tangible measurable point of reference) whereas attitudes tend to be less tangible. Accordingly, a clear advantage in terms of both reliability and validity is to be gained by questionnaire items that possess a clear empirical referent. Given the problems of validity and reliability that beset survey research in the Middle East, behavioral questions should take preference over attitudinal questions unless strong theoretical or practical considerations dictate otherwise.

A related factor that could make behavioral items preferable to attitudinal items is the fact that political and social constraints in the Middle East may make it far more difficult for attitudes to influence behavior in that area than in the United States or Western Europe. This would particularly be the case for attitudes that contravened social norms or political restrictions. A female respondent from Saudi Arabia, for example, might well express values or desires that the social constraints of her society would preclude her from expressing through overt behavior. Such attitudes would be of prime importance if the goal of the questionnaire was limited to measuring the attitudes or wishes of Saudi females. If, however, the goals were to predict likely changes in the social behavior of Saudi females, they could be extremely misleading. The time lag required for attitudes to shape values would certainly appear to be different in the Middle East than in the West.

Forsaking hard principles for the fascination of speculation, one must consider the percentage of Middle Easterners that actually possess opinions. To begin this venture into the unknown, one must distinguish between attitudes and opinions. For purposes of discussion, attitudes will be defined as generalized predispositions toward broad subject areas such as sex, religion, or race. An opinion, by contrast, would represent the use of generalized attitudinal predispositions to make evaluative preferences relating to specific events or objects (a question seeking these might be, "What do you think of this law or that piece of farm equipment?"). Opinions are more specific than attitudes and would require an evaluative choice about a specific object rather than a generalized category. An opinion would also require sufficient information to allow the individual to relate the specific object or event to the relevant set of attitudinal predispositions.

In a casual comment, one of the co-organizers of the Bellagio conference suggested that it was theoretically possible that only 18 percent of the Egyptian people possessed opinions on more than a limited number of issues. This situation, if true, could be explained by two factors. First, many population groups in the Middle East are cut off from information by illiteracy and the isolation of a rural or tribal environment. Rural environments in the Middle East, it should be noted, are infinitely more isolated from information sources than rural environments in the United States. This lack of information alone could restrict the formation of opinions beyond the immediate experience of the respondent. To adapt a concept formulated more than thirty years ago by Daniel Lerner, many Middle Eastern population groups may also have a low empathy capacity.[21] Their lack of information makes it extremely difficult for them to psychologically project themselves into circumstances or events beyond their own restricted frame of reference. Accordingly, opinions are limited not only by the lack of specific information but also by the inability of low empathy individuals to imagine or invent opinions on topics beyond their own experience.

A second factor conceivably limiting opinions among some Middle Eastern peoples is the infrequency with which many Middle Eastern population segments are required to express opinions. Females in the rural areas of most Middle Eastern states, for example, live a very restricted existence and are seldom asked their opinion on anything beyond immediate family concerns. It could be argued that they have not learned the art of forming opinions.

To the extent that Middle Eastern populations being surveyed are not in an informational or social position to possess opinions, there will be a great the risk that opinion-oriented questionnaire items will create opinions where none exists in reality. The results of such items would be invalid; far worse, they would be misleading. If such speculation is even partially accurate, a very strong argument could be made for limiting Middle Eastern questionnaire items to behavioral questions unless those people being tested possessed a reasonably high level of education. Unfortunately, speculation is speculation. As in so many areas of survey research in the Middle East, one must wander in the dark.

Response Format

Once an appropriate number of questions have been selected from the original pool to provide accurate measures of each concept included in the questionnaire, suitable response formats must be chosen for each questionnaire item to be used.[22] Selection of response formats tends to revolve around three basic issues: open vs. closed formats, forced choice vs. neutral option formats, and complex vs. simple choice formats. Comments will also be made concerning the need for experimentation in response formats.

Open format questionnaire items are simple questions that request the respondent to provide information on a specific topic. Examples of open format questions would be, "please list that aspect of your job that you find most pleasing" or "what do you consider to be the major foreign policy questions facing your country." Open format questions will frequently be followed by requests for the "second most important problem" and "third most important problem," thereby generating an array of problems as well as a rough indicator of their relative importance.

The main advantage of open-ended questions is that they provide a wealth of spontaneous information; they truly tap the richness of the region. Also, by using open-ended questions a researcher avoids the very real possibility of prejudging things that should be important to the respondents and forcing them to choose from a prestructured list whether their concerns are reflected on that list or not. Similarly, open choices are far more likely to tap dimensions of Middle Eastern behavior that may be beyond the perceptual framework of Western social theories. Open questions are one means of addressing the "unperceived concept" problem. Finally, the use of open questions avoids the need of presenting respondents with a long list of every conceivable item that might possibly be included in their answer. Such lists become particularly long and difficult when questionnaires are presented in an interview format and the interviewer is forced to read and perhaps explain each choice. Not only do such readings extend the time of the interview, a very precious item, but they also offer multiple opportunities for the interviewer to inadvertently bias the responses of the subject. In high illiteracy areas of the Middle East a large percentage of general population questionnaires will have to be administered via interviews. Open format question, although shunned in the West, must be seriously considered as one means for generating broad areas of information among Middle Eastern respondents.

What are the problems with open-ended questions? First, precisely because such qustions lack structure, answers to them may be virtually limitless in range. The researcher is thus forced to regroup the responses into manageable clusters. In effect, the researcher will have to guess what the responses mean and hope that his or her clustering of responses corresponds to reality. Particularly difficult in this regard is the fact that many of the responses lack a clear direction. The researcher may not understand if the respondent was happy or unhappy with the item listed. A recent survey in Cairo, for example, requested respondents to list what they felt to be the major obstacles to peace in the Middle East. Many respondents listed "the Palestinean situation" as their answer, without indicating whether they believed the problem to be the absence of a Palestinean state or tension in the Middle East generated by conflict among Palestinean groups. Such lack of clarity occurs very frequently. It may be alleviated in an interview format by the use of clarifications, though such clarifications themselves may shape responses.

From a practical perspective, researchers should bear in mind that all questionnaire items have to be coded if they are to be systematically analyzed. Coding takes time and effort and involves arbitrary judgments by the coder. The greater the number of open-ended questions that appear in a questionnaire, the greater becomes the number of hours that must be devoted to coding and the greater the number of errors that can creep into the data set as a result of either fatigued coders or differing subjective interpretation of response patterns if more than one individual is coding.

The advantages and disadvantages of restricted choice items are the reverse of the advantages and disadvantages of open-ended questions. Restricted choice items are focused, less time consuming and easier to code. Conversely, they run the risk of excluding important information and may inflate the importance of those choices listed in a specific questionnaire item by precluding respondents from indicating their primary concerns.

One possible solution to the dilemma of choosing between open and closed format items is to use open-ended items in an extensive pretest and then utilize the responses gathered in the pretest to construct restricted choice items. Under any circumstances, the sheer weight of coding and analyzing open-ended questions must limit their use to highly specialized objectives. The overwhelming majority of the questionnaire items in any but the briefest questionnaire will by necessity have to be cast in a restricted-choice format.

The next area of concern in selecting a response format for Middle Eastern questionnaires is weighing the relative merits of forced choice and neutral choice formats. The standard Likert scale format, by way of illustration, is a neutral choice format. Respondents are presented with a statement and requested to indicate their assessment of that statement on the basis of five choices: strongly agree, agree, neutral, disagree, strongly disagree. Individuals lacking a strong opinion on the statement provided may select the neutral option. For measures to be accurate, it is vitally important to distinguish low or neutral feelings from feelings of greater intensity. The presence of a neutral choice also precludes the danger of inventing an artificial opinion when none exists in reality.

The main defect of neutral option response formats is that the neutral option provides an escape hatch for respondents who would prefer to avoid a direct response to a particular questionnaire item or to the questionnaire in general. In specific reference to the Middle East, the number of respondents inclined to avoid questionnaire items is very high. In some cases, the number of respondents reflecting neutral choices threatens to negate the utility of unpopular scales within the questionnaire or even the entire questionnaire. Particularly problematic is the fact that it is often impossible to distinguish between respondents who truly lack an opinion on a particular statement and those pursuing an avoidance strategy.

The alternative to the neutral choice response format is to force respondents to express an opinion by eliminating the neutral option. Forced choice items carry the risk of creating opinions where none actually exists. It is important to recall in this context the earlier discussion of why opinions may not exist among many populations within the Middle East. The problem of creating opinions, then, is a very real problem that should not be dismissed out of hand. There is no simple solution to the dilemma of choosing between a neutral choice format and a forced choice format other than to make the decision on the basis of the population being surveyed and the response patterns provided by extensive pretesting.

The third problem to be considered in selecting a response format is the number of choices to be presented to the respondent on any given item. In the example of the Likert scales, respondents were provided with either four or five options, depending upon whether the neutral option was available. Some texts on questionnaire design suggest that a true measure of respondents' feelings toward an issue requires that they be allowed to record their feelings on scales ranging from seven to twenty points.[23] Social Science Research Council surveys in Europe, for example, measure party preference by presenting respondents with a multipoint scale in the shape of a thermometer and requesting them to indicate where on the hot or cold side of the thermometer their feelings toward a particular issue lie. The resulting information is far more sensitive than responses received from a simple four or five point scale.

Several Middle Eastern survey researchers with whom this problem has been discussed, by contrast, maintain that Middle Eastern subjects find it hard enough, given their cultural background and lack of familiarity with questionnaires, to make simple yes or no responses. Simplicity, they argue, is best. In their view, multiple choice formats merely confuse the subject and lead to random responses. Multiple choices also take more time and reduce the space available for other items. Because few empirical data exist on the optimal range of choices for use in Middle Eastern surveys, the only recommendation that can be made is a call for experimentation and extensive pretesting. Also, the author's personal experience suggests that long and involved questionnaire formats generally result in high nonresponse rates and confusing results. Included in this category would be questionnaire items requesting respondents to arrange a list of items in terms of their importance. Rank ordering takes excessive time and results in very high nonresponse rates. Respondents also lose interest in rank ordering a list of items once they have selected the one or two items of greatest importance to themselves.

A particularly effective response format for use in the Middle East presents respondents with a pair of balanced statements and asks them to indicate the statement that best fits their views. The questionnaire items presented in Table 8.1, for example, represent a set of fifteen such paired statements, each of which requests the respondent to choose between a pair of motivational factors relevant to the selection of a bureaucratic position.[24] In responding to the fifteen questions, the respondents will have evaluated each of six work values (money, prestige, proximity to family, location, security, comfort) with each of the other values. Equally important, an overall ranking of the importance of the six values is also easily computed. Such items have a high content validity as they refer to clear and unambiguous choices. They also have proved

TABLE 8.1
Main incentive values of Egyptian bureaucrats (low and medium level only)

Listed below are several pairs of statements. In each pair, please indicate the statement that most agrees with your preferences.

a. a high-paying job with low prestige	6.7
b. a moderately paying job with high prestige	93.3
a. a high-paying job away from friends and relatives	49.1
b. a moderately paying job near friends and relatives	50.9
a. a high-paying job in the rural areas	52.3
b. a moderately paying job in a city of your choice	47.7
a. a high-paying job that was very difficult and time consuming	74.6
b. a moderately paying job that was not too difficult or demanding	25.4
a. a high-paying job that involved a great deal of responsibility and risk	60.1
b. a moderately paying job that was very secure	39.9
a. a very prestigious job away from family and friends	85.9
b. a respectable job near family and friends	14.1
a. a very prestigious job that involved a great deal of risk and responsibility	82.6
b. a respectable job that was very secure	17.4
a. a very prestigious job that was very difficult and time consuming	89.7
b. a respectable job that was not too difficult or demanding	10.3
a. a very prestigious job in a rural area	75.7
b. a respectable job in the city of your choice	24.3
a. very secure position in the rural areas	45.2
b. a position with risks and complex responsibilities in a city of your choice	54.8
a. a very secure position away from friends and relatives	50.2
b. a position with risks and complex responsibilities near friends and relatives	49.8
a. a very secure position that was difficult and time consuming	73.0
b. a position of risk and responsibility that was not very difficult	27.0
a. a position of little difficulty away from relatives and friends	72.9
b. a difficult and time-consuming position near friends and relatives	27.1
a. a position of little difficulty in the rural areas	41.8
b. a difficult and time-consuming position in the city	58.2
a. a position near friends and relatives in the rural areas	48.6
b. a position away from friends and relatives in a city of your choice	51.4

TABLE 8.1, *cont.*

Scales: *Percentages of Unanimous Choices*

Prestige	62.8
Location	14.4
Money	4.1
Security	3.2
Relatives	1.7
Comfort	0.2

Weighted Preference Ordering* (Range 0–100)

Prestige	88
Money	50
Location	46
Security	45
Relatives	39
Comfort	35

---

*Scale scores reflect the mean score of total choices for each value over each competing value, doubled. The scale scores range between 0 and 100.

to be reliable in terms of both the internal consistency of response patterns and the reduction of nonresponse rates. Finally, the paired items offer the respondent a simplified choice between two items, thereby reducing the response time required by longer, more complex items.

As a general statement, the more time and care a research team devotes to testing diverse response formats, the better their results are likely to be. It might also be noted that questionnaires that include a variety of response formats tend to retain the interest of respondents for a longer period than do questionnaires possessing uniform response formats. They also keep respondents on their toes and offset inadvertent tendencies toward consistently high or low response patterns (response bias).

Questionnaire Size

Long questionnaires, regardless of the site of their administration, invite reliability problems resulting from boredom and fatigue. Effective limits on the size of questionnaires designed for use in the Middle East are influenced by other considerations as well. The social time required for administering questionnaires in the Middle East is extensive. Long periods must be devoted to social amenities before the questionnaire can actually be administered. Time must also be taken to explain the nature of the questionnaire and to ease the anxieties of the respondent. Social time must be added to the time respondents can reasonably be expected to devote to the questionnaire.

A second size consideration involves the length of time that a reasonable environment will be available for completion of the questionnaire. It is rare in any Middle Eastern social setting to isolate an individual on a one-to-one basis for more than half an hour without multiple interruptions from friends and colleagues, all of whom will stay awhile and express their views on the questionnaire. The longer and more time consuming the questionnaire, the more such interruptions will influence the reliability of the questionnaires. These problems are elaborated in Chapter 7. A third factor limiting questionnaire length in the Middle East is the nervousness of many authorities regarding the administration of questionnaires. The longer the questionnaire, the more nervous they become. All in all, questionnaires that take more than thirty to forty minutes to administer are likely to encounter serious problems.

The Language of the Questionnaire

To select the proper language for a questionnaire in the Middle East the researcher must choose between administering the questionnaire in the indigenous language or in a European language. The choice between French and Arabic is particularly difficult in North Africa because many population groups in Morocco, Algeria, and Tunisia use French as well as Arabic as a medium of conversation. If the questionnaire is limited to a specific population, the choice of the most suitable language will be determined by the needs of the population. If the survey includes a number of population segments, the questionnaire will in all probability have to be administered in both languages. Although administering questionnaires in more than one language imposes formidable problems of establishing uniform meanings for each questionnaire item, the only alternative is to force at least part of the sample members to complete the questionnaire in a secondary language. This approach is usually unacceptable. If it is difficult to avoid administering a questionnaire in two languages, the translation problems can be reduced by using questionnaire items that are simple and that possess explicit empirical referents.

If Arabic is to be the language of the questionnaire, the researcher must choose between modern standard (newspaper) Arabic or a regional dialect. Local dialects vary markedly from one corner of the Arab world to the other, even within a single country. Although standard newspaper Arabic is generally understood by highly educated people throughout the Arab world, the medium of conversation (and thinking) for the average individual is the local dialect. The more questionnaires move away from the dialect of the respondent, the less likely the respondent is to fully understand the questionnaire items. The selection of a language for use in the questionnaire must be between the broad applicability and comparability of standard Arabic and the greater reliability of the local dialect. The characteristics of the target population will determine the choice.

The Pretest

The basic means of alleviating the myriad problems of questionnaire design is extensive pretesting of the questionnaire among members of the target population(s). (Indeed, the need for extensive pretesting of survey projects cannot be overemphasized.) Pretesting questionnaires in the Middle East, though crucial to the validity and reliability of survey research in the region, may not be easy. The general nervousness that surrounds the administration of questionnaires in that region may cause authorities to grant permission for only a single administration. In such situations multiple pretesting of the questionnaire under ideal circumstances becomes difficult.

A more difficult problem to anticipate is the possibility that the administration of a pretest may result in unexpected repercussions and preclude the administration of the main questionnaires. In the discussion at the Bellagio conference, numerous examples of questionnaire items that upset respondents and ultimately forced cancellation of the project were cited. Pretesting is very delicate operation and should be approached with maximum caution.

The sensitivity that accrues to pretesting in the Middle East necessitates that researchers place even greater emphasis on the role of a panel of experts in evaluating the survey instruments before they are deemed suitable for pretesting among members of the target population. If pretesting is judged to be difficult because of the nervousness of the political authorities or the target population, the size of the panel of experts and the intensity of their labors must be increased proportionally.

Conclusion

This chapter was designed to assist both Middle Eastern and Western scholars with the design of survey research instruments for use in the Middle East. As the author has attempted to illustrate, the application of survey research in the Middle East is an exceedingly complex process that must be approached with infinite care, sensitivity, and patience. If survey researchers do approach their task with these attitudes, the results of their efforts may help solve the myriad social, economic, and political problems of the region. Sloppy research, on the other hand, will exacerbate the problems of the region by providing false and misleading information in the name of science.

Notes

1. The Al Ahram Survey of the Eygptian Bureaucracy was conducted during 1983 by the Al Ahram Center for Political and Strategic Studies. The project was supported by a grant from the Ford Foundation.

2. For a general review of the study of social class see, Reinhard Bendix and Seymour M. Lipset, eds., *Class, Status and Power* (New York: Free Press, 1966.)

3. M. A. Cook, ed., *Studies in the Economic History of the Middle East* (London: Oxford University Press, 1970).

4. Doreen Warriner, *Land Reform and Development in the Middle East* (New York: Royal Institute of International Affairs, 1957); Alfred Bonne, *State and Economics in the Middle East* (London: Routledge and Kegan Paul, 1955).

5. Monte Palmer, Ibrahim Fahad Alghofarly, and Saud Mohammed Alnimir, "The Behavioral Correlates of Rentier Economics: A Case Study of Saudi Arabia," in Robert W. Stookey, ed., *The Arabian Peninsula* (Stanford, Calif.: Hoover Institution Press, 1984) pp. 17–36.

6. David C. McClelland, *The Achieving Society* (Princeton, N.J.: D. Van Nostrand, 1961).

7. For a discussion of the reliability scales used in the California Psychological Inventory (CPI) see *Manual, California Personality Inventory* (Palo Alto, Calif.: Consulting Psychologists Press, 1975).

8. Interviews conducted in Teheran, 1974.

9. An extended discussion of scale length can be found in Jum C. Nunnally, *Psychometric Theory*, 2nd ed. (New York: McGraw Hill, 1978). For an application of scaling when designing and validating a survey instrument for use in the Arab world, see Mark Tessler, "Measuring Abstract Concepts in Tunisia," in William O'Barr, David Spain, and Mark Tessler, eds., *Survey Research in Africa: Its Applications and Limits* (Evanston, Ill.: Northwestern University Press, 1973).

10. Nunnally, *Psychometric Theory*.

11. Marvin E. Shaw and Jake M.Wright, *Scales for the Measurement of Attitudes* (New York: McGraw-Hill, 1967.)

12. Monte Palmer et al., *Survey Research in the Arab World: An Analytical Index* (London: Menas Press, 1982).

13. M. Saftey, M. Palmer, and M. Kennedy, *An Index of Survey Research in Egypt* (Cairo: Cario Papers, 1986).

14. The CPI contains several cultural references specific to the United States but has been modified for use in a variety of foreign languages.

15. Monte Palmer and Mima Nedelcovych, "The Political Behavior of Moroccan Students," *Journal of Arab Affairs* 3, no. 1, 1984.

16. Systematic error in response patterns is generally considered a validity problem rather than a reliability problem.

17. Nafhat Nasr and Monte Palmer, "Alienation and Political Participation in Lebanon," *International Journal of Middle Eastern Studies* 8 (1977):493–516.

18. Monte Palmer, William Thompson, and Saudi Al Nimir, "A Proverbial Approach to the Traditional-Modernity Continuum," a paper presented at the Convention of the Middle East Studies Association, 1978.

19. Sania Hamady, *Temperment and Character of the Arabs* (New York: Twane Publishers, 1960).

20. Khalil Nakib, *Bureaucracy and Development, a Study of the Lebanese Civil Service* (Ph.D dissertation, Florida State University, 1972.); Omar I. Fathaly and Monte Palmer, *Political Development and Social Change in Libya* (Lexington, Mass.: Lexington Books, 1980).

21. Daniel Lerner, *The Passing of Traditional Societies* (Glencoe, Ill.: Free Press, 1958).

22. Response formats and the utility of combining items with different response formats into a single scale are discussed in relation to Arab society in

Mark Tessler, "Problems of Measurement in Comparative Research: Perspectives from an African Survey," *Social Science Information* 12 (1973):29–43.

23. See note 7.

24. Ali Leila, El Sayeed Yassin, and Monte Palmer, "Apathy Values, Incentives and Development," a paper presented at the 1983 Convention of the International Studies Association.

9

Selecting a Sample and Interacting with Respondents

Tawfic E. Farah

In this chapter I will attempt to acquaint the reader with the principles underlying sampling theory and with the commonly used sampling designs. An effort will be made to offer examples of actual sampling strategies followed by researchers in their studies in the Arab states. The mathematical aspects of sampling are avoided. Interested readers may pursue this matter in specialized texts listed in the notes.[1]

The reason for sampling is simple: A researcher samples because he or she does not have the time or the resources to study a whole population. A population may be a group of people, speeches, houses, students, and so on. The nature of the population depends on what is being studied or the unit of analysis. If a researcher is studying food preferences of all university students in Tunis, the population is all university students (males and females) in Tunis, and the unit of analysis is the university student. A researcher may be interested in a number of characteristics of this unit, such as age, religious affiliation, family background, and so on.

Nonprobability Sampling

A researcher may decide to draw a nonprobability or a probability sample for a study. A nonprobability sample is one in which the probability of any member of the population being included in the sample is not known. It is not possible to measure the standard error of the estimate with this sampling technique. However, there is a place in research for nonprobability sampling because of the convenience and economy that may outweigh the risks involved in not using probability sampling. At times a population cannot be defined because a list of the population is not available. The data may be unreliable or dated. Census statistics are available in many Arab states but should be handled with utmost care. The most recent population census in Lebanon was made in the

136

1930s. Population statistics in some other countries are incomplete. For example, it is hard to locate the number of Shia Moslems in Kuwait's population statistics; it is simply not given. A researcher would have to contend with this challenge by using nonprobability samples. Nonprobability samples are economical and convenient, but they may be unrepresentative. There are three types of nonprobability samples: accidental, quota, and judgmental.

Accidental Sampling. An accidental sample, or hit-or-miss technique, consists of selecting the most convenient elements in a population for a study such as students in a classroom or men in a coffee shop.

Quota Sample. In quota samples, the researcher subjectively selects a certain number of respondents fitting the characteristics (quota) of the population. If the population has an equal number of men and women, the researcher selects an equal number of men and women in the sample. If it is known that 25 percent of university students are freshmen, 25 percent of the total sample should be freshmen. In quota sampling, interviewers are given the task of interviewing quota groups specified by traits such as age, religion, social class, and ethnicity. It is, of course, impossible to estimate sampling errors, and interviewers may fail to secure a representative sample. In addition, when quota sampling is used, control of the quality of the field work is very difficult. The major advantage of quota sampling is that the characteristics of the sample may be determined with a view toward the analytical needs of an investigator's research design.

Judgmental Sample. Judgmental samples are composed according to the researcher's judgment about which units should be included. Past research experience is used in making these "judgments." Usually, an experienced researcher uses this method of sampling in pretests of questionnaires or in pilot studies.

Probability Sampling

Probability sampling is superior to nonprobability sampling because every member of the population has a known probability of being selected. Probability sampling is systematic and based on mechanical procedures; it is not a hit-or-miss technique. It permits the estimation of sample error. Three main types of probability samples will be discussed: random, stratified, and clustered.

Random Sampling. Random sampling is a technique that gives each member of the population (N) an equal chance of being selected. This method, however, requires a tremendous quantity of up-to-date data from which to choose a sample. Saad Gadalla, a participant in the Bellagio conference, recounted his efforts to conduct surveys in Egypt in 1982 when the most recent census data available were from 1979. He reported that in some cases interviewers were not able to locate over 35 percent of the sample given to him by the Egyptian Department of Mobilization and Statistics because people had changed their residence, died, or given false names or false addresses. If the sample frame (information about the population) is not reliable and up to date, it is futile to even attempt random sampling.

On the other hand, researchers can obtain up-to-date computerized lists of student enrollments at many universities. These lists often detail information about each student's age, religion, year of enrollment, field of study, sex, and anticipated year of graduation. In this type of case a researcher may use random sampling. The standard method of ensuring the randomness of a sample is the use of a table of random numbers (you may generate your own if you have access to a computer), like that reproduced in Table 9.1. The operational procedure is simple. Each member of the population is listed and given a number, from zero to N. The table of random digits is entered at some random starting point. Each digit that appears in the table is read in order (up, down, or sideways—the direction does not matter, so long as it is used consistently).

Whenever the number that appears in the table of random numbers corresponds to the number of a sampling unit on the list, that sampling unit is selected for the sample. This process is continued until the desired sample size is reached. When sampling without replacement, which is usually the case, and the same number appears before the sample is completed, it is skipped. As an illustration, suppose that the student population of Qatar University consists of 7,232 full-time students. A researcher wants a random sample of 400. Each student is numbered from 1 to 7,232. You enter the table of random numbers the same as before, and the student who is numbered 6,118 on the list becomes the first member of the sample. You continue this process until 400 students are selected. If a number that has been previously selected appears a second time before the sample is completely selected, it is ignored. This gives the researcher a sample without replacement. Every sampling unit of the population has an equal nonzero probability of being included in the sample; this probability is n/N, where n stands for the size of the sample and N for the size of the population. In the Qatar example, in which the population consists of 7,232 full-time students at the university and a simple random sample of 400 was drawn, the probability of each sampling unit of the population being included in the sample is 400/7,232.[2]

Simple random sampling is often hard to obtain because lists of populations are not available in appropriate form for a researcher or the lists are outdated and obsolete. Often a researcher in the Arab world has to be innovative. The remedies vary with each case. If the list is not available, the researcher can attempt to enumerate the population from various sources of information that are available; if the list appears to be out of date, it must be checked very carefully. If the missing elements are few, they can safely be ignored. If the list is divided into groups (men and women, for example), it may be recast into one list.

Table 9.1   Random Numbers

81 83 83 04 49	77 45 85 50 51	79 88 01 97 30	87 63 93 95 17
92 79 43 89 79	29 18 94 51 23	14 85 11 47 23	08 61 74 51 69
48 40 35 94 22	72 65 71 08 86	50 03 42 99 36	08 52 85 08 40
64 71 06 21 66	89 37 20 70 01	61 65 70 22 12	89 85 84 46 06
06 94 76 10 08	81 30 15 39 14	81 83 17 16 33	42 29 72 23 19
94 61 09 43 62	20 21 14 68 86	94 95 48 46 45	79 53 36 02 95
34 85 52 05 09	85 43 01 72 73	14 93 87 81 40	79 93 96 38 63
53 16 71 13 81	59 97 50 99 52	24 62 20 42 31	97 48 72 66 48
88 46 38 03 58	72 68 49 29 31	75 70 16 08 24	26 97 05 73 51
65 88 69 58 39	88 02 84 27 83	85 81 56 39 38	06 87 37 78 48
68 69 80 95 44	11 29 01 95 80	49 34 35 86 47	87 02 22 57 51
79 57 92 36 59	89 74 39 82 15	08 58 94 34 74	39 77 32 77 09
22 45 44 84 11	87 80 61 65 31	09 71 91 74 25	28 06 24 25 93
80 45 67 93 82	59 73 19 85 23	53 33 65 97 21	97 67 63 99 61
53 58 47 70 93	66 56 45 65 79	45 56 20 19 47	69 30 16 09 05
26 72 39 27 67	53 77 57 68 93	60 61 97 22 61	33 73 99 19 87
43 00 65 98 50	45 60 33 01 07	98 99 46 50 47	87 14 77 43 96
52 70 05 48 34	56 65 05 61 86	90 92 10 70 80	99 53 93 61 28
15 33 59 05 28	22 87 26 07 47	86 96 98 29 06	93 86 52 77 65
85 13 99 24 44	49 18 09 79 49	74 16 32 23 02	18 46 23 34 27
87 03 04 79 88	08 13 13 85 51	55 34 57 72 69	07 10 63 76 35
52 06 79 79 45	82 63 18 27 44	69 66 92 19 09	92 38 70 96 92
46 72 60 18 77	55 66 12 62 11	08 99 55 64 57	00 57 25 60 59
47 21 61 88 32	27 80 30 21 60	10 92 35 36 12	24 98 65 63 21
12 73 73 99 12	49 99 57 94 82	96 88 57 17 91	28 10 99 00 27

If the groups are uneven in size and the researcher cannot economically and efficiently recast them into single list, then separate random samples may be drawn from each list. Techniques used in stratified and cluster sampling may be used. Above all, the researcher must not give up.

Stratified Samples. In stratified samples, the population is divided into two or more groups called strata, and simple random samples are taken from each stratum and combined to form the total sample. For example, suppose that in a given population, there are 500 Shia, 300 Sunnis, 100 Greek Orthodox, and 100 Druze. If a random sample of 100 persons was drawn, chances are that the proportion of one or several of these groups would be too large or too small. A stratified sample would remedy this situation by selecting 50 Shia, 30 Sunnis, 10 Greek Orthodox, and 10 Druze. These groups would be selected randomly, and the probability sample subsequently drawn within each stratum.

Sampling from different strata can be either proportional or disproportional. In proportionally stratified sampling, larger samples are taken from larger strata and smaller samples are taken from smaller strata. In a proportionally stratified sample, 10 percent of the total sample, for example, would be selected from a stratum that represents 10 percent of the population. On the other hand, disproportionally stratified samples are weighted samples; that is, the sample size from each stratum is not proportional to the population size of the stratum. Data are weighted to create the equivalent of a truly random sample. This means that if a sample has too many men or young people, then respondents in that category get counted as more or less than one respondent. For example, if a random sample of 1,500 university students in Jordan should have 700 females but has only 350, each is counted twice. Weighting, however, does not guarantee a representative sample because a researcher is still using people available for those who are not. A sample should be weighted as a last resort.

Larger samples may be selected from smaller strata than one would expect based on the size of the strata. In a disproportionally stratified sample, 10 percent of the total sample may be selected from a stratum that represents only 1 percent of the population. Disproportionate stratified samples are often used by researchers who wish to analyze a stratum intensively and to assess the differences between two or more particular strata. When a disproportionate stratified sample is used, a mean computed for the population based on the means of all strata would have to be weighted in accordance with the number in each stratum. If generalizations are to be made about the characteristics of the total population, then the sample must be reweighted. Stratified samples are often more accurate than simple random samples because stratification reduces sampling error by using knowledge about the population.

Cluster Samples. In cluster samples, the researcher divides the population into a large number of groupings or clusters and draws a random or a stratified sample of clusters. The investigator lists each of the elements in each of the sampled clusters and draws a simple random or stratified sample of units from each cluster.

Suppose then that an investigator intends to study modernizing attitudes in the Hamra district of Beirut, Lebanon, where addresses are sketchy, no single list of residents is available, and families live in large block apartment buildings. Samir Khalaf, a Lebanese scholar who took part in the Bellagio conference, accomplished this feat by drawing a careful inventory and a socioeconomic profile of each household in each apartment building in the district and selecting clusters from the list. Within each cluster they selected buildings at random and interviewed persons selected randomly within these buildings. Their sample was selected in stages, and hence it is referred to as multistage cluster sampling. Fouad Khuri, another Lebanese social scientist, also used cluster sampling. He obtained aerial photographs of the city of Beirut and pinpointed areas and households by imposing grids onto the photographs, in this way obtaining cluster samples.

Another example is provided by Ali Zaghal, a Jordanian scholar who reported on his research at Bellagio. In his study of social change in northern Jordan he utilized cluster sampling to identify the three districts he wanted to study; then he stratified his sample within each district according to the number of households in each village as follows:

Small villages	1–99 households
Middle villages	100–399
Large villages	400–699
Small towns	700–999
Middle towns	1000–1600
Large cities	Over 1600

One and three-fourths percent of the households in each strata were calculated. This gave him the subsample size in each strata. The next step, the number of localities to cover the subsamples from each strata, was calculated. By random procedure, the names of localities in each strata were selected, giving him twenty-six localities within which the total sample was composed of 660 households. In each locality, a subsample was drawn from the old generation and another from the young generation. In the three studies, the researchers overcame sampling obstacles by being creative and innovative. They did not give up.

Three points should be remembered about cluster sampling. First, the decision to call a particular aggregate of units a cluster depends on the inquiry unit. Areas such as the Hamra in Beirut, Dokki in Cairo, and Al-Rawda in Kuwait can be called clusters since they contain a number of households. The household in each case is the unit of inquiry. On the other hand, if the area is the unit of inquiry, it cannot be called a cluster. Second, clusters do not necessarily have to be natural aggregates. Artificial cluters can be made, such as when a researcher imposes grids onto maps and draws his own clusters. Third, in any one sample design, several levels of clusters may be used. These three designs of probability sampling are the most commonly used by social investigators, but they certainly do not exhaust the range of probability sampling procedures.

Sampling Error

Sampling error consists of sampling bias and random sampling error. *Sampling Bias.* Sampling bias is the difference between the statistic and the parameter attributable to systematic errors resulting from the design of the sample. An illustration of sampling bias is the well-known story of the U.S. magazine, *Literary Digest.* In 1936, this magazine polled its well-to-do subscribers on their choice in the U.S. presidential campaign between Alf Landon, the Republican candidate, and Franklin Roosevelt, the Democrat. The *Digest* predicted that Landon would beat Roosevelt in the election whereas in fact Roosevelt won the election by a wide margin. The *Digest*'s error arose from a biased sample: The subscribers to the *Digest* were well-to-do people who owned cars and telephones—an unrepresentative group during the economic depression days.

Let us assume, for example, that a researcher in the United States is going to conduct interviews over the telephone. Many phone calls will be unanswered and the researcher will be unable to reach 25 percent to 30 percent of those he tries to phone. Moreover, people who are most likely to be at home to answer their phones differ markedly from those who are not. In the United States, for example, women, the elderly, the less affluent, the unemployed, rural residents, and the less educated are more likely to be reached by telephone than are men, the young, the affluent, employed persons, urban residents, and the educated. In Kuwait, in contrast, researchers may be able to reach younger women, and in many cases those women are housemaids, who may or may not be relevant to the research study. Moreover, among those who are reached, those who agree to be interviewed differ from those who refuse. In the United States, "higher status" households and some elderly people, apparently fearful of talking to strangers on the phone, are the most likely to refuse interviews. Higher status people are most likely to refuse interviews over the phone in many Arab countries, and such people do not answer their phones—servants and maids perform this function. Hence, biased samples cannot be controlled. Increasing sample size does not reduce errors resulting from a defective sample design. Although sample bias is impossible to estimate, sampling errors can be estimated and controlled.

Random Sampling Error. Random sampling error is estimated with the standard error formula, usually at the 95 percent confidence level. Sampling errors could be errors of mean or proportion. To estimate the sampling error of a mean, the standard error formula used is

$$SE_X = \pm z \frac{s}{\sqrt{n}}$$

where SE_X is the sampling error, or standard error (the terms can be used interchangeably), Z is the approximate standard or Z score for the 95 percent confidence level, s is the standard deviation of the sample, and n is the sample size.

Sampling error of a proportion may be estimated according to this formula

$$SE_p = \pm z \sqrt{\frac{p(1-p)}{n}}$$

where SE_p is the sampling error, Z is the approximate standard or Z score for the 95 percent confidence level, p is the sample proportion, and n is the sample size. This formula shows sampling error to be a function of three factors: the confidence level, Z; dispersion in the population, $p(1-p)$; and sample size n.

The Z score at the 95 percent level, which is the acceptable confidence level in social science, is 1.96 rounded to 2 for ease of calculation. The confidence level could, of course, be increased to the 99 percent level where Z is 2.6. Increased confidence is usually gained by making more vague and general statements: safe statements that are useless in many cases.[3]

As for dispersion in the population, a rule of thumb is that the more homogeneous the population, the smaller is the sampling error. Conversely, the more heterogenous the population, the greater is the sampling error. Heterogeneity is at a maximum when p = 0.5.

The size of the sample, not the size of the population, affects sampling accuracy. Usually, increasing the size of the sample will have the effect of reducing the sampling error. Increasing sample size is how random sampling error can be controlled. As shown in Table 9.2, to reduce sampling error from 2 percent to 1 percent, the sample size must be increased fourfold—from 2,500 to 10,000.

Nonresponse Error

Nonsampling errors such as measurement errors are a concern for the survey researcher. Nonresponse is defined as those observations that are not carried out because of the reasons described in this section. However, a word of caution: If a researcher has done his or her homework well and has become known and trusted in the community, the problem of nonresponse becomes minor. If people do not respond to the researcher, it is because he or she has not done adequate preliminary work in the community. A researcher cannot simply pop into a community, a classroom, a refugee camp, or a government office and announce that he or she is there to conduct research. If a researcher is associated with a university, the barriers are not going to simply come tumbling down. People are not going to welcome a stranger with open arms and make him or her privy to their attitudes. This is true in Japan, the United States, Europe, or Timbuktu. Arabs are not inherently more private or more secretive than any other people. If a researcher is ignorant of the cultural mores and nuances of a community he or she should not conduct research in that community. His or her findings are prima facie suspect.

Ahmad Dhaher and Faisal Al-Salem conducted political culture surveys in Kuwait, Bahrain, the United Arab Emirates, and Oman. Tawfic Farah

Table 9.2   Sampling Error and Sample Size*

Sampling Error (%)	Sample Size
+ 1	10,000
+ 2	2,500
+ 3	1,111
+ 4	625
+ 5	400
+ 6	278
+ 7	204
+ 8	156
+ 9	124
+ 10	100

* Assumes 95% confidence level (z = 2), p - 5, and a
simple random sample.

conducted surveys among Palestinian children in Kuwait and Qatar. The
Yasumassa and Alice Kuroda worked with Palestinian children in the
camps in Jordan and Lebanon. Mark Tessler carried out survey research
among Tunisian students and among Tunisian adults from different
social classes. Samir Khalaf was able to interview prostitutes in Lebanon.
Saad Eddin Ibrahim and others performed a mission thought to be
impossible when they conducted their study of Itajahat Al-Ra'iy Al-'Amm
Al-'Arabi Nahwa Mas'alat Al-Wahda. Saad Eddin Ibrahim and his col-
laborators delved into politically sensitive topics. They faced plenty of
obstacles but managed to complete their work.

Every society has its peculiarities; every community has its sensitivities.
What plays in San Francisco does not necessarily play in Peoria, Illinois.
Similarly, one cannot always ask a modern-day Cairene the same things
that he or she asks a Berber in the Atlas mountains. Yet the task can
be done. Mustapha Attir, for example, found in his research in Libya

that rural and Bedouin people were very cooperative with him. They trusted him because he took time with the respondents, "warming them up" before he even started asking interview questions. He explained to them the purpose and the process of the study. He even discussed the questions with the respondents after the interview was over. People were cooperative even when he delved into sensitive personal areas. Tessler also reported that this technique proved very effective in Tunisia, where a high response rate was obtained not only among middle-class respondents but in remote rural communities and among poorly educated respondents as well.[4]

Knowing the community and the right people in the community helps the researcher to overcome some obstacles. Privacy is important to people everywhere; hence a researcher's sensitivity to people's desire for privacy and his adept handling of these ticklish matters cannot be overemphasized. People are very often suspicious of outsiders who seek to collect information, adding to the difficulty of establishing trust and responsiveness. The kinds of procedures that can be employed to allay such concern and to gain the confidence of the inhabitants of communities where surveys are being conducted are discussed at some length in Chapter 2 in this book. Sammani reports on an unusually ambitious and successful project in the Sudan, in which care was taken to involve the local community in the project and to ensure that it benefited from the presence of the researchers.

The proportion of nonrespondents varies in relation to many factors, including the nature of the research project, the agency sponsoring it, the kind of questions being asked, the skill of the interviewers, the level of trust between the interviewer and the interviewee, and the number of callbacks that can be made. Good sampling techniques cannot make up for a poorly designed and administered interview schedule, nor can estimates of the effect of nonresponse on the quality of the data and the computations that are used by some survey researchers to correct for nonresponse.

Yet despite homework in the community, a researcher cannot hope to interview everyone he or she wants to for a number of reasons:

1. Uninterviewables: people who are ill or illiterate, or have language barriers.
2. Not found people: those who have changed their addresses, are inaccessible, or are deceased.
3. People not at home or at the work place: those who happen to be absent when the interviewer calls but who could be reached on the second or third effort.
4. Refusals: people who refuse to cooperate and/or are afraid to answer certain questions. Some people are sensitive about answering questions about religious affiliations. Others refuse to answer questions about income levels and sources of income. Yet others

are dubious of questions related to politics. In many Arab societies fear of the tax collector and repressive security agencies is very real in the absence of laws that protect citizens' civil liberties.

Group Responses

Women and men are social animals; they live in herds. A researcher finds it almost impossible to talk to someone alone when conducting a survey; everybody seems to have an opinion that he or she wants to share. A researcher who asks questions in a market place becomes the show, and everybody volunteers answers. It is very difficult, indeed impossible, to corner a respondent alone especially in a crowded place or a small village or town. What does a researcher do in such cases? How does a researcher handle and account for group responses? How does this affect one's sampling techniques and the integrity of the whole research design? What is group response? When the sampling unit is the individual, then the researcher is logically interested in this one person's opinion, attitudes, preferences, or values. However, these are very hard to obtain in the field in many cases. For example, a researcher would find it very difficult to walk into a house in an Egyptian village and interview an individual in a private room or a corner of a room. There are always other people present. They answer for the individual and volunteer their own opinions and their own answers. Saad Gadala, director of the Social Research Center of the American University in Cairo, does not find a problem with this phenomenon as long as the researcher is aware of it when analyzing the data. Opinions and attitudes of the individual interviewed are not a product of his or her thinking alone but also rather of the thinking of other members in the household or the community. To illustrate, a researcher who interviews a woman in rural Egypt about family planning is apt to receive different answers, depending on who is present. This is to be expected. The husband's answer will be different from the mother-in-law's, the mother's or the sister's. If the woman is asked how many children she would like to have or whether she is using contraceptives, she will give a different response in front of her mother-in-law than the one she will give if the researcher talked to her alone. Similarly, when women are interviewed by themselves, and husbands are interviewed by themselves, their answers may differ; when husbands and wives are interviewed together, they give a different set of responses.

In Saudi Arabia, Naiem Sherbiny and Saad Ibrahim reported that during their field work among Bedouins, friends, relatives, and colleagues of the interviewee would volunteer answers, comments, and discussion of the question asked specifically of the interviewee. The researchers found that they could not avoid this problem without awakening hostility so they changed the research design with a clear conscience, deciding that the group response was indeed better than the individual response.

Sometimes a researcher has to break out from the straightjacket of the strict rules and canons of sampling theory.

Conclusion

Sampling is an art. A researcher is not going to become a good sampler by sitting in an office designing samples. He or she has to venture out in the field, get dirty hands, and be rebuffed, shocked, and dejected. Sampling is not learned in graduate school or methodology textbooks; it is learned by doing—by sampling. Good basketball players are not developed in classrooms by studying basketball theory but on the courts shooting baskets. Researchers will make many mistakes, many hits and errors; field research is not easy, certainly not in the Arab world. The obstacles are there, but they are not unsurmountable.

A researcher has to be sensitive to people and to their needs to become a good researcher. People value their privacy in Samoa and San Francisco. The tax collector is loved in neither Morocco nor Marseilles. People are not all that different. An Arab is not necessarily more suspicious and more secretive than anyone else. The information is available for those who know how to get it.

Finally, as social scientists we have a lot to be humble about despite the sophistication in sampling techniques and the magnificent tools (computers) available for investigators. Survey findings, of course, can be revealing and accurate, and they will almost never disappoint a researcher who does not take the numbers too literally. This is a plea for the reader to become a more skeptical consumer of surveys, regardless of how well designed are the research and sampling techniques. Any security in sampling is false security.

Acknowledgment

In writing this chapter, I have depended on the discussions and comments of the participants at the Bellagio Conference and Tawfic Farah and Faisal Al-Salem, *Research Methods in the Social Sciences* (Kuwait: Kuwait University, 1977), Chap. 4.

Notes

1. Hubert Blalock, *Social Statistics* (New York: McGraw-Hill, 1960), Chap. 22; Isidor Chein, "An Introduction to Sampling," in Claire Sellitz et al., *Research Methods in Social Relations* (New York: Holt, Rinehart & Winston, 1959); and William Cochran, *Sampling Techniques* (New York: Wiley, 1963).

2. David Nachmias and Chava Nachmias, *Research Methods in the Social Sciences* (New York: St. Martin's Press, 1976), p. 262; and Leslie Kish, *Survey Sampling,* (New York: Wiley, 1965) pp. 39–40.

3. This discussion depends heavily on Dickinson McGaw and George Watson's, *Political and Social Inquiry* (New York: Wiley, 1976) p. 364.

4. Many of these studies are found in Tawfic Farah, *Political Behavior in the Arab States* (Boulder, Colorado: Westview Press, 1983), and Monte Palmer et al, *Survey Research in the Arab World: An Analytical Index* (London: Menas Press, 1982).

10

Toward Scientific Cumulativeness: Operational Needs and Strategies

Mark A. Tessler

With a few notable exceptions, survey research in the Arab world lacks the integrated and cumulative character that has contributed to its importance in Western societies. Many survey researchers in the Arab world operate in a comparative scientific vacuum. They have relatively few opportunities to participate in or contribute to collective and cumulative scholarly endeavors, wherein individual studies are conceived and carried out with a view toward adding incrementally to the accuracy and sophistication of knowledge generated by investigators working as an integrated and self-conscious scholarly community.

Obstacles to scientific cumulativeness are most serious at the operational level, and this chapter is devoted to such considerations. A related epistemological concern, also discussed at the Bellagio Conference, will be summarized briefly by way of introduction. Many of the scholars assembled at Bellagio noted the dominance of Western concepts and models in Arab social science. They also asked questions about whether this situation is consistent with the production of maximally accurate and satisfying knowledge about the Arab world. In the view of many, the exaggerated importance of foreign paradigms contributes to and is reinforced by low levels of scholarly integration.

Survey researchers and other social scientists working in the Arab world frequently use studies carried out in the West as their principal point of analytical reference. These investigators often formulate the conceptual parameters of their research with a view toward addressing issues articulated and given prominence by Western students of social change and development. Given the universal character of scientific inquiry, work of this sort is appropriate in many instances. Yet a more original and authentic Arab contribution is also needed for an adequate understanding of Arab society. Analytical insights derived from such a contribution would also enhance the quality of scholarship and knowledge concerned with other regions of the world.

Arab intellectual discourse with established Western paradigms and analytical models is not undesirable. Effective social science welcomes the introduction of new and foreign ideas. The problem is that patterns of interaction and exchange in this case tend to be disproportionately unidirectional. There is an absence of symmetry: Arab scholars feel the impact of external stimuli but find comparatively few opportunities to make a significant mark on research endeavors concerned with universality as well as specificity. Equally significant, there is insufficient scholarly autonomy. Students of the Arab world have inadequate opportunities to develop alternative models for understanding their own society, for pulling together the diverse strands of their individual studies in such a way that the whole begins to exceed the sum of the parts and new ground is broken in the search for guides to understanding and action.

Low levels of scholarly integration in the Arab world are linked interactively to the disproportionate influence of imported concepts and models. A central problem is the weakness of Arab social scientists as a unified community—not as individual scholars possessing intellectual sophistication and methodological expertise but as an integrated community capable of imposing patterns of complementarity on the respective and individual efforts of its members. This situation does not reflect inertia and disinterest on the part of individual Arab social scientists; it is rather the result of numerous practical problems, some of which are discussed in this chapter. There was also a lively discussion at Bellagio about the degree to which the political and economic circumstances of many Arab countries exacerbate the problem by limiting the opportunities and resources available to scholars, especially those in the social sciences. A final obstacle is an epistemological context that leads Arab social scientists to seek a dialogue with their Western counterparts but does not attach equal significance to cooperation among Arab scholars themselves. Thus, on the input side, the dominance of foreign scholarly paradigms is an intellectual impediment to scholarly integration and cumulativeness.

On the output side, the number and influence of studies conceived and executed fom a perspective that draws upon the specificity of the Arab world remain limited in part because Arab social scientists do not constitute a unified intellectual community. Survey researchers and other investigators in the Arab world may be generally aware of one another's work, but for the most part they conduct their studies in isolation. This reduces the influence of innovative and original Arab thinkers; although it does not diminish it entirely, it nevertheless restricts the opportunities to evaluate and refine such contributions by making them the focus of multiple investigations or coordinated empirical studies. More generally, this fragmentation reduces opportunities to plan and carry out coordinated or complementary studies of any kind. Thus, low levels of scholarly integration help to perpetuate the dominance of external scholarly influences. They militate against the kind collective effort that is essential if there is to be an authentically Arab dimension to social research in the Arab world and if such research is to achieve its goals of better understanding and the provision of more useful information.

Though cumulativeness is an essential ingredient for any sustained scholarly endeavor, its absence in the Arab world should not be overstated, especially at the conceptual or intellectual level. Similarly, Arab (and associated foreign) social scientists are increasingly finding opportunities to articulate and define the unique aspects of the intellectual contributions they aspire to make. Such work is often carried out at international conferences and workshops. Sponsors include the League of Arab States and various Arab countries, national and international Arab institutions—like the Beirut-based Center for Arab Unity Studies, the Cairo-based Al-Ahram Center for Strategic Studies, and the Tripoli-based Arab Development Institute—and even concerned individuals who organize programs like the Bellagio Conference. Much more work of this sort is needed, and efforts need to become more institutionalized. Nevertheless, Arab social scientists are aware of the need to create a community of investigators capable of making contributions that are original and authentic and whose accuracy and completeness will continue to evolve in an incremental fashion. Their activities represent important initial steps in the direction of promoting scholarly integration and laying a foundation for scientific cumulativeness.

To proceed further it is necessary to overcome serious operational obstacles. This need is especially important for social scientists who wish to include survey research among the analytical tools available to them for study of the Arab world. As far as survey research is concerned, these obstacles include (1) inadequate inventories of the research that has already been conducted; (2) the lack of norms that stimulate replication and complementary studies; and (3) an absence of data archives or other institutionalized mechanisms for sharing data and encouraging fuller exploitation of existing data files. In each of these areas, problems are exacerbated by the paucity of viable and permanent institutional structures devoted to encouraging more and better survey research. Such institutions could take the lead in finding solutions to specific operational problems. They could also unify research endeavors in critical areas, so that the results of individual studies would more frequently complement one another and add incrementally to the accuracy and completeness of social scientific knowledge.

There have been accomplishments in some of these areas, but on balance continuing obstacles outweigh progress, and this is likely to remain the case for the foreseeable future. In the present chapter I discuss in more detail some of the operational problems that militate against scientific cumulativeness so far as survey research is concerned and then suggest areas in which action can and should be taken to improve the situation. The principal goals of the chapter are to encourage the acceleration of efforts already under way and to stimulate initiative in additional directions.

Efforts to foster cumulativeness should not be undertaken only by overarching institutions, structures that work to produce intellectual unity and scientific integration from the top. Much can also be done by social scientists working alone or in small groups, who might think of their efforts as part of a grass-roots movement to bring a measure of cumulativeness to the scholarly community of which they are a part. Stimulating such efforts is an equally important goal of this chapter. The purpose here is to increase levels of awareness and sensitivity among both indigenous and foreign scholars who carry out survey research in the Arab world, to offer suggestions about specific activities these practitioners of survey research might undertake, and to encourage them to devise and experiment with additional and more original strategies for conducting research in a fashion that contributes maximally to the incremental improvement of scientific information.

A companion chapter has been prepared for readers wishing a fuller introduction to the meaning and importance of cumulativeness, as well as to those aspects of the scientific method from which considerations of cumulativeness derive.

Inventories and Analytical Indices

Although survey research in the Arab world is of comparatively recent origin and still is conducted only infrequently in some Arab societies, hundreds and probably thousands of survey projects have been carried out by indigenous and foreign scholars working in the Arab Middle East. Collecting and making available information about these surveys are necessary for there to be significant progress toward scientific cumulativeness. Replication cannot take place unless present-day scholars have adequate knowledge about previous studies, including both methodological information about their design and conduct and substantive information about their findings. The same is true even if a direct replication is not desired, if the goal is rather to carry out a complementary study that will address questions and gaps that have come to light as a result of the earlier work. With such information, the potential merits of replication and complementary studies can be considered, and, where it is deemed appropriate, surveys can be conducted to assess the accuracy of previously reported findings and/or to determine the applicability of these findings in new social settings. Moreover, just as new studies enrich the value of knowledge produced by previous research, the more recent studies will themselves increase in value to the extent that their conclusions can be laid alongside those of earlier investigations. Alternatively, without adequate knowledge about prior research, or in many cases without any knowledge that the research was even carried out, the road to replication and cumulativeness is closed.

Institutional Sources of Information

At present, the store of available knowledge about previous survey research in the Arab world is limited. Many surveys have been conducted under the auspices of universities, public policy institutes, and market research companies; and, with patience and perseverence, information about these surveys can be obtained from the sponsoring institutions. The American University of Beirut has perhaps the longest tradition of survey research in the Arab world, establishing its reputation with the work of Edwin Terry Prothro and Levon H. Melikian in the 1950s. The American University in Cairo (AUC) also has a long tradition of including survey research among the tools by which its social scientists carry out their studies, and AUC's Social Research Center has been particularly active in this respect. Another important institution in Egypt is the National Center for Sociological and Criminological Research, which has been operating since the 1960s. Some of the national center's research can be found in a journal it publishes, *The National Review of Social Sciences;* studies conducted at AUC are often reported in its monograph series, *Cairo Papers in the Social Sciences.*

Although precise statistics are not available, the greatest quantity of survey research may have been carried out in Lebanon and Egypt, followed by Tunisia. Credit for Tunisia's prominence may to a considerable degree belong to the University of Tunis' social science annex, the Centre d'Etudes et de Recherches Economiques et Sociales (CERES). CERES has been operating since the 1960s, and the scope of its work was expanded under a grant from the Ford Foundation. Through the publication of its journal, *Revue Tunisienne des Sciences Sociales,* CERES has done a better job than most institutions in providing a vehicle through which information produced by its own researchers and others working in Tunisia may be obtained. Among the other institutions that deserve mention are the Survey Research Center of the University of Kuwait, Morocco's Institut National de Statistique et d'Economie Appliquee (INSEA), and the Development Studies and Research Centre of the University of Khartoum, Sudan. Each publishes summaries of past and current research activities and lists a fair number of surveys among the works cited. Kuwait University also publishes *Journal of the Social Sciences,* an Arabic-language journal that includes articles based on survey research. Morocco's INSEA publishes its own review, which is written principally in French but contains some articles in Arabic.

In principle, it should be possible by contacting these and other relevant institutions to obtain general information about a wide array of past survey projects and then to acquire detailed descriptions of those particular studies that may be relevant to a researcher's own proposed investigation. In practice, however, this is often difficult. The collection, standardization, and distribution of such information are often rudimentary and on occasion nonexistent. Moreover, the available summaries are sometimes prepared with a view toward advertising an institution's accomplishments rather than toward encouraging and facilitating either replication, the analytical integration of findings from new and completed work, or other efforts aimed at fostering cumulativeness. But at least such centers and their journals and reports are a place to begin searching for the information about previous work that is necessary for serious and sustained scientific endeavors.

If scholars and administrators associated with major research centers can be persuaded to approach more systematically the task of providing information about their survey (and other) projects, they will make an important contribution toward scientific cumulativeness and the incremental improvement of social scientific knowledge. Ideally, they should collect and make available detailed information about studies conducted in the past. But even if they do no more than systematize and regularize their efforts in the future, and develop them in a context that recognizes and responds to the need for replication and cumulativeness, they will do much to ameliorate a major operational obstacle to the realization of survey research's full potential.

Individual Efforts and Contributions

Apart from the production of survey inventories by major research centers in the Arab world, there remains the problem of identifying the much larger number of surveys carried out by private individuals and small research teams. A thorough review of plausible social science journals is the logical place to begin the search for information about these studies, but this can be tedious. Moreover, many studies are published in obscure outlets or go unpublished altogether, sometimes the result of lethargy on the part of the investigators and sometimes of the vagaries of academic publishing. Sometimes, too, publication is discouraged by a nervous government, which fears that dissemination of the research will raise questions it is unable to answer.

Even when a published account is available, it frequently does not contain enough information to guide a replication or other efforts to plug findings into a cumulative scientific endeavor. Sometimes constraints imposed by journals and their editors are responsible for this situation—a state of affairs not unknown in the United States and other countries where survey research is more common. Sometimes such information is deliberately glossed over by the author (or at least that is the way it often appears). Researchers, who realize that practical difficulties associated with survey research in the Arab world require many compromises and that the resulting data may not be as rigorous as they would wish, or as they may naively imagine all survey data collected in the United States and Europe to be, sometimes prefer giving little information to revealing the limits of their work. But, in fact, almost all social research involves compromises and trade-offs. Real confidence in research findings is much more likely to be established through replication and multiple investigations, even if each single study is of necessity imperfect, than through the conduct of a small number of supposedly definitive and error-free studies. Finally, scholars often fail to see their own research as a vital link in a chain of cumulative investigation. Many are only dimly cognizant of the need to report on their research in a way that enables it to make a contribution to the fulfillment of this task.

All of this adds up to a serious obstacle to scientific cumulativeness in those areas where survey research is or can be widely employed. Sufficient information is simply not available about the work that has been done to date and is being done at present. Nor does there appear to be an adequate generalized recognition of the need to provide such information, one that might stimulate the search for ways to overcome this obstacle.

Nevertheless, some important individual contributions have been made in dealing with the problem of information collection and dissemination, and a few may be mentioned, both to indicate sources presently available and to suggest the kind of work that more scholars may be motivated to undertake in the future. One important contribution is the work of Egyptian social psychologist Louis Meleika. Meleika is currently bringing out the fourth volume of his *Readings in Social Psychology in the Arab World,* which is published in Arabic by the Egyptian National Office of the Book and is highly interdisciplinary in character. In each volume, Meleika brings together reports of surveys and other empirical social scientific studies conducted throughout the Arab world. Some chapters are original, solicited research reports, and some of these are syntheses by an investigator of a series of research projects in which he or she has been involved. Other chapters are reprintings, where necessary translated from a European language. Meleika's self-conscious goal is to facilitate communication among Arab scholars and to promote replication and the analytical integration of findings. Meleika has also made an important original contribution to the quest for cumulativeness in the area of psychological testing. He has translated and/or adapted over a dozen standardized psychological tests developed in the West, when necessary modifying them for use in Arab society and then establishing their cross-cultural validity based on empirical studies in at least some Arab environments.

A similar kind of contribution is made by the semi-annual *Journal of Arab Affairs* (JAA), established by Tawfic Farah in 1981. Interdisciplinary in character, the journal nevertheless gives preference to social science and especially to empirical studies. A large proportion of the articles published are in fact reports of surveys carried out in Arab countries. Though the journal is published in the United States, its editorial board is composed overwhelmingly of scholars residing in the Arab world, and fourteen Arab institutions are represented. Coupled with Farah's regular travels to the Arab world to maintain contacts and solicit articles, this makes the journal one of the most broadly based and truly integrative endeavors devoted to disseminating social science information about the Arab world.

Another journal that deserves brief mention, even though it is published in the United States and is not devoted to the Arab world, is the *Journal of Social Psychology* (*JSP*). Modeled on natural science journals, in which the importance of replication is considered self-evident and the provision of information that permits progress toward cumulativeness is the raison d'etre of scholarly journals, the *Journal of Social Psychology* has for over forty years been publishing short interdisciplinary reports of survey research and other empirical studies. Moreover, the journal has long had a policy of giving preference to cross-cultural studies, meaning investigations conducted outside the United States and Europe even if such studies are not actually comparative and involve only a single society. Indeed many of the leading practitioners of survey research in the Arab world have published in *JSP* over the years. The journal also devotes considerable space to cross-cultural notes—abbreviated communications dealing with methodology and findings. All of these considerations, as well as the editor's broad definition of social psychology, make *JSP* an important source of information about surveys conducted in Arab societies, a vehicle for disseminating such information in the future, and a model and stimulus for more focused efforts to provide the information base necessary for cumulativeness in survey research in the Arab world.

Another kind of effort to provide this information base is the recent compilation and publication of two major analytical inventories. The first, *Survey Research in the Arab World: An Analytical Index,* is the work of Monte Palmer and several colleagues and was published in London by Menas Press in 1982. Prepared under a grant from the Arab Development Institute, the book presents substantive and methodological information about 361 survey research projects. Two sample pages from Palmer's inventory appear in Fig. 10.1, which shows both the kind of information assembled and the form in which it is presented.

In compiling information for the index, Palmer and his associates reviewed virtually all English language and many French language journals in the social sciences. In addition, they visited a number of universities in the Arab world and elsewhere to consult collections of local periodicals, they interviewed Arab scholars in an effort to identify other potential entries, and they reviewed both the holdings of major data archives in the United States and dissertations on file with University Microfilms. This investigation produced a list of works carried out by 309 investigators, of whom 202 are Arab. The distribution of studies by country is as follows:

Algeria	4%
Egypt	23
Iraq	2
Jordan	3

Kuwait	2
Lebanon	10
Libya	3
Morocco	9
Palestinians	6
Qatar	1
Sudan	3
Syria	2
Tunisia	18
Yemen	1
Cross-national	13

Palmer reported that for a large number of the surveys identified, little or no methodological information was available. Information was also generally absent about the location and availability of the data and the sponsor of the research. Finally, relying on secondary sources in a number of instances, the inventory appears to contain a number of errors. Despite these limitations, however, the analytical index makes a significant contribution. The volume is certainly much more notable for the information it contains than for what is absent, especially in view of its originality and innovative nature. Further, the inventory directs readers seeking more detail to the relevant sources. Finally, the utility of the index is enhanced by its classification of studies by location and topic, the latter involving fourteen substantive categories. With these assets the index will be an extremely useful for those survey researchers who seek to identify previous studies with a view toward better informing their own research and/or developing their investigations so as to contribute to the quest for scientific cumulativeness.

The second analytical index is being compiled by social scientists at the American University in Cairo and will be published as a special issue of *Cairo Papers in the Social Sciences*. The Egyptian index summarizes about 300 survey projects covering more than two decades of work. Information was gathered by identifying and visiting virtually all academic and other institutions believed to have sponsored any survey research. The surveys are categorized according to seventy-two primary topics, and categories are then subdivided as a function of nineteen subtopics.

Future Needs

Despite this laudable effort, probably only a small proportion of the surveys conducted in Egypt have been identified and recorded. In a preface to the Cairo index, Monte Palmer expressed this point in the following terms:

Egyptian survey researchers have, unfortunately, hidden their light under a basket. No one appreciates, including the Egyptians themselves, the tremendous quantity of data available for the analysis of Egyptian society.

FIGURE 10.1
Sample pages from inventory of survey research projects in the Arab world

```
COUNTRY:  Egypt
SUBJECT:  Population
```

****
```
INVESTIGATORS: Gadalla, Saad
TITLE:   Is There Hope:  Fertility and Family Planning in a Rural Egyptian
         Community

DATE OF ADMINISTRATION: 1968-70
LANGUAGE OF QUESTIONNAIRE:   Arabic (Colloquial)
MODE OF ADMINISTRATION: Interview Schedules
SURVEY NUMBER: 35
```
****

GROUPS SURVEYED	CATEGORY OF GROUP	SAMPLE SIZE
General	Households	457

```
MODE OF SELECTION: Representative Sample
RATE OF RESPONSE:  99.5%
```

THEMES/HYPOTHESES

Objectives: development of a systematic investigation of population growth and
fertility control in Egypt; to gain insight into the processes of dynamics of
population change.

FINDINGS

Includes information about socio-demographic characteristics (age, sex
structure, education, etc.); cultural norms about reproduction (ideal family
size, etc.); contraceptive use; the nature and scope of the fertility problem.
In his last chapter, "But There is Hope," the principal investigator gives an
optimistic view toward the future.

METHODS

Freedman S model of factors affecting fertility (1967) was adopted as the main
theoretical framework for the study. Interview schedules were pretested
several times. Senior researchers did field checking on the accuracy of
collected data of 5% of the interview schedules, and questions were designed in
such a way as to request the same information in different forms at different
stages of the interview.

SOURCES

Gadalla, Saad, IS THERE HOPE: FERTILITY AND FAMILY PLANNING IN A RURAL
EGYPTIAN COMMUNITY, Social Research Center, American University in Cairo Press
and Carolina Population Center, Chapel Hill, 1978.

COMMENTS

The survey was done in Shanawan and Kafr Shanawan and Kafr El Amra. Study
sponsored by U. S. Department of Health, Education and Welfare.

Source: Monte Palmer et al., *Survey Research in the Arab World: An Analytical
Index* (London: Menas Press, 1982).

FIGURE 10.1, *cont.*

COUNTRY: Kuwait
SUBJECT: Politics

****
INVESTIGATORS: Salem, Fysal
TITLE: Political and Social Socialization in Kuwait

DATE OF ADMINISTRATION: 1966-67
LANGUAGE OF QUESTIONNAIRE: NP
MODE OF ADMINISTRATION: Interview Schedule
SURVEY NUMBER: 296
****

GROUPS SURVEYED	CATEGORY OF GROUP	SAMPLE SIZE
Middle School Students	Ages 10-16	500

MODE OF SELECTION: Random
RATE OF RESPONSE: NP

THEMES/HYPOTHESES

The survey attempted to measure questions of national identification, hierarchy of loyalty patterns (family, state, religion, Arab nation), personal and national values.

FINDINGS

1) The overwhelming majority of the respondents are strongly concerned about the development of Kuwait. 2) The overwhelming majority of respondents gave their first loyalty to religion. Loyalty to the state (Kuwait) was second and loyalty to the extended family was third. 3) In terms of political information, T. V. came first; radio second; peers third; father fourth; mother fifth; school sixth.

METHODS

Random selection of 10 middle range schools from a total of 123 schools. Further random selection from enrollment lists of students attending the 10 schools for a total sample of 500 male and female respondents ranging from 11 to 16 years of age. Respondents were interviewed by specially trained students. Questionnaires contained both open and closed items.

SOURCES

Salem, Fysal, "Political and Social Socialization in Kuwait," JOURNAL OF THE SOCIAL SCIENCES (Arabic), Vol. 8, No. 3, October 1980.

The 300 projects analyzed in the present volume represent, in all probability, little more than the tip of the iceberg. As a result of inadequate communication channels and publication outlets, most survey research projects remain hidden.

The same is undoubtedly true with respect to other Arab countries. Thus, despite several valuable initiatives, much more work is needed if adequate information about surveys carried out in the Arab world is to be collected and made available.

With the number of surveys steadily increasing, the problem will become even more serious in the future. It will be necessary for both individuals and institutions to become more aware (and convinced) of the importance of scientific cumulativeness and to make self-conscious efforts to help construct the necessary foundation of information. Individual practitioners of survey research can play a role by being careful to report the kinds of information that will assist others, especially in the scientific community, in making use of their data and findings. They must struggle to place this information where it will be reasonably visible or at least accessible to those who are searching for it.

Institutions can increase their contribution, already significant in some instances, by encouraging these same practices among researchers working under their sponsorship and by taking steps to routinize and provide support structures for collecting, standardizing, and disseminating the information thus made available. If they can also serve as a clearing house for information about surveys over which they do not have direct jurisdiction, commissioning inventories patterned on those identified or in some other way assisting practitioners of survey research to fulfill their responsibility to distribute information about their studies, these institutions can make an even greater contribution to scientific cumulativeness. Some of this work can perhaps be done by innovative individuals working on their own, such as the Palmer group that operated under a grant from the Arab Development Institute. More generally, however, continuity and standardization will be maximized if suitable institutions decide to devote resources to this endeavor. Interinstitutional connections can also be used to broaden the scope of both information collection and dissemination.

Efforts in this area will produce important benefits for survey researchers in the Arab world. It will enable them to profit much more fully than is presently possible from the lessons and mistakes of past research. Even more important, it will permit them to fashion studies with a view toward their analytical integration into an emerging body of social science knowledge and thereby to contribute to an incremental improvement in the quality and utility of that knowledge. The precise kinds of information about completed studies that should be collected and made available to achieve these goals need not be elaborated definitively at present. Concerned practitioners may establish and improve the contents of their inventories in light of their own growing experience. A useful and appropriate agenda with which to begin, however, is offered here; the twenty categories of information were adapted from the analytical index of Palmer and his associates. Although the list is incomplete, it is already quite ambitious. Palmer reported that in some categories information was not available for a substantial majority of the projects his team identified. But the list is nevertheless a satisfactory point of departure for those individuals and institutions that would undertake to prepare inventories and indices in the future, and it is especially appropriate as a guide for those practitioners of survey research who recognize the need to provide systematic and complete information about the investigations they themselves conduct.

1. Name of investigator(s)
2. Sponsor of the project
3. Country and locality of research
4. Dates of data collection
5. General topic of survey
6. Major objectives or hypotheses (including major variables and variable relationships)
7. Summary of findings
8. Population and target groups
9. Estimated population size
10. Methodology of sample selection (random, cluster, stratified, etc.)
11. Sample size
12. Response rate
13. Size of interview schedule (number of items)
14. Types of items (forced choice, open ended, etc.)
15. Method of administration (personal interview, mail questionnaire, etc.)
16. Language of administration
17. Operational definitions and measurement procedures
18. Estimates of validity and reliability and method of assessment
19. Source of additional information and published reports
20. Location and availability of data

Replications, Complementary Studies and Intersocietal Research

Replication is essential for extending the utility of previous and present research and is a keystone in the edifice of cumulativeness. Each time results from one study are confirmed by a subsequent investigation, confidence in the accuracy of findings from the first survey increases. Further, in most cases, the generalizability of these findings increases as well. In other words, there are gains with respect to both internal and external validity. Moreover, these gains apply not only to the original study, making its contribution more important than had hitherto been the case; they also apply to and enhance the value of the replication as well.

Alternatively, if the results of the first study and the replication are not consistent, one of two conclusions may be drawn; and though additional research may be necessary to determine which of the two is warranted, both are important and either will advance the quest for cumulativeness. The first possible conclusion is negative: that one of the studies is in error, having introduced some undetected operational or methodological distortion that ultimately produced inaccurate findings. Or possibly, though inaccurate in different ways, something of this sort may have occurred in the conduct of both studies, making the conclusions of both erroneous. Although the result of this situation is not new or better-quality knowledge, it is, nevertheless, a reduction of error through the identification of false information. Knowledge that had been accepted, or that at least had been taken seriously and regarded as likely to be accurate, is called into question. This is an important contribution to the search for accuracy and for the reduction of error—basic aspects of scientific cumulativeness—even if additional replications will be necessary before researchers can determine whether the errors and distortions belong to the original study, the replication, or both.

The second potential contribution of conflicting findings concerns a delineation of the locus of applicability of established social science knowledge. Findings may be accurate without being universally applicable, a point that is discussed at length in Chapter 11. They may pertain under some conditions but not under others, and a replication that establishes that research results derived in one social environment cannot be derived in different milieux contributes measurably to the determination of conceptual boundaries. Again, the full potential of such a contribution is unlikely to be realized with a single replication. Rather both the original study and the replication, taken together, become a stimulus to additional research. After all, one or both studies may have been flawed, causing their findings to conflict. If the studies had been accurate—and this can be judged only by further replication—the findings might have applied under both sets of conditions or under neither. A collective and incremental approach to the production of social scientific knowledge is necessary to sort out all these possibilities, which of course is the very direction in which it is being argued that survey research must move to achieve its full potential. Judged from the vantage point of the first replication, however, a failure to reproduce the results of an earlier investigation need not necessarily be taken as an indication that there is an error somewhere. There is also an excellent chance that one has begun to identify the parameters of applicability of findings that obtain in some social settings but not in others.

Information about prior research is a necessary condition for replication and other approaches to incrementalism and cumulativeness. Equally critical is a broader recognition of the need for cumulativeness and for research norms that encourage activities that contribute to this goal. In fact, especially in academic circles, prevailing norms and the distribution of rewards often discourage such programs of research by branding them as lacking in originality. Prestige, and with it grants, promotions, and other opportunities and rewards, is all too often judged to be merited not by those who do the patient and routine work of testing, verifying, and refining existing ideas but rather by those who claim to be embarking on brilliant new ventures, ones that aspire to make conceptual breakthroughs or to devise novel ways of looking at and understanding familiar intellectual problems. Work of this type is extremely worthwhile, of course, and when successful it has the potential to make a scientific contribution of enormous importance. But there is often a tendency, in the Western world as well as in the Arab world, to think that such contributions can and should be the rule rather than the exception and to forget that even conceptual breakthroughs and brilliant intellectual innovations only attain their potential worth if they inspire others and become themselves a stimulus to replication and complementary studies. Such notions not only set unreasonable expectations for individual researchers; they also do a disservice to the scholarly community as a whole. By contrast, norms that encourage replication and active borrowing from past investigations—that encourage individual researchers to be guided by past studies and to relate their findings to these studies as explicitly as possible—are very much needed if replication is to take place on the scale that a concern for cumulativeness demands.

Examples of Replications

Despite the problems of inadequate information and a frequent lack of encouragement, many social scientists nevertheless have carried out surveys that build directly on the foundation of previous work, and, though imperfect, these studies illustrate the kind of research that needs to be undertaken more frequently in the future. A particularly good illustration is Farah's 1976 replication in Kuwait of a study of university student affiliations originally conducted by Melikian and Diab in Lebanon in 1958. Not only does Farah's study build directly and explicitly on previous work, but it also is related to an earlier investigation done in the Arab world. It thus goes beyond the preoccupation of those replications whose goal is to determine whether or not "Western" theories apply in the Middle East.

Farah's findings differ from those of Melikian and Diab in several significant respects. For example, religion was a less important focus of social identification among university students in Lebanon (including non-Lebanese students) than among university students in Kuwait (including non-Kuwaiti students). This difference raises interesting questions about the causes of the variance, which, if they can be answered, will produce a more elaborate and satisfying understanding of the factors that shape group affiliation among Arab students. It might be argued that the resurgence of religion and especially Islam, particularly after 1967, accounts for this difference; alternatively, it might be suggested that the difference is attributable to the dissimilar social and political environments of Lebanon and Kuwait. Given that Melikian and Diab replicated their own study in Lebanon in 1971 and found that religion was even less important than determined in the original study, the evidence available to date supports the latter rather than the former interpretation. More study will have to take place before any conclusions can be drawn with greater certainty, but the example nevertheless shows how multiple studies and replications contribute to an incrementally improving body of knowledge and toward a more complete understanding of the phenomenon under study.

With respect to another dimension of its findings, the results produced by Farah's study were identical to those reported by Melikian and Diab. In both cases, politically oriented Palestinian students had a different hierarchy of group affiliations than other students, and in both cases they ranked citizenship or national origin (i.e., Palestinian) as most important, more than family in the Lebanese case and more than religion in the Kuwaiti case. In each study, too, non–politically oriented Palestinians did not differ from other students in this way. Thus, in this instance, the contribution of the replication is both an increase in the confidence accorded to each set of findings and a more thorough knowledge of the different conditions under which these findings apply.

There is not space here to do more than mention these surveys in passing, by way of illustration. Those wishing more information should consult the original studies, which have been brought together and reprinted in *Political Behavior in the Arab States,* edited by Farah and published by Westview Press in 1983. In any event, considerable work remains to be done before survey research will provide anything near a completely satisfactory description and explanation of group affiliations among university students in the Arab world. Nevertheless, this battery of research neatly illustrates how progress can be made toward scientific cumulativeness and how replication is central to the enterprise. It is worth noting, in conclusion, that Farah and a colleague, Faisal Al-Salem, have extended this work by studying group affiliations among children, exploring still further the locus of applicability of established research findings.

Some replications involve surveys designed to examine in the Arab world hypotheses and findings that have already been the subject of considerable investigation in countries where survey research is more common. Replications of this kind help to determine whether there are cultural limits to particular propositions. They serve to delineate the areas in which it is necessary to develop separate, more specific models of behavior for understanding Arab society and in which, alternatively, Arab specificity is less pronounced. One example is a study by the present author of determinants of personal political involvement in Tunisia, in which it was found that variation in participation levels was accounted for by many of the same independent variables shown to be salient in other societies. This study is discussed more fully in Chapter 11.[1]

Another such replication is a study by Iliya Harik, one of the participants in the Bellagio conference, in which he investigated the "two-step flow of communications" hypothesis. Well known in the West, the hypothesis emphasizes the role of local "opinion leaders" in forming mass attitudes, as key links in transmitting information from political elites and generalized societal sources to the average citizen. Harik tested this hypothesis in rural Egypt and found that the proposed pattern occurred on only a limited scale. Although local opinion leaders served as mediators of information and ideas for a small segment of the public—mostly persons who had little access to the mass media—a more common pattern was for messages to reach the public directly and effectively.[2]

Complementary Studies

Complementary or parallel studies, rather than direct replications, involve different individual researchers working on a common problem or exploring similar variable relationships with discrete data bases and/or in dissimilar settings. These researchers have not developed an explicit plan for their parallel research projects, and it is unusual for them to make a focused attempt at the direct integration of findings. Yet each researcher is conscious of an emerging body of work in the area under study and each aspires to add incrementally to that body of knowledge. His or her goal may be any of the principal concerns of cumulativeness, including increased confidence, greater generalizability, and knowledge about the locus of applicability of established research findings.

The study of political support and political alienation is one area in which one finds this kind of complementarity in survey research in the Arab world. Some of the author's work on political behavior in Tunisia explored the relationship between this dependent variable and individual levels of socioeconomic status, on the one hand, and the character and orientation of the political regime, on the other.[3] Two other coorganizers of the Bellagio conference, working with colleagues, have also investigated this issue. Tawfic Farah and Faisal Al-Salem examined determinants of political trust in Kuwait,[4] and Monte Palmer and Nafhat Nasr, a Lebanese scholar who was also at Bellagio, explored determinants of alienation, including socioeconomic status, in Lebanon.[5] All three studies further examined the relationship between political alienation and various forms of political activity; the Kuwait and Lebanon studies were particularly comparable because both focused exclusively on university students. One of Palmer's students, Mima Nedelcovych, also conducted a study among Moroccan university students, investigating some of these same issues.[6] By bringing together the findings of these and other complementary studies, it is possible to begin to answer questions about the experiences and conditions affecting citizen political orientations in the Arab world. It is also possible to see what additional work is necessary and how, if carried out successfully, such work would contribute incrementally to steadily improving descriptions and explanations. And with better information about other researchers' studies and with improved avenues for communication among survey researchers working separately on related topics, the potential for making such a contribution would improve even more.

Because studies in the field of population and fertility involve a high degree of complementarity, that field may be the area in which progress toward cumulativeness has been the greatest. Saad Gadalla, director of the AUC Social Research Center and a participant at Bellagio, has been one of the Arab world's pioneers in this area. His work has explored relationships between fertility, on one hand, and both individual demographic attributes and national policies and programs, on the other.[7] Studies dealing with these relationships have also been carried out by others in Egypt, such as Nadia Halim, who found that variations in fertility are related to socioeconomic status, education, profession, and place of origin;[8] in Morocco, where a survey of over 3,000 ever-married women under fifty years of age found that improvements in health, nutrition, and education were all likely to increase fertility;[9] and in Jordan, where a national fertility survey of over 5,000 ever-married women under fifty found an association between fertility and such independent variables as age at marriage, duration of marriage, residence, socioeconomic status, and education.[10]

Similar batteries of complementary studies related to population issues focus on such dependent variables as preferred family size, patterns of contraception use, and receptivity to family planning programs. Again, these individual studies are not always as mutually comparable as might be desired. There is room for improvement in designing and conducting research in a manner that will increase comparability among discrete investigations and facilitate their collective analytical integration. Nevertheless, much progress has been made in the field of population and fertility, and work in this area can serve as a model for the kind of cumulative effort that needs to be undertaken in many fields where survey research is increasingly in use. An important stimulus for cumulativeness and comparability in the area of population research has come from international development agencies. Without their financial assistance and their requirements of evaluation research, work in this field might be much more fragmented.

Intersocietal Studies

Although less common in the Arab world, intersocietal studies involving coordinated investigations in several countries represent an important way in which progress toward cumulativeness can be made. In a sense, they are like replications: Though they may be carried out either simultaneously or sequentially over a period of time, survey researchers design and execute a program of research in one society and then repeat the operation in a second society or in several others. Coordinated studies of this type possess important advantages when compared to individually crafted replications. They also have several drawbacks.

The principal advantage of coordinated studies obviously lies in the maximization of comparability and the potential for integrating findings.

Studies in different societies can be made virtually identical, so as to reduce greatly any extraneous sources of variance when trying to assess the locus and extent to which findings are generalizable; this includes constructing matched samples and employing survey instruments that are identical or equivalent. This degree of comparability and control, though not impossible, is much more difficult to achieve in discrete replications, because there is no coordinated planning and because a far larger number of scholars is involved.

Intersocietal studies also permit greater comprehensiveness and analytical flexibility in the selection of research sites. For example, some investigations may derive theoretical payoffs by working in several highly similar societies, (e.g., in military regimes or in monarchies). Comparative studies of this type are said to involve a "most similar systems" research design. Others, by contrast, may be able to profit analytically by taking a "most different systems" approach to the selection of research sites. The choice pertains essentially to alternative strategies for seeking to control societal attributes in order to compare more rigorously relationships among variables conceptualized and measured at a level of analysis below that of the society.

A most similar systems design is often especially useful when intersocietal differences in variable relationships are anticipated. Since the attributes with respect to which the societies differ will be limited, it is easier to determine the system level properties that account for these differences and, thereby, to specify in conceptual terms the locus of applicability of the relationships investigated. Alternatively, a most different systems approach may be most worthwhile if findings are the same in each society. Given that similar patterns and relationships will have been determined to exist under widely differing conditions, the contribution to generalizability and external validity will have been maximized.[11] In any event, the important point is that coordinated intersocietal studies permit flexibility and enable researchers to take such considerations into account when designing a project. Finally, in contrast to individual replications, coordinated intersocietal research offers the possibility of investigation on a much wider scale, wherein information is gathered in a much larger number of countries and the contribution to any and all of the goals of cumulativeness is accordingly much more substantial.

Intersocietal survey research is expensive and difficult to organize—one of its drawbacks and a principal reason that it has not been widespread in the Arab world. A disadvantage of another kind, not inherent but nevertheless present in many instances, is the considerable gap between those who design the survey and those who execute it, with the attendant possibility of inadequate control over data collection at the operational level. An extreme example, unsubstantiated but circulating for many years, is the rumor that some students hired to conduct interviews for an important early cross-national survey in six Middle Eastern nations sat in cafes and filled out questionnaires on behalf of fictitious respondents. Though probably apocryphal, and not a problem that is limited to intersocietal research, this persistent report nevertheless illustrates a danger that may attend surveys that cast their net over an extremely broad area and are unable to monitor closely work on the ground.

Finally, coordinated intersocietal investigations are less satisfactory than multiple discrete replications as mechanisms for establishing confidence in research findings. This is because of the possibility that errors or biases introduced into one part of the study will be carried through to the entire program of research. In other words, the replications do not constitute independent trials; with the same intellectual and operational canons employed throughout, it is not the case that information produced by one investigation is being tested by laying it alongside that produced by others. Other investigators may conduct research in the future that will address this issue and thereby either increase or decrease confidence in the findings of the original project. But such independent assessments of accuracy and internal validity are not present in the intersocietal study itself, despite the fact that it has examined the same phenomenon in several societies and possibly reached similar conclusions in each instance.

If carried out with the care that one would demand of any credible survey research project, coordinated intersocietal studies can make a very important contribution to the quest for scientific cumulativeness, and individuals and institutions need to be encouraged to expand their efforts in this area. A few recent studies may be mentioned briefly to show what can be done and to stimulate additional work. The published accounts of these studies contain much practical information about the conduct of intersocietal research as well, and thus they may be profitably consulted by those who wish more detail about the design and conduct of this kind of work. Finally, these studies show the difficulties, as well as the benefits, associated with intersocietal survey research.

Examples of Intersocietal Studies

Perhaps the most ambitious intersocietal study to date is a ten-society investigation sponsored by the Center for Arab Unity Studies in Beirut and directed by Saad Eddin Ibrahim, one of the organizers of the Bellagio conference. The major purpose of this survey was to assess popular support for Arab nationalism and for various political formulas that might give practical expression to desires for Arab unity and also to chart inter- and intra-societal variation in citizen attitudes in this domain. Over 5,500 individuals were interviewed. Among the conclusions were that support for Arab unity is widespread, that it is nevertheless comparatively weak in Morocco, Lebanon, and Sudan, and that a loose confederal arrangement linking individual Arab states is the political structure preferred most frequently.[12]

Though the survey was sponsored and conducted by a respected Arab scholarly organization, only half the countries belonging to the League of Arab States authorized it to be conducted in their territory. It was carried out in Egypt, Kuwait, Jordan, Lebanon, Morocco, Qatar, Sudan, Tunisia, and Yemen, and also among Palestinian Arabs. Respondent selection was at times a problem. It was not possible to draw national random samples in any of the countries, and stratified quota samples were accordingly constructed. In cases in which internal validity is maximized, these and other kinds of analytical samples can add considerably to the rigor of a study. But in the present instance there were important intersocietal variations in the samples, exacerbated by the fact that the mean response rate was only slightly over 70 percent, and this reduced the comparability needed to ensure that national differences are not based on spurious associations. A related problem concerns the representativeness of the samples, both because of the way they were constructed and because educated and urbanized sectors of the population were overrepresented, although not to the same degree in all countries. A partial justification for the overrepresentations was a desire to focus on opinion leaders. In any event, despite these and other problems, the effort of the Ibrahim team is a major pioneering study, which it is hoped will stimulate additional intersocietal research projects.

A second example is a six-nation study of over 1,800 university students, executed by Russell Stone and Clement Moore. The study brought together data collected between 1963 and 1966 in Morocco, Tunisia, Lebanon, Turkey, Iran, and Pakistan. All of the countries are Muslim and in or proximate to the Middle East. Only three, however, are Arab, which, as the previous discussion of most similar system and most different system designs suggests, has both analytical advantages and analytical drawbacks. Among the principal findings of the Stone and Moore study are that Middle Eastern students anticipate mobility to elite status as a result of their university education; that most desire careers in the liberal professions, although there are notable intersocietal variations in this regard; and that there is also considerable intersocietal variation in the class origins of university students, with Tunisian and Moroccan universities containing the children of farmers much more frequently than do universities in the other countries.[13]

Moore also joined with Arlie A. Hochschild to perform a different analysis of the data on student attitudes from Tunisia and Morocco. This effort provides yet another example of the kind of coordinated intersocietal studies that can be profitably undertaken, and it also illustrates some of the advantages of this kind of research. One of the investigators' concerns was religiosity and its relationship to political orientations, and among their findings was the absence of any significant aggregate differences in religiosity—as measured by observance of Ramadan and daily prayers and by each respondent's self-evaluation—between university students in Morocco and Tunisia.

This ability to compare directly subjects from different countries, rather than to compare only findings, is one of the most important benefits of comparative intersocietal survey research. In this way, the direct impact of system-level independent variables on dependent variables conceptualized and measured at the individual level can be assessed. In the case at hand, individual religiosity is not affected by those systemic attributes that differentiate the social and political climate of Morocco from that of Tunisia in the 1960s, a finding not without significance given how different the two countries were at the time of the research. There were intersocietal differences in other areas, however, indicating that system-level properties do have some explanatory power and do account for variation along some of the dimensions under investigation in the study. Specifically, in contrast to levels of religiosity, the relationship between religious and political orientations was not the same in the two settings. In Morocco, the less religious a student was, the more likely he or she was to be interested in politics. In Tunisia, on the other hand, the relationship between low religiosity and high political interest was not present, and in fact there was a positive correlation between high religiosity and aspirations to play a political role in the future.[14] Thus, in sum, comparative analysis involving the examination of relationships among variables conceptualized and measured at different levels of analysis was made possible by the intersocietal character of the research.

Intersocietal survey research is probably most advanced in the area of population and fertility. Moreover, though there have been some projects of this type limited to the Arab world, many have involved comparative work in which an Arab society was only one among a number of worldwide sample sites. One comparative study of cultural values and population policies, for example, was carried out in Egypt but also involved investigations in Mexico, Kenya, and the Philippines. In Egypt, about 750 respondents were interviewed between 1976 and 1978 to determine the impact on fertility and family planning behavior of such cultural considerations as religion, women's status, and fatalism.[15] Another Egyptian study, in which 500 married women were interviewed in 1978–1979, was part of a cross-national project involving eight other countries.[16] An additional example comes from Morocco, where over 5,000 women were interviewed in the late 1960s about the impact of urban-rural income and educational inequality on practices and values relating to fertility. The research was part of a project involving parallel studies in Turkey and Taiwan, as well as Morocco, and among its findings were that increased education is an important vehicle for reducing fertility among rural women and, more generally, that economic development tends to reduce fertility only if it brings about changes in the prevailing social structure.[17]

The listing of these examples should not give the impression that replications and coordinated intersocietal studies are reasonably common. Although other examples could also be given, the number of such studies carried out with an explicit commitment to cumulativeness is still very small and much more work of this type needs to be done if survey research is to realize its full potential.

Coordinated intersocietal studies are unlikely to become common until more and better structural support exists for social science research in the Arab world. Additional resources will also be necessary. To an extent, small teams of dedicated researchers, determined to work together and to coordinate their efforts, can actually accomplish a lot in the area of comparative and cross-national survey research. Scholars from or with experience in different societies can meet to fashion a joint research strategy, and then each can return to his or her base and preside over the collection of data. It will thereafter be necessary to find opportunities and facilities for the integrated analysis of data. Although such undertakings are ambitious, they can be done. Nevertheless, it is doubtful that efforts of this kind will be more than sporadic and exceptional for the foreseeable future. Coordinated intersocietal research will assume significant proportions and become regular and routinized only when research institutions located in the Arab world decide to devote more time, people, and money to such endeavors. A few pioneering studies have shown what can be done if institutions recognize the importance of such research and decide to act: It remains to be seen whether this will occur.

Replicating One's Own Research

Individual scholars can and should make their biggest contribution— and can place themselves squarely within the tradition of intersocietal survey research—by giving greater attention to the possibility of conducting complementary studies and replications. Moreover, such replications need not only build on the base of earlier work done by others; it may also build on the base of a scholar's own previous research. Saad Gadalla did something of this sort in one small-scale project, for example, by having one of his students interview the wives of household heads he himself had interviewed five years earlier.[18]

A different kind of coordinated research project, far larger and much more ambitious, involves an individual scholar's efforts to build sequentially and incrementally on the base of his own previous work. This project is an on-going investigation of political socialization among primary school pupils being carried out by Michael Suleiman, a U.S.-based political scientist of Palestinian origin, who was also a participant in the Bellagio conference. Aspects of this program of research are discussed in Chapter 5. Suleiman began his work in Egypt in the early 1970s, starting with the content analysis of text books in order to look at differences in the norms and values communicated to pupils before and after the Nasser regime.[19] His work has gradually expanded to three other countries: Sudan, Morocco, and, recently, Tunisia, and it has assumed an increasing important survey research dimension. In 1979 and 1980, he collected survey data from a sample of 1,700 Sudanese pupils, in both the north and the south of the country, and from a sample of 1,400 pupils in Morocco. In both cases he focused on third through sixth graders. Suleiman has more recently returned to Morocco, where he extended his survey research to a sample of 550 teachers in seventy primary schools in five different cities, and he has continued to collect information on textbooks and to conduct interviews with Moroccan educators responsible for their preparation. In 1984, Suleiman began work in Tunisia, where he encountered a number of obstacles (see Chapter 5). In the future he hopes to extend his project to additional countries.

Suleiman is interested in the ideas that children acquire about citizenship and political authority and in the role played by governments and schools in inculcating these ideas. Among the particular norms and values with which he is concerned are those associated with power, leadership ability, deference to authority, nationalism, political efficacy, pride in government, political participation, and the political status of women. Suleiman's project is notable for the way it has evolved and become increasingly sophisticated, not only by adding incrementally to the data base and to the number of research sites but also by expanding the structure of the investigation each time he undertakes new field work and data collection activities. It is also notable for its multimethod approach, demonstrating that survey research may sometimes be most effective when combined with other kinds of social science tools. In addition to employing both content analysis and systematic survey research, Suleiman has conducted unstructured interviews with many government officials and school administrators, gathering still more information and gaining additional insights into the process of political socialization.

Finally, as far as the survey component of the project is concerned, Suleiman is bringing together data from countries that differ in interesting and potentially important ways, and this approach will yield significant scientific payoffs when all the data are eventually analyzed. Although the choice of research sites has been dictated by practical as well as analytical considerations, the societies studied differ from one another with respect to such attributes as ethnic homogeneity, political structure, regime orientation, and educational policies and accomplishments. Data from these countries thus provide the base for a most different systems research design—one which will enhance the case for generalizability and external validity if similar conclusions emerge from the analysis of each data set. Alternatively, if different findings emerge from some or all of the cases, it will permit specifying in conceptual terms the locus of applicability of dissimilar patterns and relationships by incorporating system-level variables into the analysis.

A final example is the author's own replication of his study of social and political attitudes in Tunisia. After an interval of six years, a second sample was constructed using the same variables of sample stratification employed in the original investigation. This yielded two highly similar data bases, differing only with respect to the time of their collection, and comparability was further enhanced and rigor added by matching individuals from the two samples, selected in 1967 and 1973. To achieve this, each respondent from the 1967 sample was paired with a respondent from 1973 who possessed similar attributes on a large number of personal and demographic variables, including age, gender, education, profession, income, and place of residence. It was possible to match most respondents from the two samples in this way, and for each year there was a strong correlation between the entire battery of respondents and the subsample composed only of individuals included in the matching operation. Thus, though only the matched pairs were employed in those parts of the analysis involving comparisons of the data from the original study and the replication, the matching procedure enhanced internal validity without seriously reducing generalizability and external validity.

Replications of this sort can easily be undertaken by individual scholars and, though they may appear to be lacking in originality, they can in fact make very significant analytical contributions. Notable among their strengths is the provision of data from both the original study and the replication. Like coordinated and intersocietal studies, but unlike most of the replications of another investigator's research previously discussed, it is possible not only to compare findings from surveys conducted at different points in time (and space) but also to compare respondents themselves. The analytical potential is expanded greatly when an investigator has data from the original study as well as from the replication, rather than a report that simply summarizes findings that he or she can contrast with those of a subsequent study.

An example of the kind of analysis this permits may be taken from that part of the author's study dealing with changing attitudes toward the status of women. The Tunisian government was much more active in promoting new norms and behavior patterns concerning women in the early 1960s than in the early 1970s, and by directly comparing responses to questions about women's status from 1967 and 1973 it was thus possible to make some assessments of the normative impact of changing governmental policies. But, since changes in the political environment did not necessarily affect the views of different categories of citizens in the same way, it was also important to disaggregate the data and to contrast attitudinal differences between 1967 and 1973 among particular subcategories of the samples. In Table 10.1 responses to a question about the relative importance of education for boys and girls are shown to illustrate how the degree of attitudinal change over time, attributable in part to shifts in government policy, varies as a function of educational level and gender. The table does not present the entire analysis, and readers seeking more information about the relevance of these findings should consult the published reports of this

Table 10.1   Percentage of Respondents Agreeing that

Education is as Important for a Girl as it is for a Boy

	1967	1973	1967	1973
	Men	Men	Women	Women
Educational Level				
High	80	75	95	80
Middle	58	37	80	70
Low	41	19	65	60
Total	59	42	84	73

research.[20] The goal here is to illustrate what can be done by a single individual who replicates his own earlier research and to encourage other survey researchers to consider such replications.

In conclusion, both research institutions and individual survey researchers should seek opportunities to conduct replications, complementary studies, and coordinated intersocietal studies. Such work can be exciting, but it may not be as stimulating as the fashioning of some bold conceptual or methodological departure. Nevertheless, additions to the quality as well as the quantity of social science knowledge require that such investigations be carried out much more frequently than has heretofore been the case in the Arab world.

Secondary Analysis and Data Archives

Existing data sets are rarely analyzed to the extent of their capacity, and secondary analysis of previously collected survey data thus offers an important avenue for increasing social science knowledge. Even in countries where survey research is common, many data files that contain information on a wide range of variables are utilized only to prepare a few focused research reports. The data themselves are thereafter placed on a shelf. Secondary analysis of existing data files is rarer still in the Arab world, where only a handful of projects based on such work has been published.

Benefits of Secondary Analysis

Several potential benefits can be derived from secondary analysis of existing survey data. First, topics on which a data file may contain information but in which persons who collected the data may not have been interested can be explored. It is common for survey researchers to ask many questions beyond those of immediate interest, reasoning that since they have done the work of selecting a sample and contacting respondents they might as well gather as much information as possible. After all, they argue, it is not always possible to determine in advance all the variables on which it might subsequently prove useful to have information. In fact, however, most of this additional information is rarely exploited; a reasonable estimate is that for a majority of studies little more than half of the items on the interview schedule are incorporated into the principal analyses. The rest of the information is stored for future use, and, with rare exception, it remains in storage permanently, never becoming the basis for subsequent investigation.

Whether this information should have been collected in the first place depends largely on whether it was inexpensive in terms of time and money and required no compromises in the project's principal analytical preoccupations (such as making a survey instrument so long that respondent fatigue weakens the reliability of the data collected). In any event, even if such information involves costs, its collection is common and likely to remain so. Therefore, it is appropriate to consider whether an existing data file contains useful information that may be extracted through secondary analysis. And, if there is reason to believe that this in the case, the objectives of social science can be advanced by taking the data off the shelf and exploiting their potential.

A related consideration is that an existing data set may contain valuable information about some issue or problem that was not salient at the time the study was carried out. As such issues come to the fore, or alternatively as scholars become more aware of the need to study topics they had heretofore tended to ignore, social research may benefit greatly by the use of existing data files which, serendipitously, contain information on variables pertinent to the new topic.

Some examples based on the present author's survey research in Tunisia involve analyses carried out after a lapse of some years that investigated the Islamic resurgence in Tunisia and elsewhere and issues of women and political development. Although neither analysis was anticipated when the data were originally collected, it proved possible to say something useful about both topics without collecting additional data, by designing and executing a secondary analysis of the existing data file. In the case 'of Islamic orientations, it was possible to document an increase in personal observance among all categories of respondents and in support for greater societal conformity to Islamic codes among certain categories but not among others, for the most part among respondents from the more disadvantaged sectors of society.[21] In the case of women and political development, the data were reanalyzed with gender introduced as both an independent and a specification variable in an attempt to account more fully for variations in citizen political orientations. The findings are too complex to summarize briefly. Suffice it to say that important differences between the political attitudes of men and women were found, but that the magnitude and even the direction of these gender-linked differences varied greatly as a function of social class and aggregate political environment.[22]

Although it can be extremely valuable to reanalyze social science data as new insights emerge and as new questions about familiar topics develop, such reanalyses will rarely be as "neat" as those in which the questions under investigation guide the study from the outset. Existing data files may not contain all the information desired or may be based on samples selected with a view to maximizing analytical considerations pertaining to the study of other issues. In the investigation of gender and political attitudes in Tunisia, for example, sex had not been a criterion in selecting respondents, and it was thus necessary to hold other variables constant to ensure that gender-linked attitudinal variations did not constitute spurious correlations. In this case, male and female respondents were matched, in a fashion similar to that discussed with respect to the 1967 and 1973 samples, and most of the analysis was limited to the restricted data base that resulted from this operation. Although internal validity and analytical rigor were thus maximized, a tradeoff had been necessary: not all the available data had been used and a sacrifice was accordingly made in external validity, meaning that confidence in the generalizability of the findings will depend more heavily than ever on their confirmation in subsequent replications. Nevertheless, though fewer compromises would have been necessary had new data been collected, the example illustrates the benefits of secondary analysis. Underanalyzed data were exploited more fully and made to yield interesting insights about an important topic. And these insights were obtained without the expensive and time-consuming task of collecting new data. In addition, with attention to methodological issues, rigor was preserved. Finally, it was possible to benefit from the unique attributes of the existing data file, in this case its longitudinal character spanning two very different governmental regimes, attributes that would be difficult to duplicate even if a researcher expended the effort necessary to collect new data.

Secondary analysis is not an alternative to the construction of new data files, and ideally ones of ever-improving quality as well. But it is a very valuable complement to the conduct of original survey research. Moreover, going far beyond these examples, the real potential of such work lies not in the secondary analysis of one's own data but in gaining access to data collected by others and making these files the foundation of investigations based on reanalysis. At present, the sharing and dissemination of survey data that would be necessary to promote such activity on a meaningful scale are virtually absent in the Arab world.

Obstacles to Secondary Analysis

In addition to wider recognition of the potential value of secondary analysis of existing data, several obstacles must be surmounted if such work is to become more common. First, the reluctance of many researchers to share the data they have collected must be overcome. One source of such reluctance is probably the researchers' insecurity—an awareness of the data's limitations and a desire to prevent others from learning of their inadequacies. (Insecurity of this sort is by no means limited to the Arab world, of course.) In fact, this sort of reluctance is rarely justified: If the data are so poor that their problems genuinely deserve to be hidden, then they should not be analyzed at all, not even by the individual(s) who collected them. They should be discarded, survived only by a report on why they were poor so that others may avoid the same difficulties. Ideally, in the interest of greater accuracy and methodological cumulativeness, the social science research community should encourage published summaries of such "failures," rather than attaching negative sanctions to the admission that a project was unsuccessful. In any event, the data should not be used to produce substantive reports or publications, and they should not be considered an available existing data file. Alternatively, however, if the data are imperfect but useful, possibly containing no greater proportion of error than most other data sets, they deserve to be analyzed and to be shared. Those who possess such data sets must overcome their doubts, and possibly their naïveté about the flawlessness of other files, and agree to make their data resources available to others for secondary analysis.

Another reason why researchers are sometimes reluctant to share data is fear of misuse, and here they may legitimately exercise caution. It is reasonable to require credible assurances that the data will not be used in ways that betray confidences or threaten the welfare of respondents. It is also appropriate to be concerned that data not be misused by national or even foreign agencies. Institutions that are repressive or exploitative or otherwise injurious to the public welfare certainly should not be abetted by receiving survey data collected by social scientists. Such concerns were expressed frequently by the practitioners of survey research assembled at Bellagio.

Judgments about whether a topic is truly sensitive or dangerous and about whether an individual or institution seeking data is trustworthy must ultimately rest with the individual researchers who have collected and stored the data. Considerations of this sort must be given serious attention when data sharing is discussed and when individual scholars decide whether or not to make the information they possess available to others. At the same time, in contrast to governments that may classify documents to hide mistakes, effective scientific research requires a degree of openness and a reasonable balance between caution and common sense on the one hand and responsible access to information on the other. Individuals possessing data must struggle to find this balance, avoiding the extremes of secretiveness and paranoia and of naïveté and opportunism. Similarly, those seeking to acquire data for secondary analysis—and increasing activity of this sort would certainly benefit the scientific community—have a right to expect responsiveness in return for credible demonstrations of legitimate scientific concern and scholarly good faith.

The Need for Data Archives

Beyond the reluctance of individuals to share their data, and the related fact that some may also hesitate to request access to existing data files given a normative climate that makes this practice unorthodox and even suspicious, there is a major barrier of another kind—the absence of institutional structures that support the sharing and secondary analysis of existing data resources. Known as data archives, such institutional arrangements are common in the United States and Europe but virtually absent in the Arab world.

Some data archives are specialized whereas others process data dealing with subjects ranging across the social sciences. Some are small operations, serving a relatively restricted community of users, whereas others, such as the University of Michigan–based Inter-University Consortium for Political and Social Research (ICPSR), are supported and utilized by dozens of universities and hundreds of social scientists throughout the United States and elsewhere. The ICPSR distributes data for secondary analysis through its member institutions, each of which designates an official representative (OR) to the consortium. This local OR coordinates interinstitutional relations and attends annual meetings at which ICPSR policy is set. In addition to acquiring ICPSR data for scholarly purposes, some universities request data for use by their students in courses devoted to methodological training or even the investigation of certain substantive subjects. A fair number of data-based doctoral dissertations written in the United States also make use of data from the ICPSR or some other archive.

Data archives receive and store data sets collected by various private scholars and institutions and make them available to legitimate users for diverse analytical purposes. But such institutions can be and often are far more than simple repositories; they perform a number of important functions and encourage the use of data files in their possession. In so doing, they make a very important contribution to scientific cumulativeness. The larger and more institutionalized archives, of course, perform more of these functions and on a larger scale.

Data archives serve as clearing houses for information as well as for data. They prepare and distribute documentation showing what data are available, in effect both advertising the files that scholars may acquire and promoting more general awareness of the potential advantages of secondary analysis. A related consideration is the visibility they give to the surveys of individual scholars or research teams, including mention of their work in regularly updated inventories of holdings. This recognition can stimulate survey research in general and a willingness to make one's data available for secondary analysis in particular. For this reason, some major data archives are actually offered more data than they can effectively process, some of which they must accordingly decline (sometimes because the quality or utility of the data are inadequate) and some of which they accept but maintain in "uncleaned" form and identify only on supplementary lists. In any event, the provision of information, visibility, and legitimacy is an important contribution made by survey data archives.

Cleaning and standardizing data are other contributions made by major archives. By taking data collected and coded according to many different formats, occasionally containing such diverse irregularities as inadequate or confusing documentation and entries for which there is no code or for which the coding system permits more than one interpretation, data archives often devote considerable time and effort to correcting errors and ambiguities and to putting data in a more readily usable form. Such operations, known as "cleaning," greatly facilitate the ability of borrowers to use the data and to avoid problems that might lead to erroneous conclusions or, at least, require many hours to solve. Some data archives also standardize coding schemes on common variables, like profession and socioeconomic status. This standardization is particularly helpful when an investigator is borrowing more than one data set, each of which was originally coded in a different manner. It means the data can be more easily integrated, and it simplifies the analysis of the data by standardized computer programs. Cleaning operations are so expensive and time consuming that archives rarely have the resources to bring all the data files they acquire up to desired standards. For this reason, cleaning is often done in stages, and in listing its holdings an archive will indicate whether each file is fully cleaned, partly cleaned, or uncleaned. Even if incomplete in many cases, cleaning and standardizing are important services that data archives perform.

Data archives may also be appropriate vehicles for managing financial aspects of data sharing. Either by providing a structure through which government or foundation resources can be channeled or by raising their own moneys through user fees or membership dues, they can accumulate the financial base necessary to support all manner of relevant activities. Publicizing the availability of data and cleaning the files acquired are only two among many such activities. Data archives can also maintain a technical staff capable of advising and assisting prospective borrowers, and some of these staff members may also undertake original empirical research aimed at refining the methodology of secondary data analysis. Similarly, such institutions can organize periodic seminars and workshops devoted to the discussion of relevant issues, not all of which need to be methodological, and can even undertake to provide training in the collection and analysis of survey data. Although some of these activities go beyond archiving and promoting secondary analysis, such services are offered by the U.S.-based ICPSR and some other data archives and, given the concentration of resources and expertise, there is no need to insist on a rigid distinction between the needs of original survey research and those associated with the secondary analysis of existing data.

With adequate resources data archives can initiate projects of data collection, whose sole purpose is to provide information for secondary analysis. In such instances, data are collected by an institutional staff that has no specific analytical preoccupations and no intention of using the data themselves. Such collections are sometimes called omnibus surveys: They gather a wide range of information from a representative sample with the expectation that a large number of researchers will be able to exploit profitably portions of the data. Such surveys can also be replicated at regular intervals, yielding unusually good longitudinal data sets that, again, will be available to any legitimate user interested in one or more of the topics covered in the survey. In this manner, an archive can use its resources not only to distribute existing survey data for secondary analysis but also to create data for this purpose.

Not all of these functions are performed by large numbers of data archives in the United States and Europe, and some of the activities are performed by other research institutions in the Arab world. Nevertheless, there are no active and full-service data archives in any Arab country—at least that the authors have been able to discover—and only the most minimal of institutional encouragement and support for any secondary analysis of existing data files. The absence of such institutions is a serious obstacle to the full utilization of data resources, and the presence of such institutions would undoubtedly contribute to the conduct of more and better survey research in many other ways as well.

Establishing Ethical Standards

A final contribution that data achives can make concerns the determination and application of ethical standards governing the dissemination of existing data files. Archives in Western societies are not called upon to play this role, and of course an individual who collects data remains responsible for determining whether or not they should be shared with an archive in the first place. But once such data have been made available for wider use, it remains important to respect donor wishes about the conditions under which they may be obtained and, more generally, to fashion criteria for evaluating requests for access in light of the potential for misuse. Whether regulation by such criteria should be minimal in the name of scientific openness or whether, conversely, there are real dangers that must be avoided even if this means forgoing analytical benefits is a decision to be made by donors and users. In any event, data archives would provide a structure for making such determinations, for reviewing them periodically, and for enforcing decisions and sanctioning violators by barring them from obtaining data in the future.

In addressing issues of ethics and responsibility in social science research, archive-oriented institutions might also be in a position to see that available data benefit subjects and respondents as well as survey researchers. This, too, is comparatively uncharted territory. Nevertheless, to the extent possible, it is desirable that data be analyzed not only in terms of abstract intellectual preoccupations, or even more applied goals defined by researchers rather than subjects, but also in terms of intellectual and practical preoccupations of respondents themselves or of the community and society of which they are a part. Thus, for example, foreign scholars working in an Arab society, or even Arab scholars working in a country other than their own, might be encouraged to deposit a copy of their data for use by persons closer to the needs and wishes of the people studied. Indeed a few foreign scholars report that they have sought to turn their data over to representatives of the societies in which they have conducted survey research but found no structure willing or able to make use of them. Similarly, it might be desirable for researchers to offer a copy of their data to representatives of the community studied, or of the school, factory, clinic, or so forth in which they have conducted their data-gathering operations.

Translating these noble but vague sentiments into concrete action raises difficult intellectual and practical questions. To many subjects and their representatives, unskilled in data analysis or even the logic of social science inquiry, the data would be meaningless. Other researchers would have to perform analyses on their behalf and develop answers to the questions they might choose to ask. Under such circumstances, subjects might find well-intended attempts to enable them to share the fruits of research to be more trouble than they are worth, and under such circumstances subjects would not be gaining independent control of information. Also, respondents might object to sharing this information with their community leaders because it could lead to their manipulation or exploitation, the precise opposite of the objective motivating the venture. Whether these and other problems can be solved remains to be seen, but it is a valid principle that researchers should seek avenues for sharing the information they collect with those who provide it in the first place. Whenever possible, subjects as well as researchers should benefit from survey research, and subjects themselves should be given an opportunity to define the benefits that hold the highest priority for them. If any progress is to be made in dealing with these issues, and in implementing strategies that seem desirable and workable, institutional and administrative support will be necessary. This is an important additional function that data archives may be able to perform.

Integrated Secondary Analysis

The confidence merited by a study can be assessed not only by replicating the experience with a new investigation and comparing the respective findings; the accuracy and precision of a study can also be assessed by acquiring the data from the original study and submitting them to reanalysis. The validity and reliability of measures and indicators can be assessed or reassessed, for example, and variable relationships can be explored using different statistical techniques and/or with new variables held constant or incorporated into multivariate analyses. In other words, much can be done by those who doubt the validity of the study's reported conclusions, and the interest of scientific accuracy is ideally served by placing data in the public domain and permitting skeptics to see if they can find flaws in the procedures that produced the suspicious results. If they can, errors or at least limitations will have been discovered, thereby contributing to scientific accuracy. If they cannot, confidence in the existing knowledge will be increased. In practice, few studies are so important and controversial that they inspire others to devote much time to such reanalyses. But the interest of science is nevertheless served by the potential for such operations and by their conduct when deemed appropriate. This is yet another scientific benefit that results from making existing data files available for secondary analysis.

A final possibility for productive work in this area is the integrated secondary analysis of multiple existing data files. This analysis involves bringing together a number of previously collected data sets, selected because the surveys on which they are based were conducted at a series of points in space and/or time which, taken together, strengthen the analytical potential of the study by permitting the incorporation of system-level variables. The logic here is that of genuine comparison, based on work at multiple levels of analysis and analogous to that previously discussed. Attributes of the social environment within which each data set was collected—such as its level of development, degree of ethnic or cultural pluralism, government orientation, legal system, co- lonial history—are coded and thus rendered variable properties in the integrated data file constructed from the diverse surveys. The explanatory power of any of these system-level variables can accordingly be assessed. Further, their ability to account for variance relative to the individual level independent variables employed when analyzing data from a single social system or a single point in time can be evaluated. Finally, multivariate statistical techniques permit examining patterns of interaction among variables conceptualized and measured at different levels of analysis.

Although such work is rare even in Western societies, it could become much more common if a substantial range of existing data sets was made available for secondary analysis. If this were to occur, integrated secondary analysis would permit far more elaborate and sophisticated investigations of social phenomena than usually occur in single survey studies. The larger the number of points in space and time from which data are brought together, and the greater the variance on a wide range of system-level attributes that they collectively encompass, the greater will be the analytical potential of the research. In seeking to explain individual level behavior with respect to such dependent variables as fertility, religiosity, or group affiliation, for example, attention can be paid to individual level variables like education and gender and also to whatever system-level attributes characterize and differentiate among the group of societies in which the data files were collected.

An example is a research project that the author and a Tunisian colleague are currently planning. Though only in the design stage and limited to only three data files drawn from the same society, it may be used to illustrate the character and the potential of integrated secondary analysis of multiple existing data sets. The dependent variables in the proposed study are religious orientation, which includes levels of personal piety and beliefs about the extent to which social and political life should be guided by Islamic laws and principles; political orientations, including views about the importance of democracy defined in terms of popular control of leadership selection and organized competition among diverse political institutions and ideologies; and the interrelationship between individual attitudes about religion and politics. In the broadest sense, then, the goal of the proposed analysis is to discover determinants of differences in religious orientation, of differences in political outlook, and, most important, of variations in the way that individuals conceive of the connections between religion and politics. To use a highly simplified classification scheme for this brief illustrative account, individuals may favor either more liberal or more fundamentalist conceptions of Islam and either more centralized or more pluralist modes of political organization. Taken together, these orientations give rise to four categories of interaction between religious and political attitudes and accounting for variance across these categories is the kind of objective that will guide the inquiry.

Sources of variance on this and other dependent variables will be sought be examining the impact of many individual level variables, including educational level and type, place of residence, gender, economic and professional status, and age. The data sets to be assembled for the project were collected in Tunisia at three separate points in time, during periods when Tunisia was marked by major differences in political and ideological climate, and these aggregate system-level differences will be treated as independent variables as well.

The data sets to be employed are from 1966, 1973, and 1983. In the first year, Tunisia was governed by a mobilization-oriented, single-party, socialist regime. The emphasis was on religious reform and modernist interpretations of Islam, and traditional Islamic groups and leaders were on the defensive. In the second year, the country was more oriented toward laissez-faire economics and less interested in political mobilization. It was also beginning to experience an Islamic revival. By the last year, Tunisia was moving haltingly toward multiple political parties, after having experienced some political disturbances. It was also characterized by a well-developed Islamic tendency movement, which had become an important part of the political scene. By combining data from the three time periods, these latter categories of variable attributes may also be included in the analysis, with a view both toward assessing their explanatory power and toward accounting for variance on the dependent variables as fully as possible. Thus, for example, the impact on individual religious and political attitudes of government ideology and of the position of Islamic groups in the overall environment can be examined. Further, the data can be disaggregated as a function of individual level variables, like education, age, and gender, taken in combination if desired, so as to delineate in conceptual terms any variations in the nature or intensity of relationships between individual level dependent variables and system-level independent variables. Finally, the specification effects associated with these system-level variables can be examined. In this part of the analysis, the degree to which relationships between the dependent variables and individual level independent variables differ as a function of system-level properties will be examined. This brief account should give an idea of both the structure and analytical power of the integrated secondary analysis of multiple existing data files.[23]

Projects of this sort can be made much more elaborate if data are available. Ideally, it would be desirable to execute the kind of project outlined here with data from one or several additional societies, for which longitudinal data are preferably available as well. This approach would increase the number of system-level independent variables that could be explored, possibly increase the amount of variance on many of these variables, and, perhaps most important, increase the ability to examine one system level variable with others held constant. The degree to which such analytical benefits are actually obtained would depend ultimately on the number and character of the societies represented in the data file constructed from discrete individual surveys. Nevertheless, if data bases of adequate dimensions can be assembled, it will be possible to undertake sophisticated projects of integrated secondary analysis, in which variables measured at two or more levels of analysis can be considered both independent of one another and in combination. Rather than simply comparing and attempting to integrate *findings* from various discrete studies, comparison and analytical integration would take place during the course of the data analysis itself, adding greatly to the methodological rigor, theoretical elaboration, and explanatory power of the investigation.

Combining Existing and Original Data Sets

It is also possible to combine replications and other new data collection efforts with the integrated secondary analysis of existing data files. Many of the advantages discussed, and specifically the ability to compare subjects rather than findings and to build system-level variables directly into the analysis, can be realized if an investigator not only replicates another researcher's survey but obtains for his or her own utilization the raw data from the previous study.

An example in which original survey research is combined with secondary analysis of existing data is the study in which Stone and Moore examined attitudes of university students from six different countries. Moore had conducted surveys in Tunisia and Morocco, and the data from these surveys were then analyzed in combination with those from four other states—Lebanon, Turkey, Iran, and Pakistan. As noted, the latter three countries are not Arab, although they are Muslim and Middle Eastern. The data from Lebanon, Turkey, Iran, and Pakistan were collected by a West German public opinion research organization under contract to the U.S. Information Agency. Among the findings from the combined data set reported by Stone and Moore is that although most Middle Eastern university students aspire to careers in such professions as law, medicine, engineering, and science, the two countries of the Maghreb are channeling considerable numbers of students into teaching careers, indicating governmental planning for economic development. The two Maghreb countries have also been more active in promoting university education among students from the rural areas, suggesting that future elites in the Maghreb are more likely to favor agricultural reform and development of the rural sector.

The Stone and Moore study does not constitute truly integrated secondary analysis in that the six data sets were not actually merged. Each was rather analyzed in a parallel fashion, with the authors reporting their findings about attitudinal distributions and relationships on a country-by-country basis. Since differences among students grouped by country are reported and the possible origins of these differences are discussed, the study does have an important comparative dimension. Because country differences are not treated as variable properties, however, the analysis does not include system-level variables. Whether a more truly integrated analysis, rather than parallel ones accompanied by a comparison of findings, would have led to different and more elaborate insights cannot be guessed. Perhaps not. Nevertheless, the study is of interest to the present discussion because it illustrates an additional variation on the theme of secondary analysis. In this case, the investigators utilized but did not rely exclusively on existing data files assembled by others. And in adding data of their own for an expanded analysis, they contributed survey files generated for reasons external to the six country comparative project they subsequently undertook; they did not carry out their data collection efforts with an eye toward replicating earlier studies or toward combining their data with other, existing files. Thus they in effect undertook the secondary analysis of multiple existing data files, some of which they themselves had previously collected and some of which they obtained elsewhere.

This discussion illustrates some of the ways that research based on multiple existing data sets can be carried out. Sometimes an investigator may obtain data from a series of discrete prior studies having common intellectual preoccupations and then conduct secondary analysis of a data base constructed by merging these various files. On other occasions, a data base of this sort may be assembled by a team of scholars working together, each of whom contributes data from his or her own previous survey research. The study of religion and politics being planned by the author and a Tunisian colleague is structured in such a way. In still other instances, an investigator may obtain one or several existing data sets and then conduct a replication to create a data base composed of multiple surveys. Also, as discussed in the last example, an investigator may sometimes undertake the secondary analysis of his own or her own data, originally collected for different purposes, while simultaneously obtaining additional files to be analyzed in combination with these data sets.

This list does not exhaust the range of analytical possibilities. The main purpose of the present discussion is to encourage future investigators to be alert to the possibility of secondary analysis of multiple existing data files and to stimulate these researchers to think creatively about ways to design and carry out such analyses. It is also to encourage them to consider merging these data files whenever possible and to conduct integrated secondary analyses. Such research holds out the possibility not only of utilizing more fully available but underexploited data resources but also of moving survey research in the Arab world toward more complete, sophisticated, and useful analytical insights.

Acknowledgment

The author acknowledges with gratitude the careful reading this and the following chapter received from David Gibson.

Notes

1. Mark Tessler, "The Application of Western Theories and Measures of Political Participation to a Single-Party North African State," *Comparative Political Studies* 5 (1972): 175–191.

2. Iliya Harik, "Opinion Leaders and the Mass Media in Rural Egypt: A Reconsideration of the Two-Step Flow of Communications Hypothesis," *American Political Science Review* 65 (September 1971).

3. Mark Tessler, "Regime Orientation and Participant Citizenship in Developing Countries: Hypotheses and a Test with Longitudinal Data from Tunisia," *Western Political Quarterly* 34 (1981): 479–498, and Mark Tessler and Jean O'Barr, "Gender and Participant Citizenship in Tunisia," *Journal of Arab Affairs* 3 (October 1982): 47–84, reprinted in Tawfic Farah, ed., *Political Behavior in the Arab States* (Boulder, Colo.: Westview Press, 1983).

4. Tawfic Farah and Faisal Al-Salem, "Political Efficacy, Political Trust, and the Action Orientations of University Students in Kuwait," *International Journal of Middle East Studies* 8 (July 1977): 317–328. See also Faisal Al-Salem, "Political

and Social Socialization in Kuwait," *Journal of the Social Sciences* (Kuwait) 8 (October 1980).

5. Nafhat Nasr and Monte Palmer, "Alienation and Political Participation in Lebanon," *International Journal of Middle East Studies* 8 (1977): 493–516.

6. Mima Nedelcovych and Monte Palmer, "The Political Behavior of Moroccan Students: Democratic Indicators in a Quasi-Democratic Environment," paper presented at the 1980 annual meeting of the Midwest Political Science Association.

7. Saad Gadalla and Mahanna Sohair, "Cultural Values and Population Policies: The Egyptian Case," American University in Cairo, Social Research Center, 1978.

8. Nadia Halim, "Social and Psychological Factors Affecting Fertility," *National Review of Social Sciences* (Egypt) 12 (January 1975): 199–206.

9. Rabinder Kumar Sharma, "Fertility Determinants in Urban Morocco," dissertation, University of Pennsylvania, 1975.

10. Hanna Rizk, "Fertility Trends and Differentials in Jordan," in James Allman, ed., *Women's Status and Fertility in the Muslim World* (New York: Praeger, 1976).

11. For a fuller discussion, see Adam Przeworski and Henry Teune, *The Logic of Comparative Social Inquiry* (New York: Wiley, 1970).

12. Saad Eddin Ibrahim, *Directions of Arab Public Opinion Toward the Question of Unity* (Beirut: The Center for Arab Unity Studies, 1980).

13. Russell Stone and Clement Moore, "Anticipated Mobility to Elite Status Among Middle Eastern University Students," *International Review of History and Political Science* 10 (1973).

14. Clement H. Moore and Arlie A. Hochschild, "Student Unions in North African Politics," *Daedalus* (Winter 1968): 38–42.

15. Gadalla and Sohair, "Cultural Values."

16. Khattab Hind, "Patterns and Perceptions of Menstrual Bleeding: The Egyptian Case," American University in Cairo, Social Research Center, unpublished report, n.d.

17. Amit K. Bhattacharyya, "Role of Rural-Urban Income Inequality in Fertility Reductions: Cases of Turkey, Taiwan and Morocco," *Economic Development and Cultural Change* 26 (October 1979).

18. Nazek Nozzeir, *Family Planning Knowledge, Attitudes and Practices,* M.A. thesis, American University in Cairo, 1970.

19. Michael Suleiman, "Values and Societal Development: Education and Change in Nasser's Egypt," in Farah, *Political Behavior,* 1983.

20. Mark Tessler, "Women's Emancipation in Tunisia," in Lois Beck and Nikki Keddie, eds., *Women in the Muslim World* (Cambridge: Harvard University Press, 1978), and Mark Tessler, "Tunisian Attitudes toward Women and Child-rearing," in Allman, *Woman's Status.*

21. Mark Tessler, "Political Change and the Islamic Revival in Tunisia," *Maghreb Review* 5 (January-February 1980): 8–19.

22. Mark Tessler and Jean O'Barr, "Gender and Participant Citizenship."

23. Some findings from the 1983 survey about the relationship between religious and political orientations are reported in Elbaki Hermassi, "La societe tunisienne au miroir islamiste," *Maghreb Machrek* 103 (January-February 1984): 39–56.

11

Cumulativeness and the Logic
of Systematic Social Inquiry

Mark A. Tessler

This chapter offers an introduction to systematic social science research and specifically to those elements of the scientific method from which derive a concern for cumulativeness. It is intended primarily for readers whose familiarity with the canons of social inquiry is limited, including those in the Arab world. Unless practitioners of survey research have a solid understanding of the intellectual foundations of their craft, they will be unable to employ investigatory tools in ways that produce useful knowledge of acceptable quality. This chapter makes a start at introducing readers to those intellectual foundations. It seeks to familiarize them with some of the concepts and vocabulary central to social research and to stimulate further inquiry into the logic and goals of the scientific method.

A problem discussed at the Bellagio conference was that some practitioners of survey research in the Arab world have an inadequate understanding of the scientific method. This deficiency reduces their ability to determine when and how survey research may be used productively and, conversely, when it is not an appropriate research strategy. As discussed in Chapter 7 by Barbara Ibrahim, surveys of poor quality and limited utility have sometimes been the result, a situation of course not unique to the Arab world. Problems are compounded if it is added that good research should not only answer questions of immediate interest but should also contribute to the collective and on-going effort of the social science community to produce a body of knowledge that is steadily becoming more accurate and more complete. This concern for scientific cumulativeness—for the incremental improvement of information that enables us to understand and manage our social environment—demands an even greater knowledge of the logic of social research. The present chapter not only introduces the nature of the scientific method and its application in the Arab world, but it also explains why scientific investigation is preoccupied with cumulativeness.

Given its focus on intellectual considerations and the logic on inquiry, the present chapter might well serve as a useful introduction to the discussion of operational needs and strategies in Chapter 10. The chapter on operational issues, however, was placed first for two reasons. First, the present chapter covers material that will be familiar to at least some readers, including some in the Arab world. It may thus be reasonably treated as a sort of optional addendum to the principal contribution dealing with the issue of scientific cumulativeness. Second, the material contained in the present chapter is more difficult and abstract. It may therefore be more comprehensible to uninitiated readers—including those for whom English is a second language—if read after a comparatively straightforward account of practical considerations, which will familiarize readers with some of the issues involved.

Scientific and Nonscientific Knowledge

"Science is the study of those judgments about which universal agreement can be obtained,"[1] according to one scholar's definition, and of necessity this implies a concern with multiple investigations, replication, and an incremental and cumulative approach to the production of knowledge. Scientific inquiry is based on objective judgments, meaning sense-related perceptions that produce knowledge that is "intersubjectively transmissible." Science aspires further to produce from these observations and perceptions insights that have general rather than specific applications, which are nomothetic rather than ideographic in character. These definitional components of science imply that the work of a single investigator becomes maximally useful and derives ultimate worth when integrated into a more diffuse body of research carried out by a community of scholars.

Accounts of the scientific method sometimes put off the uninitiated by an excessive use of jargon. But terms like "intersubjectively transmissible" and "nomothetic" are simply conveniences for differentiating between forms of knowledge and inquiry that fall within and without the purview of science. They establish an intellectual foundation with which to comprehend that science, by its very nature, requires a concern with cumulativeness.

Studies of epistemology and the logic of inquiry classify types of knowledge and methods of knowing in a variety of ways, routinely differentiating between scientific information and other kinds of judgments. An Arab scholar attending the Bellagio conference recently discussed four ways of knowing.[2] The first is tenacity, wherein "truth is known because . . . people have always known it to be true." Folk-knowledge and other forms of traditional wisdom are considered time tested and above all self-evident. Such established assertions about reality may also provide a foundation from which new and original knowledge may be deduced.

A second source of knowledge is authority, by which information is viewed as accurate because it comes from a source considered trustworthy and competent. A statement may be believed because it is made by or is attributable to a respected individual, one whose wisdom has previously proved convincing or useful. The transmission of religious knowledge and the credibility of proffered interpretations of religious doctrine rely heavily on authority. Thus, if one wants to know what is true and right, one may consult those authorities—either the individuals themselves or the texts they have communicated—whose secular wisdom or spiritual powers make their judgments believable. The credibility of an authority, though it may be enhanced by past performance and continuing demonstrations of special skills, is ultimately a matter of faith, about which individuals may reach dissimilar conclusions.

A third way of acquiring knowledge is intuition or, so far as religion is concerned, revelation. "The great philosophers—Descartes, Spinoza, Al-Ghazali, Ibn-Tufail and others—describe the process as a natural light thrown upon the hearts of men. Hence they see what nobody has ever seen and hear what nobody has ever heard."[3] It does not matter whether one actively initiates the search for some intuitive insight, calling upon intellectual powers of imagination and creativity, or whether one simply finds information placed in his or her consciousness. In either case, the knowledge is acquired through the exercise of the intellect alone, with the added provision that in religion there is faith that divine powers have chosen to place the knowledge in the individual's mind.

Scientific knowledge is a fourth category, which stands out against the preceding or any other system of classifying nonscientific and subjective modes of inquiry. In scientific investigation, objective observations are made and replicated. Unlike the preceding categories, science is concerned exclusively with description and explanation. Other methods of knowing may produce explanations and descriptions, but they are also capable of producing value judgments—statements about good and bad or right and wrong.

Although value judgments are not amenable to universal agreement—they are not intersubjectively transmissible—and hence cannot be produced through the scientific method, scientific research is nevertheless influenced by values in many ways. The enterprise of science is inescapably embedded in a normative context. An individual scientist's selection of a topic or problem to address in his or her investigation is a value judgment. Science is concerned with how information about this topic is produced but is silent on the issues of whether the topic should be studied and of whether it is important or insignificant. These subjective judgments must be reached by some other way of knowing.

Other important connections exist between scientific and nonscientific knowledge, between objective and subjective judgments. For example, many scientific insights and hypotheses begin with intuition, with the scientist temporarily functioning as a philosopher. Indeed, the effective exercise of creative intellectual intuition, of what is sometimes called the scientific imagination, is usually essential if scientific knowledge is to be valuable. Judgments arrived at through rigorous scientific study can be useful and important; however, they can also be trivial or obvious. The production of knowledge that is worthwhile as well as scientific depends to a considerable extent on an investigator's ability to bring imagination and creative insight, as well as methodological precision, to the research.

Despite the connections between scientific and normative information, science remains a separate and distinct category of knowledge. Though influenced and given meaning by subjective considerations, scientific investigation is based on principles of objectivity, which in turn make findings intersubjectively transmissible and amenable to universal agreement. Similarly, no matter how brilliant, intuitions and educated guesses can only be transformed into scientific judgments in this manner. Exercise of the scientific method requires objective testing of hypotheses and ideas and inspection and replication of these tests by other scientists.

A subject that has considerable meaning to many Arab and Muslim scholars is the relationship between Islam and various forms of knowledge. As in all religions, Islam's truths are derived and transmitted through intuition and authority. Moreover, again like other religions, orthodox Islam regards its judgments as taking precedence over those acquired through the scientific method. Indeed, the very use of the term *scientific* to describe this secular quest for knowledge, including sociological knowledge, is often rejected. Finally, because Islam's foundations are a divinely revealed legal code and a divinely guided historical experience that may be interpreted to explain events and show appropriate behavior in virtually every domain of human experience, there is little room in fundamentalist Muslim conceptions for a compartmentalized distinction between coexisting domains of religious knowledge and scientific knowledge. As Dhaher summarized this point of view,

> Islam states that all knowledge was revealed to man with the advent of the Koran. . . . All that had been discovered is considered explained by the Koran . . . [which] eliminates the need to understand, study or explain events or to perceive causal relationships between events. The holy men of Islam are referred to as "men of science," showing that the two are synonymous, that learning is Islamic learning and only that. In the Koran one finds the statements: we have not omitted anything and we have calculated everything. These statements have the force of edicts against scientific inquiry, should one choose to interpret them as such.[4]

Muslims have long disagreed about the appropriateness of such fundamentalist conceptions of Islamic doctrine and about whether they have been adhered to sufficiently to create an actual, as opposed to a potential, conflict between science and Islam. Many observe that Islam has in fact stimulated scientific and intellectual activity, thus giving rise to brilliant civilizations following its emergence as an operative legal and normative code. Others, in contrast, call for a critical reexamination of the relationship between traditional religious values and the contemporary needs of Muslims and Arabs. Though they note that allegations about Islam's hostility to science have historically been advanced by cynical foreigners, as part of an attempt to legitimize colonial and imperial endeavors, they nevertheless believe that self-criticism is necessary. They suggest that fidelity to Islam, or rather to certain fundamentalist interpretations of Islam, may indeed have hindered modernization and scientific advance in the Arab and Muslim world.[5]

Pious Muslims will probably continue to debate whether contemporary and secular social science conflicts with religion, hence necessitating a choice between rejection of the former and acceptance of a more liberal interpretation of the latter, or whether religion and secular science can and should respect and complement each other. Those seeking to conduct social science research in Muslim environments should be cognizant of these interpretations and debates, not only to avoid offending local sensitivities but also to make themselves more critically aware of the normative assumptions guiding their own investigatory efforts.

To report that scientific knowledge is different than other forms of knowledge is not to argue that it is superior. Judgments not rooted in an experience all can share, whose accuracy cannot be assessed by those who might otherwise remain unconvinced, are not necessarily either untrue or unimportant. Further, objectivity defined as the potential for universal agreement through unobstructed replication of sensory-based observations is not an absolute guarantor of either accuracy or significance. But though it would be unreasonable (and unscientific) to claim that objective and scientific knowledge is better than subjective and nonscientific knowledge, the two kinds of judgments are qualitatively different, and the distinction between them is essential for an understanding of scientific inquiry.

Judgments such as "God is merciful," "my child is beautiful," and "evil will be punished in the next world" illustrate subjective and nonscientific knowledge. Depending on how each conclusion was reached, it could constitute information derived through tenacity, authority, or intuition. In any case, these statements are all examples of knowledge that is not intersubjectively transmissible; they are not based on observations that anyone can make solely through the application of his or her senses and hence they are not amenable to replication and universal agreement. Again, this is not to deny that the three statements deal with matters important to many individuals. Nor does it suggest that science has anything to contribute to debates about whether each statement is true or false. Certainly there is no presumption that a statement is false simply because it is not scientific. But whatever the potential worth and accuracy of the preceding pieces of information and of similarly subjective statements, they are examples of the kind of judgment with which science as an enterprise does not and cannot concern itself.

Alternatively, "grass is green," "the Earth is flat," and "the sun revolves around the Earth" are scientific statements; they are derived from sensory-based observations of continuous phenomena that all observers are capable of making. So too are statements like "the speed of light is 286,272 miles per second" and "the sun is 93 million miles from the Earth." Though acquired through the use of instruments that aid the senses, this information is based on observations that any scientist (and most others) can be trained to make, and hence it is amenable to universal agreement. Since two of the statements are false, but for centuries were widely held to be true, these examples also demonstrate that objectivity and universal agreement can be in error. Sensory illusions and generalized misinterpretations of sensory data are dangers in science, and inaccuracies may go undetected for years, possibly forever. Although such inaccuracies should keep scientists from attributing to their insights any natural superiority over other forms of knowledge, the quest for objective knowledge is a fundamental and essential part of the task of understanding and prospering in the world.

The sort of information science aspires to contribute requires a particular kind of investigatory effort, one in which individual contributions attain their full value through integration into an incremental and cumulative endeavor. Confidence in scientific findings increases when they are shown to agree with other data, and movement toward universal agreement thus progresses to the extent that observations, experiments, and other forms of inquiry are replicable and replicated. Findings must be reproducible. The potential for distorted perception and faulty interpretation, though never completely removed, declines significantly as the judgments of one observer are reproduced by others. Information amassed by one scientist merits confidence to the extent that others who might be suspicious of error or bias have had an opportunity to make their own investigations and have had their doubts dispelled as they reached similar conclusions. At the most basic level, this concern for replication gives science its cumulative character. This is a fundamental part of the connection between cumulativeness and a method of knowing based on universal agreement and intersubjective transmissibility.

Nomothetic Knowledge

Science seeks agreement on matters of general concern, on attributes and patterns of behavior that pertain to classes or subclasses of phenomena rather than to unique events or to individual members of a given population. This is the concern for nomothetic rather than ideographic insights, the other half of science's concern with cumulativeness. Though the individual is frequently the unit of analysis in social science, especially in survey research, each individual is observed or studied in order to draw conclusions about individuals in general or at least about certain categories of individuals in general. The same is true for other units of analysis, such as social aggregates and structures like factories, schools, clinics, and villages. Even when only one or a few cases are investigated, the objective is almost always to learn something about factories, schools, clinics, or villages in general or at least to acquire nomothetic information about certain kinds of factories, schools, clinics, or villages.

Information about how a single individual looks or behaves, or about what he or she believes, may well be objective and intersubjectively transmissible, but the goal of science is not to describe or explain the characteristics of a single case. Such discrete observations are the building blocks of scientific inquiry, and science proceeds by collecting such facts. But individual cases are examined in order to obtain information that may be combined with facts about other members of the same class of units, and the goal of such analyses is to discover patterns of broad applicability and/or to delineate the locus of applicability of these nomothetic insights.

Individual cases may be a more central preoccupation when putting to use the results of scientific investigation, when applying and seeking to derive benefit from generalized patterns of nomothetic knowledge. The use of insights derived from medical research is an obvious example. Individuals who are sick or who have received medical treatment for an illness are studied in an attempt to discern general patterns about the behavior of the disease or the treatment, and this general knowledge is in turn valuable because it can be used to understand better and to treat more effectively the malady of a suffering individual. But the knowledge that science values and seeks to acquire is itself nomothetic. If a given observation were truly ideographic, that is, if nothing of a general nature could be learned from a particular case, then that case would not be of interest to an investigator concerned with the production (as opposed to the application) of scientific knowledge.

The quest of science for knowledge that is nomothetic and hence generalizable beyond a single case carries a concern for cumulativeness in two interrelated respects. First, replication is necessary to determine the extent of a particular phenomenon across space or time. This concern is sometimes called "population extensiveness." A pattern of behavior or thought is of interest because it is reasonably generalizable. But exactly how widely does it apply? In an example from survey research in the Arab world, researchers observed in Lebanon in 1957–1958 that the social identity of students at the American University of Beirut formed a hierarchy of group affiliations, with the strength of reference group attachments ordered in the following manner: family, national (ethnic) origin, religion, citizenship, and political party affiliation.[6] This finding is already nomothetic in that it is generalizable to a class of individuals— university students in Lebanon (including those from other Arab countries). But is the observed pattern more widespread than that? Does it apply in Kuwait, for example, or in the Arab world as a whole, or even more broadly than that? Such questions about population extensiveness cannot be answered unless the study is replicated, unless the same or other investigators collect information about the phenomenon from other populations and integrate the findings from the original study and these diverse replications.

A related concern is for generalizability across time, as well as across space, and again replication and cumulativeness are central. Patterns of behavior and thought are not necessarily constant; even the aggregated physical characteristics of the members of a society, such as height and weight, may differ today from what they were in the past. Assessing these possibilities and determining the temporal as well as the spatial parameters of scientific findings are parts of the quest for nomothetic knowledge. Here again, replication and the integration of findings from discrete but interrelated studies are necessary. In the study of social identities in Lebanon, the original investigators, Levon H. Melikian and Lutfi Diab, replicated their study after an interval of fourteen years.[7] As discussed in Chapter 10, other scholars, notably Tawfic Farah,[8] repeated the investigation among university students in Kuwait, among children in Kuwait, and among Arab students in the United States. Each of these studies was designed and carried out to assess the generalizability across space and/or time of findings from the original research project. Still another survey research project that investigated social identities, and which accordingly provides data that contribute further to the production of nomothetic knowledge about group affiliations in the Arab world, was conducted by the author among Arabs (Palestinians) in Israel.[9]

The second of the two interrelated reasons for a connection between cumulativeness and the quest of generalizable insights derives from a need to specify the parameters, or locus, of scientific findings. This concern will be elaborated more fully when discussing the distinction between description and explanation in the next section. Briefly, though science welcomes findings of universal applicability, observations about many of the phenomena with which scientific investigation is concerned vary from one social or physical environment to another. Accurate and worthwhile scientific contributions, ones that enhance the available store of useful knowledge, must therefore often be pursued by seeking multiple descriptive or explanatory insights and by then specifying the attributes of the environments within which each applies. In other words, several nomothetic statements may be necessary to characterize fully an element under investigation, and the utility of such statements depends on the investigator's ability to determine the conditions governing the applicability of each.

Some examples from the author's survey research in Tunisia illustrate this concern, as well as the place of replication and cumulativeness in carrying out the enterprise. One study dealt with the generalizability of research findings about the determinants of political participation among individual citizens. In studies conducted in Western nations, researchers have shown (and reconfirmed in numerous replications) that political involvement tends to increase as a function of social status variables, such as education and income, and also as a function of certain personality attributes, such as sociability and efficacy. Confidence in the applicability of these behavior patterns beyond developed Western polities had increased somewhat as a result of several comparative studies involving developing nations in Asia, Africa, and Latin America,[10] but many more replications were needed and the matter had not been investigated in any Arab country or in any single-party state. During the 1960s, when Tunisia was governed by an effective mobilization-oriented single-party regime, the author investigated determinants of citizen political involvement to ascertain, inter alia, whether patterns observed in the West and in some developing countries existed in an Arab country governed by a single-party regime.[11] In this instance, the findings from earlier studies were reconfirmed, adding to the generalizability and population extensiveness of the observed relationships.

The study extended the range of sociocultural and political circumstances under which the previously observed patterns may now be said to apply, although full confidence in this assertion will require additional replications. If the established patterns had not been manifested in single-party Tunisia, however, something of equal value would have been learned. Such a finding would have been an important addition to efforts to delineate in conceptual terms the locus of applicability of known determinants of political participation. In other words, there would have been an incremental addition to knowledge about the conditions under which certain socioeconomic status and personality attributes do and do not tend to increase political involvement. Moreover, to the extent that the locus of applicability of particular findings can be specified in conceptual terms, in terms of systematically defined variable attributes, this additional information will contribute directly to a fuller understanding of the observed phenomenon. Variable attributes that differentiate among social environments in which given behavioral patterns do and do not apply may properly be regarded as constituting some of the determinants of those patterns; as a result, they are necessary components in any complete explanation of the latter phenomena.[12]

A slightly different example is the replication of the Tunisian survey after an interval of six years, when the machinery of the country's political party had fallen into disarray and by which time the socialist ideology that had previously guided the regime had given way to a more conservative and laissez-faire approach to national development. Under these conditions, the relationship between social status and political participation was rather different, so that the results of this replication were indeed a refined understanding of the way that patterns and determinants of political behavior vary as a function of a state's political and ideological climate. In the case at hand, the author found that individual political involvement tended to decline in the aggregate and that variations in individual participation levels were no longer associated with levels of social status, thus establishing some of the contextual factors affecting the generalizability of the original findings.[13] More important than the specifics of the example, however, is the larger analytical point: The generalizability of nomothetic knowledge is assessed not only in terms of quantitative estimates of population extensiveness but also by discovering the specification or conditional variables that determine its applicability or inapplicability. This is also part of the reason that replication and a preoccupation with cumulativeness are of fundamental importance.

A final illustration can be derived from differences in findings reported by the various studies of group affiliation and social identification summarized earlier. For example, religion ranked relatively low in importance in the original study in Lebanon, and it declined ever more in the subsequent replication. Further, religion was found to be a comparatively unimportant focus of identity among Arabs in Israel. On the other hand, studies conducted among university students in Kuwait and among children in Kuwait found that religion occupies the highest position in the hierarchy of group affiliations of most respondents. Similarly, religion ranked first among most Arab students surveyed in the United States. Assuming that each of the investigations was carefully done and that its findings are accurate, the juxtaposition of these interrelated investigations begins to offer a picture of how the contribution of religion to social identification is distributed across time and space. Even more, this comparative analysis of findings from interrelated studies can contribute to scientific cumulativeness by defining in conceptual terms the characteristics of social environments in which religion is relatively important and those in which it ranks lower in hierarchies of group affiliation.

In summary, systematic investigation requires replication and the integration of findings from discrete studies into a communal scholarly endeavor for three reasons. First, confidence in the accuracy of knowledge that is objectively derived and intersubjectively transmissible increases to the degree that observations and insights produced by one investigator are reproduced by others. To the extent that those who are skeptical of these observations and insights have had an opportunity to gather empirical evidence of their own, which will either repudiate the original findings or allay the skepticism, there occurs movement in the direction of universal agreement. Replication is thus the essence of the process by which science strives for confidence in the accuracy of knowledge it produces.

Second, findings are useful—both as contributions to understanding and as guides to action—to the extent they are nomothetic in character and hence of reasonably general applicability. Levels of generalizability and population extensiveness can be established only by replication. Even if a single study could somehow embrace the entire universe of cases to which the knowledge being sought was potentially applicable, something that in reality is almost never possible, the need to establish generalizability across time as well as space would continue to make replication essential.

Third, assuming that much, and probably most, important nomothetic knowledge is less than universally applicable, replication is required to examine findings discerned in one kind of environment under other conditions. Cumulativeness thus involves an attempt to determine contextual parameters, to delineate in terms of major defining attributes the conditions under which a given scientific insight is and is not valid.

The importance of replication and cumulativeness in scientific research does not mean that a study is worthwhile only if it explicitly seeks to contribute to one or more of these three goals. Although the concern for cumulativeness must be recognized and must serve as the central preoccupation of the community of scholars working in any area, individual investigators may often find it fruitful to orient their work in some new direction. They may be guided by some original insight or novel preoccupation. Such departures are not to be discouraged; they are an additional way in which intuition interacts with and ultimately guides empirical research, and without such departures science would eventually become an inbred enterprise devoid of creativity and condemned to refining but not expanding knowledge. Yet innovations of this sort, however valuable they may be in breaking new intellectual ground, must themselves ultimately be evaluated in terms of accuracy and applicability through replications and complementary studies. In other words, if they bear fruit, innovative investigations, though not linked to prior studies, will nevertheless fulfill their promise and achieve maximum utility by setting in motion a new chain of interrelated research efforts. Although innovation is welcome and indeed essential at the level of the individual study, replication and a concern for cumulativeness thus remain an essential requirement for the scientific community as a whole.

Variance, Description, and Explanation

Science is used to produce both descriptive and explanatory knowledge, and the distinction between these two categories of information introduces another dimension of the scientific enterprise that reinforces a concern for cumulativeness. At the simplest level, descriptive statements are statements of fact. They are sometimes described as "what statements" because they undertake to characterize physical or social reality by telling what it is like. Alternatively, explanatory statements are sometimes known as "why statements." They begin with descriptions but go further, attempting not only to report what the world is like but also to explain why it is that way.

A central organizing principle in social science is the idea of variance, or difference, and this notion helps to delineate the practical significance of the distinction between description and explanation. In almost all cases, and certainly in those involving survey research, systematic social science investigation is concerned with the study of differences, either actual or potential. Some cases are characterized by one pattern of behavior or thought, and other cases are characterized by a different pattern. In other words, there is variance among the cases. Among individuals to be studied through survey research, for example, some people may be more religious than others, some may read newspapers frequently while others read them less often, or some may engage in family planning practices while others do not. In each instance, there is variance among the cases, and the object of social science research is either to describe or to explain this variance.

Descriptions involve discerning the distribution of variance, determining which of the possible behavior patterns characterizes each case under study and then delineating the distribution of the entire group of cases across the range of possible behaviors. With respect to religiosity, for example, description-oriented research would be concerned with determining whether each individual is more religious or less religious (or religious to an intermediate degree) and then reporting on the proportion of cases that falls into each category. Explanation, by contrast, is concerned with the determinants as well as the distribution of variance, the causes of higher and lower levels of religiosity in this case. Apart from a description of who is religious and who is not, or of what level or kind of religiosity characterizes each case, explanation-oriented research asks about the factors that impact upon some individuals but not others and lead the former but not the latter to behave in a particular way, to possess a given level or type of religiosity in this instance.

The logic of variance is central to surveys and other kinds of social research, even though it is not always made explicit. If a phenomenon in which an investigator is interested does not vary, actually or at least potentially, then neither descriptive nor explanatory research is needed. If all persons were religious to exactly the same degree, for example, or in exactly the same way—because religiosity were a concept that by definition had no variance associated with it—then descriptive studies seeking to chart the distribution of religious intensity would be pointless. It would not be necessary to conduct an investigation to determine the relative proportion of more and less religious individuals; by definition, all would be known a priori to be equally religious.

Again, social research is stimulated by potential as well as actual variance. A study may find little or no variance with respect to a given concept it has chosen to investigate; this finding is not necessarily without scientific value, however. As long as the cases are capable of varying with respect to the phenomenon, variance not being excluded by the properties that define the concept, then research aimed at describing whether and how a particular population of subjects differs is worthwhile. It will provide information that could not have been obtained without the research. Alternatively, if the phenomenon is such that even the potential for variance is lacking, we can describe its distribution throughout a population without empirical research. It will be known without any research that all subjects are similar or identical.

A few examples may be useful to illustrate how survey research in the Arab world has been used to describe variance and to relate this discussion to considerations of cumulativeness. In the mid-1960s, researchers at the American University in Cairo interviewed 3,000 Egyptian newspaper buyers to study media consumption habits. The investigation provided information about the distribution of preferences for different newspapers and magazines, both domestic and foreign, about the relative frequency with which different publications were purchased and read, and about the degree to which various kinds of articles were preferred. The results provided a detailed description of Egyptian behavior in relation to the printed media at the time of the study.[14]

A 1966 survey of family planning practices among urban Moroccans sought to provide descriptive information about variance among individuals with respect to behavior patterns of social significance. A total of 5,269 husbands and wives were interviewed in nine cities, each of which was subdivided by neighborhood type for the purpose of sampling. The findings, each of which summarizes the distribution of responses to an item on the interview schedule, include the following: Eighty-seven percent of all wives and 92 percent of all husbands had never practiced birth control, fewer than half of the respondents reported knowing that pregnancy could be prevented, and the number of children considered ideal was, on the average, 3.3 for wives and 3.1 for husbands.[15]

Population studies constitute one of the relatively few substantive areas in which similar surveys have been carried out at many different points in space and time. As discussed in Chapter 10, they are something of a model for the conduct of coordinated studies and/or replications in the pursuit of cumulativeness in other areas. Comparability among investigations does not always exist in as full a measure as might be desired. The demographic categories sampled or the survey instruments employed sometimes differ in significant ways. Nevertheless, the existence of many relatively comparable studies in the area of population dynamics and family planning does constitute important movement in the direction of cumulativeness. Examples of other population studies that contribute to this quest for cumulativeness—for knowledge that is accurate and nomothetic and whose locus of applicability is known—are surveys carried out in Tunisia and Jordan. The Tunisian investigation was conducted by the National Office of Family Planning and Population in 1975. A total of 2,361 Tunisian women were interviewed, and respondents reported much greater familiarity with contraceptive methods and family planning programs than had been found in Morocco a decade earlier.[16] In the second study, the National Fertility Survey of Jordan interviewed 5,214 ever-married women to accumulate descriptive information about age at the time of first marriages and about preferred family size and knowledge of contraceptive methods.[17]

A discussion of the attempts to integrate these and other diverse but interrelated studies, and of those attempts that must be made in the future, is beyond the scope of the present chapter. The concern here is to emphasize the importance of replication, incrementalism, and cumulativeness in the conduct of survey research in the Arab world and elsewhere. Generally, surveys are of maximum value when conceived and executed with a view toward producing findings that can be assessed in light of an emerging body of information produced by an on-going battery of empirical investigations. Some individual studies can themselves possess considerable population extensiveness or can embrace a temporal span of some duration. For example, a cross-national survey of population issues was carried out in Tunisia and Morocco between 1972 and 1974. According to the 2,326 women surveyed, family planning activities were more common in Tunisia than Morocco, the IUD was more popular in Tunisia whereas the pill was more common in Morocco, and women who used each device tended to have the same sociological characteristics in both countries.[18] But even studies limited to a single locale or a single point in time can contribute to a collective and cumulative enterprise. They can participate in the effort of social science to achieve the goals of scientific cumulativeness by investigating questions and employing methods that promote the analytical integration of their findings with those of other studies.

The importance of cumulativeness is even greater in research whose goal is explanation rather than description. Explanations, too, are maximally useful when they apply across space and time and when they are tested under diverse conditions so that it may be determined exactly when they do and do not apply. As with descriptions, the foundation of explanation-oriented investigation is the idea of variance: Survey research and many other kinds of social scientific inquiry seek to explain variance.

In explanatory studies the quest for "what statements" is replaced by an attempt to produce "why statements." Rather than being concerned exclusively with how differences among subjects are distributed, the delineation of these distributions becomes the first step in a more elaborate research process that seeks to discover the causes or determinants of variance, to understand why the differences occur. A phenomenon whose variance is to be explained is usually referred to as a dependent variable. This variance defines the observed effects or responses, whose causes or stimuli must be uncovered through empirical investigation. Factors that produce this variance, that account for the fact that individual subjects differ in either a quantitative or a qualitative fashion, are called independent variables. The central preoccupation in explanatory research is the discovery of independent variable–dependent variable relationships. Social science structures its explanations of why a given phenomenon—

religiosity, preferred family size, attitudes toward birth control, political participation—varies as it does throughout a population of individuals or other appropriate units of analysis in terms of such relationships.

The variance described in each of the immediately preceding examples may be thought of as defining one or several dependent variables. An explanation-oriented study would take observed variance on the relevant dependent variable as a point of departure and would then examine the relationship between it and any number of potentially pertinent independent variables. This approach has been used in many survey research projects in the Arab world. In the case of communications media consumption, for example, a study in Tunisia found that newspaper readership varied as a function of education and income. More specifically, increased education and increased income both increased the frequency of newspaper readership.[19] Another study found that age and gender are also critical independent variables in explaining variations in readership levels; male gender and younger age tend to give rise to higher levels of media consumption and thus to account in part for differences among individuals in newspaper readership.[20]

Explanations will be satisfying and useful only if the foundation of social science information on which they are based is sound, and here again a concern for cumulativeness is critical. In the first place, the information must be accurate, and, as previously emphasized, confidence that results are valid increases directly as a function of replication and the reproduction of findings. Such accuracy is often described as "internal validity." Further, as also previously stressed, it is essential to know the extent to which findings may be generalized across space and time. This is sometimes described as "external validity." Finally, it is necessary to be informed about the locus of applicability of established variable relationships, to be able to delineate systematically the conditions under which they apply.

These important reasons for a concern with replication and cumulativeness apply to both description and explanation-oriented research. But in explanation-oriented inquiry there is an additional aspect of the issue of cumulativeness as well, one equally significant. Beyond accuracy and generalizability, there is the critical matter of completeness, of what is sometimes called "analytical elaboration." Few dependent variables worthy of being the focus of an investigation are influenced by only one independent variable. Single-factor causation, in other words, is rare. Therefore, even after one or several pertinent independent variables have been identified and their relationship(s) to the dependent variable delineated, a considerable amount of unexplained variance remains, and the research process must be carried forward.

Single studies can and usually do deal with more than one independent variable. Nevertheless, there are almost always gaps in the completeness of explanatory variable relationships delineated by a single study, no matter how ambitious it may be. Moreover, it is common for a single investigation to focus deliberately on a limited and manageable portion of the problem of accounting for variance on the dependent variable and to leave for others, or for a future study, the task of exploring other important aspects of the problem. In any event, though subsequent studies undertaken from this perspective will not be concerned with strict replication, but rather with expanding the sophistication and complexity of the explanation of a common phenomenon, the quest for cumulativeness is again a central preoccupation. Explanations are satisfactory to the extent that most relevant causal agents have been identified and their impact on the dependent variable properly charted. The provision of this kind of information is a collective task. Individual research projects must be designed with a knowledge of the results of previous studies and an ability to identify gaps in the present state of knowledge. They must then be constructed and carried out so as to fill some of these gaps and thereby to enhance the completeness of available explanations.

In addition to focusing on multiple independent variables, studies must also consider the interrelationships among these determinants as they interact with one another so as to produce variance on the dependent variable. For example, given independent variables may bear a necessary but not a sufficient relationship to a particular dependent variable. In other words, each affects the dependent phenomenon but only when an additional stimulus is present. Alone, none is sufficient to produce variance on the dependent variable, but each is nevertheless a necessary condition for change on this variable in that it has an impact when accompanied by another independent variable, which is thus also necessary but insufficient alone.

An example of this kind of analytical pattern is found in the author's previously mentioned study of political participation in single-party Tunisia. Individual political involvement was the dependent variable, and level of socioeconomic status and level of personal efficacy were the two independent variables explored in the study. Socioeconomic status (SES) levels were measured by education and income, although many other lifestyle attributes were shown to be associated with this measure. Efficacy refers to a range of personality attributes, including sociability, self-esteem, and confidence in the future. As previously mentioned, the independent variables were selected because other studies had indicated their relevance in accounting for variance in individual political participation levels, and one goal of the study was to replicate earlier research to determine whether and under what conditions findings were generalizable.

In addition, however, the study was concerned with analytical elaboration, with examining potential patterns of interaction among the independent variables and determining how these patterns structured the impact of each on the dependent variable. Both SES and efficacy levels were categorized as high, middle, and low, and the percentage of respondents active in politics (mostly within the local committees of

Table 11.1   Percentage of Politically Active Individuals

Within Groups Differing in Socioeconomic Status and Efficacy

	Socioeconomic Status			
	Low	Intermediate	High	Total
Efficacy				
High	100	43	41	44
Intermediate	0	22	38	26
Low	0	7	40	9
Total	5	20	39	25

Tunisia's Destourian Socialist party) were then computed for each of the nine categories formed by considering the two independent variables in combination. The findings, which appear in Table 11.1, reveal that an increase from low to middle levels on either independent variable alone is not sufficient to produce an increase in political participation. Alternatively, when both increase from low to middle levels, political participation levels go up. Thus, at this level, both independent variables are necessary to increase participation and neither is sufficient. Increases from medium to high levels reveal a different pattern. Participation goes up either when SES alone is high or when efficacy alone is high. Moreover, when both are high it goes up no more than when there is an increase on only one of the independent variables. Thus, at this level, both independent variables are sufficient, and neither is necessary to bring about a rise in the level of political involvement.

More sophisticated analytical methods are available for examining multivariate relationships, of which the preceding is but a simplified example. However, the point to be retained at present is that adequate explanation requires an on-going effort aimed at the incremental construction of models of social behavior that answer questions about why a given phenomenon varies as it does—models or explanations that become increasingly complete and elaborate as a result of the cumulative character of social science research. Most individual studies will be of limited value unless they respond to the need for cumulativeness in scientific investigation, unless they are fashioned with a view toward participating in and contributing to this collective scholarly endeavor. Conversely, the aggregate value and utility of information produced by the social science community itself depend on the degree to which individual investigators accept this challenge and succeed in integrating their work into the body of existing scholarly knowledge. Researchers must therefore undertake studies that (1) increase confidence in the accuracy of existing findings or discover previously undetected errors; (2) establish the external validity and population extensiveness of observed behavior patterns and variable relationships; (3) determine as well the locus of applicability of these findings; and (4) refine present understanding by making existing explanations more elaborate and complete.

Notes

1. Norman Campbell, *What is Science* (London: Dover Publications, 1952), p. 27.

2. Ahmad J. Dhaher, "Selecting Respondents for Social Research in the Middle East," paper presented to the 1984 annual meeting of the American Political Science Association meeting, Washington, D.C. Dhaher's discussion is based on Fred N. Kerlinger, *Foundations of Behavioral Research* (New York: Holt, Rinehart and Winston, 1964), pp. 5ff.

3. Dhahar, "Selecting Respondents."

4. Ibid.

5. See, for example, Sadik J. Al-Athem, *Self Criticism After the Defeat* (Beirut: Dar al-Taliah, 1968), pp. 126–166. For a broader survey, see Fouad Ajami, *The Arab Predicament* (New York: Cambridge University Press, 1981), passim.

6. Levon H. Melikian and Lutfi Diab, "Group Affiliations of University Students in the Arab Middle East," *Journal of Social Psychology* 49 (1959): 145–159.

7. Levon H. Melikian and Lutfi Diab, "Stability and Change of Group Affiliations of University Students in the Arab Middle East," *Journal of Social Psychology* 93 (1974): 13–21.

8. Tawfic Farah, "Group Affiliations of University Students in the Arab Middle East (Kuwait)," *Journal of Social Psychology* 106 (1978): 161–165; Tawfic Farah and Faisal Al-Salem, "Group Affiliations of Children in the Arab Middle East (Kuwait)," *Journal of Social Psychology* 111 (1980): 141–142; and Tawfic Farah, "Group Affiliations of Arab University Students in the United States," in Tawfic Farah, ed., *Political Behavior in the Arab States* (Boulder, Color.: Westview Press, 1983), pp. 33–36. The volume containing the last article also includes reprints of the two preceding studies and the two articles by Melikian and Diab.

9. Mark Tessler, "Israel's Arabs and the Palestinian Problem," *Middle East Journal* 31 (1977): 313–329.

10. For example, Alex Inkeles, "Participant Citizenship in Six Developing Countries," *American Political Science Review* 63 (1969): 1129–1141.

11. Mark Tessler, "The Application of Western Theories and Measures of Political Participation to a Single-Party North African State," *Comparative Political Studies* 5 (1972): 175–191.

12. This point is discussed more fully in Adam Przeworski and Henry Teune, *The Logic of Comparative Social Inquiry* (New York: Wiley, 1970).

13. Mark Tessler, "Regime Orientation and Participant Citizenship in Developing Countries: Hypotheses and a Test with Longitudinal Data from Tunisia," *Western Political Quarterly* 34 (1981): 479–498.

14. Saad Gadalla, "Readership of Newspapers, Magazines and Books in the U.A.R." (Cairo: American University in Cairo, 1966).

15. "Urban Morocco," *Studies in Family Planning*, no. 58 (New York: Population Council, 1970). For a recent summary of survey-based population studies in the Middle East, see Frederic C. Shorter and Huda Zurayk, eds., *Population Factors in Development Planning in the Middle East* (New York: Population Council, 1985).

16. Mounira Chelli, "National Inquiry on Family Planning, 1975–1978," *Actes du Colloque de Demographie Maghrebine*, vol. 2 (1978).

17. Hanna Rizk, "National Fertility Sample Survey for Jordan 1972: The Study and Some Findings," *Population Studies of the United Nations Economic and Social Office in Beirut* 5 (July 1973): 14–31.

18. Jean Lecompte and Alain Marcoux, "Contraception and Fertility in Tunisia and Morocco," *Studies in Family Planning*, vol. 7 (1976).

19. Mark Tessler, "Cultural Modernity: Evidence from Tunisia," *Social Science Quarterly* 52 (1971): 290–308.

20. André Boyer, "The News in the Maghreb," Thesis of III'e Cycle, University of Paris II, 1976.

Appendix A:
Participants in the
Bellagio Conference

Mustafa O. Attir
Arab Development Institute
Tripoli, Libya

Alya Baffoum
University of Tunis
Tunis, Tunisia

Omayma Dahhan
Jordan University
Amman, Jordan

Ahmed Dhaher
Yarmouk University
Irbid, Jordan

Tawfic Farah
Middle East Research Group
Fresno, California USA

Saad Gadalla
American University in Cairo
Cairo, Egypt

Rita Giacaman
Bir Zeit University
West Bank

Ann Lesch
The Ford Foundation
Cairo, Egypt

Nafhat Nasr
American University of Beirut
Beirut, Lebanon

Cynthia Nelson
American University in Cairo
Cairo, Egypt

Monte Palmer
Florida State University
Tallahassee, Florida USA

M. O. El Sammani
University of Khartoum
Khartoum, Sudan

Naiem Sherbiny
The World Bank
Washington, D.C. USA

Fredj Stambouli
University of Tunis
Tunis, Tunisia

Iliya Harik
Indiana University
Bloomington, Indiana USA

Barbara Lethem Ibrahim
The Ford Foundation
Cairo, Egypt

Saad Eddin Ibrahim
American University in Cairo
Cairo, Egypt

Sharif Kanaana
Bir Zeit University
West Bank

Samir Khalaf
American University of Beirut
Beirut, Lebanon

Michael Suleiman
Kansas State University
Manhattan, Kansas USA

Mark Tessler
University of Wisconsin-Milwaukee
Milwaukee, Wisconsin USA

El-Sayed Yassin
Center for Political and Strategic
    Studies
Cairo, Egypt

Ali Zghal
Yarmouk University
Irbid, Jordan

Huda Zurayk
American University of Beirut
Beirut, Lebanon

About the Authors
and Contributors

Mark A. Tessler teaches political science at the University of Wisconsin–Milwaukee and is a faculty associate of the Universities Field Staff International.

Monte Palmer teaches political science at Florida State University.

Tawfic E. Farah is director of the Middle East Research Group and editor of the *Journal of Arab Affairs*.

Barbara Lethem Ibrahim is a program officer with the Ford Foundation in Cairo.

Iliya Harik teaches political science at Indiana University.

Saad Eddin Ibrahim teaches sociology at the American University in Cairo and is a senior researcher at the Al-Ahram Center for Political and Strategic Studies.

M. O. El Sammani teaches economics at the University of Khartoum.

Naiem A. Sherbiny is a senior economist at the World Bank.

Michael W. Suleiman teaches political science at Kansas State University.

Huda Zurayk teaches demography and statistics at the American University of Beirut.